PENGUIN CANADA

THE NAKED INVESTOR

JOHN LAWRENCE REYNOLDS has written extensively on financial and investment matters and has collaborated with former cabinet minister Brian Tobin and Air Canada CEO Robert Milton to produce acclaimed books on politics and business. His book *Free Rider: How a Bay Street Whiz Kid Stole and Spent $20 Million* won the National Business Book Award and was optioned as a motion picture. *Shadow People*, his study of prominent secret societies throughout history, was published in several foreign countries and is currently being developed into a television series. Reynolds has been honoured with an award from the Foundation for the Advancement of Canadian Letters, and has won two Arthur Ellis Awards for best mystery novel, as well as a National Magazine Award. He lives in Burlington, Ontario.

JOHN LAWRENCE
REYNOLDS

THE
NAKED
INVESTOR

WHY ALMOST
EVERYBODY BUT YOU
GETS RICH ON YOUR RRSP

PENGUIN
CANADA

PENGUIN CANADA

Published by the Penguin Group

Penguin Group (Canada), 90 Eglinton Avenue East, Suite 700, Toronto, Ontario, Canada M4P 2Y3
(a division of Pearson Canada Inc.)

Penguin Group (USA) Inc., 375 Hudson Street, New York, New York 10014, U.S.A.
Penguin Books Ltd, 80 Strand, London WC2R 0RL, England
Penguin Ireland, 25 St Stephen's Green, Dublin 2, Ireland (a division of Penguin Books Ltd)
Penguin Group (Australia), 250 Camberwell Road, Camberwell, Victoria 3124, Australia
(a division of Pearson Australia Group Pty Ltd)
Penguin Books India Pvt Ltd, 11 Community Centre, Panchsheel Park, New Delhi – 110 017, India
Penguin Group (NZ), cnr Airborne and Rosedale Roads, Albany, Auckland 1310, New Zealand
(a division of Pearson New Zealand Ltd)
Penguin Books (South Africa) (Pty) Ltd, 24 Sturdee Avenue, Rosebank, Johannesburg 2196,
South Africa

Penguin Books Ltd, Registered Offices: 80 Strand, London WC2R 0RL, England

First published in Penguin Canada paperback by Penguin Group (Canada),
a division of Pearson Penguin Canada Inc., 2005
Published in this revised edition, 2007

3 4 5 6 7 8 9 10 (WEB)

Copyright © John Lawrence Reynolds, 2005, 2007

Author representation: Westwood Creative Artists
94 Harbord Street, Toronto, Ontario M5S 1G6

Manufactured in Canada.

LIBRARY AND ARCHIVES CANADA CATALOGUING IN PUBLICATION

Reynolds, John Lawrence
The naked investor : why almost everybody but you gets rich
on your RRSP / John Lawrence Reynolds. — Rev. ed.

Includes bibliographical references and index.
ISBN 0-14-305543-7

1. Retirement income—Canada—Planning. 2. Registered Retirement Savings Plans.
3. Financial planners—Canada. I. Title.

HD7129.R488 2007   332.024'0140971   C2006-906220-X

Visit the Penguin Group (Canada) website at **www.penguin.ca**

Visit the website of John Lawrence Reynolds at **www.wryter.ca**

Special and corporate bulk purchase rates available; please see
www.penguin.ca/corporatesales or call 1-800-810-3104, ext. 477 or 474

For my sister Alice Boucher
And to the memory of Kent Shirley

No lesson seems to be so deeply inculcated by the experience of life as that you should never trust experts. If you believe the doctors, nothing is wholesome. If you believe the theologians, nothing is innocent. If you believe the soldiers, nothing is safe. They all require to have their strong wine diluted by a very large admixture of insipid common sense.

—LORD SALISBURY, LETTER TO LORD LYTTON,
JUNE 15, 1877

Experto credite
(Trust one who has gone through it)

—VIRGIL, 70–19 BC

CONTENTS

PREFACE TO THE REVISED EDITION

Before *The Naked Investor* appeared in January 2005, my wife expressed concern about my safety. "They'll write nasty letters," she warned. "They may even get violent. This could be the most dangerous book you've ever written."

"They" were the target of the book's most vehement criticism: brokers and financial advisors focused more on earning commissions than on building their clients' RRSP portfolios, mutual fund managers charging excessive fees for underperforming investments, industry associations that claimed to promote investor interests while protecting their members' fiefdoms, and your everyday embezzler, fraud artist, and well-coiffed pickpocket.

The book, after all, had not been written as an entry to exclusive Bay Street cocktail parties. I made the text intentionally provocative as a means of warning readers that the growth and security of their RRSP/RRIF investments risked being influenced by the greed of commission-paid advisors. When the investments proved unsuitable and often disastrous for the investor, little recourse was at hand to correct the situation. I prepared myself for late-night telephone calls from raspy-throated brokers, threats to the safety of our cat, and serious questions about the legitimacy of my birth. But they never arrived.

In their place, I was stunned to receive congratulations and expressions of gratitude from a wide cross-section of the people I appeared to be attacking. Advisors and brokers wrote emails and letters, contacted me by telephone, and approached me at book signings and speeches, all to thank me for drawing attention to various abuses and questionable practices in their industry. Their comments ranged from formal expressions of gratitude to earthy and humorous observations such as

> *Dear Mr. Reynolds:*
> *Your book*—The Naked Investor—*is disgusting. The sad truth is that I believe all of your examples because, as an Investment Advisor, I could add a few of my own experiences.*
> *My question—how many copies do I have to buy to get a price at which I can afford to send [copies] out to clients?*

Patricia Lovett-Reid, the high-profile Senior Vice-President of TD Waterhouse Canada, praised my book and its often scathing assessment of her industry. "Some have suggested that this book slams the investment industry because it recounts stories of investors who have fallen prey to self-serving advisors," Ms. Lovett-Reid wrote. "Nevertheless, reading this book puts you in a position to better protect yourself, clearly outlining the questions you need answers to, and advising you how to go about ensuring your advisor is working for you."

A few members of the Nova Scotia legislature actually played press agent for *The Naked Investor* during a debate on the province's new securities act. Howard Epstein, representing Halifax Chebucto, rose in the House to say,

> I suggest you want to read a book that was just published this year about the mutual fund industry in Canada and it's called *The Naked Investor* by one John [Lawrence] Reynolds. Any of you who have money invested in mutual funds, after reading this book will just want to slit your throats.[1]

Throat-slitting was hardly my intent, and a provincial Hansard rarely boasts the readership of the Book Review section of *The Globe and Mail*, but a good review is a good review.

Reviews in the mass media proved even more enthusiastic if slightly less prestigious. In his *Financial Post* column Jonathan Chevreau suggested that his readers "Buy two copies: one for [yourself] and one for a friend or relative." Benj Gallander and Ben Stadelmann, who dispense investment advice as The Contra Guys [contratheheard.com], noted in their column:

> If you count yourself as a Canadian investor—particularly at the lower end of sophistication—who values advice from a financial adviser, this book will surely strengthen an already good relationship, and empower the individual to rectify a bad one. Call it a Dr. Phil-pill for investors.

Life is strange. It takes a book on investing to establish a link between me and a tall, bald multi-millionaire with a Texas twang.

Before I strain my elbow by patting myself on the back, I should mention that one of the industry's most astute and respected observers held back his praise in order to fire broadsides at a couple of the book's points. Dan Hallett runs an independent investment research firm providing services to financial advisors out of his Windsor, Ontario, offices. In an October 2005 article in his monthly newsletter, headed Good Book Proves Everyone Biased, Hallett criticized me for using the term late trading rather than market timing in Chapter 5 ("It Shouldn't Be Complex—It Should Be Open.") Late trading, Hallett noted, is illegal, whereas market timing—defined by Hallett as "taking advantage of stale prices created by time zone differences"—is not. I believe, and he admits, that this amounts to splitting hairs. Hallett states the difference is basically one of degree. Late trading, as Hallett defines it, consists of allowing trades to be made in domestic mutual funds after the markets have closed and prices have already been determined; market timing, according to Hallett, takes advantage of time zone differences. The semantic difference may be foggy but the unfairness of it, to retail investors whose money provides the means for such shenanigans, is clear. In any case, the nomenclature has been changed in this edition. The fact remains, however, that a small group of power insiders earned millions of dollars in schemes unavailable to the investors who contributed to the assets of the mutual funds in question. The fund companies could have stopped it, but they did not.

Hallett also questioned my reference to a wrap account (Chapter 6) that added a 2.5 percent fee atop the 2.5 percent already charged by mutual funds. Did it really exist? When I provided my source, he agreed that it was "what most people would consider to be a reliable third-party source," but castigated me for not placing "a couple of phone calls to people in the industry" to confirm that such a product does not exist despite the "reliable third-party source." "This perfectly illustrates my … point about bias and scrutiny," Hallett remarked, suggesting that my bias against wrap accounts prevented me from performing more detailed detective work.

I admit my bias against wrap accounts, and Hallett would surely agree that I have a good deal of company in this regard. I am also prejudiced, just for the record, against those quarters within the industry that ignore the most outrageous aspects of certain practitioners, all the while mouthing their dedication to providing essential investment guidance and being responsive to the needs of their clients.

Paul Bourque, the personable Senior Vice-President, Member Regulation, of the Investment Dealers Association (IDA), was understandably not pleased with some commentary on the IDA's structure and operations in the first edition, and his observations are noted in this one.

Not Quite a Tsunami, But No Longer a Ripple

The first edition of *The Naked Investor* might not have created a wave of investor outrage, but it certainly rode a rising crest. Based on reader responses, it often appeared that every second purchaser of the book or some member of his or her family had suffered a loss in his or her RRSP attributed to an asymmetrical situation favouring the advisor. "Asymmetry," in this case, means in the beginning the investor has the money and the advisor has the knowledge; in the end the situation is vice-versa.

Dozens of readers contacted me to relate instances of money being deducted from their retirement savings accounts while wealth was being added to the bank accounts of advisors and their employers. Although degrees of honesty may not exist, degrees of investor abuse do, and among the worst is combining the two most inappropriate mutual fund categories, deferred sales charge (DSC) and segregated funds, with abuse of the elderly—and "abuse" is the appropriate word here.

The experience of "Beth Green," who wrote from the gentle environment of Prince Edward Island, was one example. She recounts her tale in Chapter 4 ("Mutual Funds: You Win, They Win; You Lose, They Still Win") of this edition. The snakes-and-ladders game played by various securities commissions, ombudsmen, and industry regulators is almost humorous, but only because it does not involve your money.

A few events coincided with the appearance and subsequent impact of *The Naked Investor* in January 2005. The May 31, 2005, Town Hall meeting in Toronto brought together the CEOs of the Investment Dealers Association (IDA), the Mutual Fund Dealers Association of Canada, and the Ontario Securities Commission, along with the Ombudsman for Banking Services and Investments, in front of 500 interested, and often angry, investors and commentators.

The IDA divested itself of its dual role of representing both aggrieved investors and the investment industry, choosing instead to serve as a regulatory body exclusively, something the first edition of this book proposed. And the gurus whom I criticized in the first edition ("Celebrity Bingo") have wandered off into the sunset or, in one case, marched off to Parliament Hill as an elected MP.

Did *The Naked Investor* influence any of these events? Some observers believe it did. Perhaps, but *plus ca change* ... Regulatory agencies funded by the investment industry continue to function as though either ignorant of or removed from investor outrage. Sandra Gibson, so furious at their behaviour that she insisted on stepping out from behind a pseudonym ("Hillary Cornell") in the first edition, provides a superb example of the industry's hypocrisy. Read her account of the Investment Dealers Association (IDA) ordering an advisor to return thousands of dollars in fees illegally applied to client accounts through a nicely descriptive process called *regorging*. Are the regorged fees returned to the clients whose assets were drained? No, they are retained by the IDA for its own use. You can read the details in Chapter 3, "Brokers and Advisors: Whose Money Is It Anyway?"

One alarming new chapter is launched with Larry Elford's views of the industry from his position as a former high-flying stockbroker/advisor. Do four out of five brokers/advisors bend or break the rules to maximize their own earnings and deprive clients of growth in the process? Elford claims they do and offers disturbing evidence that this may be the case.

An even more unsettling tale involves an investment company with offices coast to coast whose history has been clouded with charges by clients and regulators alike. The story includes an apparently orchestrated plan to move client assets from quality third-party mutual funds into poorly performing proprietary mutual funds for the express purpose of enriching the investment company's executives and staff ... the firm's effectiveness at silencing critics on a website and in a national newspaper … and a litigious branch manager who brooks no negative comment from any source. Potential connections led to the tragic death of a former employee after he made statements to a provincial securities commission alleging illegal activities conducted by the branch manager. What followed was a draconian search-and-seizure order that defies many articles of the Canadian Bill of Rights.

How can a profession that claims most clients will prove inept at making their own investment decisions wash its hands of responsibility so abruptly when its own counsel proves disastrous? The investment industry will assert that every employment sector must endure its share of bad apples, and that targeting it exclusively is unfair. But is it? I simply ask that they admit there are bad advisors, just as there are bad cops, bad doctors, and, yes, bad writers. Identify them, expose them, penalize them, and, if necessary, drum them out of the club.

A Toast to Good Investment Advisors

Of all the revelations that arrived with the first edition of *The Naked Investor,* the one that should please and encourage the investment industry generally is this: The majority of RRSP owners recognize that they need qualified assistance in making good decisions, and they will reward and remain loyal to those advisors who do their job fairly, honestly, and competently. Since *The Naked Investor* is based upon experiences and anecdotes, here are two to illustrate the point:

My express admiration and appreciation for two financial advisors in the book generated remarkable reactions. The unorthodox views (and exceptional performance for his clients) of Hans Merkelbach, described in Chapter 7, include his observation that he did not want or need more clients, thank you very much. This gentle reproof failed; at last count Merkelbach had added more than $10 million to client assets under his management. Based on his annual fee of 1 percent of assets under management (Merkelbach returns commissions to his clients), he earned substantially more money from *The Naked Investor* than I did.

A second encouraging note to advisors was the response of people one evening in February 2005 in my hometown of Burlington, Ontario, where I did a reading sponsored by a local bookstore. After I praised my own advisor's assistance in building the assets of RRSPs owned by my wife and me, a man in the audience asked for his name and telephone number. "See me when I'm finished," I suggested, "and I'll pass it along to you." At the end of the session about a dozen people rushed toward me with pencils poised, eager to record the name of the advisor whose wisdom and service I admired so openly. People are seeking honest, productive investment advice, and this should be reassuring news for dedicated investment specialists.

This edition of *The Naked Investor* includes updated statistics on mutual fund performance, accounts of investor abuse by unscrupulous advisors, and cautionary tales about what to expect and what to avoid in building your RRSP to a maximum (and reasonable) level. Added to this edition is a shift in primary focus from the antics of individual advisors to the more systemic outrages of the industry generally. The too-much-smoke-to-be-no-fire tales of some Assante branches in past years replace the guru section, along with concerns regarding the apparent general intolerance of investor complaints by government and regulatory agencies. In some ways, this revised approach reflects terms employed by mutual fund managers to describe their technique of choosing companies as investment targets. "Bottom-up" means the fund managers ignore wider issues to locate individual firms that promise growth and earnings regardless of their industry or geographic location. "Top-down" identifies a method that surveys a specific industry category from which candidates will be selected.

The original *The Naked Investor* employed a "bottom-up" approach to problem areas by beginning with examinations of specific cases of investor abuse. This edition repeats that approach, but as the wave of outrage builds and RRSP investors demand more openness from their advisors, it becomes clear that many problems can be solved by addressing systemic weaknesses; these include the lack of a national securities agency in Canada, the pressure placed on staff of larger investment firms to build their commission-based sales, and the general weakness of Canadian law in dealing with white-collar crime.

One aspect of this edition has not changed from the first. I would prefer to identify here those firms whose actions are the subject of criticism, but in the interest of fairness this cannot be achieved without providing the companies an opportunity to present their own views of the cases in question. I respect this premise, and the lawyers who review this text insist upon it. Unfortunately, with the exception of Assante, whose current CEO provided an extensive interview, none of the firms approached to comment on charges being made against them responded to my requests by telephone, email, or postal communications. Absent their response, their identities must be concealed, a factor that I trust does not dilute the impact of their actions as related by aggrieved clients. Another barrier to total openness concerns the use of "gag orders" preventing either side from commenting on the settlement of a dispute. Many investors wanted their stories told complete with details of negotiations and funds returned but were restricted by confidentiality clauses—with the delightful exception of Jocelyne Robidoux, whose tale opening Chapter 8 represents a milestone of sorts in investor revenge.

The two most common adjectives used to describe *The Naked Investor* were "shocking" and "revealing." I have endeavoured to ensure that these descriptions continue to apply to this revised edition. Thanks to those who provided new data, directions, and encouragement for this edition, especially (among others whose identity must remain concealed) Jonathan Chevreau, John de Goey, David Chilton, Jocelyne Robidoux, Dan Hallett, Larry Elford, Ken Kivenko, Cyril Fleming, and Jim Roache.

One last thought to retain before, during, and after reading this book:

Never forget whose money it is.

INTRODUCTION

In the spring of 2000 a middle-aged couple decided to obtain independent financial planning advice. The couple had accumulated substantial RRSP investments, owned an almost mortgage-free home, operated a personal corporation that generated more tax benefits than profits, and was looking for assistance in managing their assets.

The husband wanted to concentrate on writing books and tapering off a lucrative career as a marketing consultant. The wife wanted to expand her time gardening and pursuing other interests. Both wished to travel more widely, launch Registered Educational Savings Plans for their grandchildren, establish a cash-flow strategy, and deal with certain nagging debts, including one built up within the personal corporation and secured by the equity in their home.

The couple's chartered accountant had provided excellent advice over the years and continued to do so. But the husband believed a fresh eye could always uncover new opportunities and options. Over the years, the couple had encountered a financial advisor at social functions for an arts group they supported.

"Come in and visit me some time," the advisor suggested. "I'll do an analysis of your situation and make a proposal. If you don't like our ideas, it won't cost you a cent. If you do like them, and let us handle things, the analysis fee is $750."

"We can't lose," the husband said to his wife a few days later, showing her the advisor's business card. She noted an alphabet of letters after the advisor's name. "Let's go downtown and talk to him, see what he suggests," the husband said.

She agreed, and during three visits over the next month, each visit extending more than an hour, they provided the advisor with copies of their income tax statements, details of their RRSP investment portfolios, and information he requested that seemed to have little connection with their concern about solving cash-flow problems, such as, "How much life insurance do you carry?" and "What are the terms of your wills?"

A week or so after the couple's visit, the advisor called to say his report was ready. When could they come down to review it?

At the advisor's office, the husband and wife were surprised to be handed copies of an inch-thick computer-generated report, many of the pages bright with multicoloured pie charts. They sat stunned while the advisor flipped quickly past the charts as though they were more decorative than informative. He then summarized the lengthy report as follows.

"Sell all your bonds now—they're too risky."

The bonds in the couple's RRSPs were all federal- and provincial-guaranteed, with maturity dates extending from 5 to 10 years into the future. Purchased in the early 1990s when interest rates were relatively high, the bonds had proven an excellent investment, and their market value represented about half of the couple's total RRSP value.

"Sell all the mutual funds you have accumulated over the years."

These were primarily value-based and indexed funds investing in major Canadian corporations and managed by companies such as AIM-Trimark, Templeton, and Dynamic.

"Move into growth-oriented mutual funds, the ones that are technology-based—that's where to build wealth in the future." The advisor provided a list of such funds, noting that they were "no load—all your money goes into the fund instead of into sales commissions." All the funds, however, charged high management fees with a deferred sales charge (DSC) extending over seven years. (The explanation and implication of these terms are provided in Chapter 4.)

"Purchase $400,000 each in new term insurance with a 20-year guarantee on premiums."

The couple already carried policies totalling $300,000 in benefits, and their children were grown, with families of their own. The annual premiums for the new policies approached $10,000. No explanation for these recommendations was provided beyond the comment, "This is what you need to build your retirement nest egg."

The couple thanked the advisor for his assistance, asked for time to ponder the recommendations, exited his office as swiftly as possible, and drove home, appalled at his proposals. None addressed their original concerns. Moreover, reviewing his report and their most recent RRSP statements that evening, they estimated that the advisor stood to earn from $30,000 to $40,000 if they implemented every proposal in the plan. The money would accrue to the advisor from the following:

1. The Sale of the "Risky" Government Bonds

Commissions as high as 2 percent are not uncommon in bond markets. These commissions, earned by discounting the bond price, are rarely if ever reported to the investor and would have placed about $5000 in the advisor's pocket.

2. The Purchase of High-MER (read: "expensive to own") Mutual Funds by the Advisor

Paid for with cash from selling the existing mutual funds in the couple's RRSPs, the new funds would have paid the advisor as much as $15,000 in sales commissions.

3. The Payment to the Advisor, by the Mutual Fund Companies, of Trailing Fees

These would be paid annually for as long as the couple retained the new mutual funds. The husband estimated these payments at $2500 each year; over five years, about $12,500 would have flowed into the advisor's pocket.

4. Sales Commissions on the $800,000 Life Insurance Policies

Estimated at $8000 in the first year.

The couple informed the advisor that they would not be following his recommendations and refused his several telephone pleas to give him a chance to "rethink things a little differently."

Within a few weeks of the couple's encounter with the "independent" financial advisor, stock markets began to fall. The value of mutual funds recommended by the advisor, heavily weighted toward high-tech and health services companies, suffered the worst. Had the couple invested their entire RRSP savings accrued over 25-plus years, as the advisor proposed, perhaps 80 percent of its value would have vanished with the market decline. It took over three years for prices to begin a recovery, but by mid-2004 they had still not achieved their earlier value. Whenever and if ever they returned to the price levels of early 2000, the couple would have lost at least several years of potential growth.

When tech stock prices began sliding, so did interest rates, which meant the value of the couple's bonds increased with every rate reduction (bond prices move in the opposite direction to interest rates). Had the couple sold their bonds when the advisor prompted them to, several thousand more dollars in potential earnings would have been lost.

Nothing the advisor did or proposed was illegal or even, in some quarters, considered ill-advised. The fact remains, however, that if the couple had followed his counsel, he would have been at least $30,000 wealthier. Meanwhile, the value of the couple's RRSPs would have been reduced by hundreds of thousands of dollars and they would have little recourse to recover their losses. An attempt to do so would take years of investigation and substantial upfront legal fees.

While industry organizations claim to protect small investors and work to replace losses as a result of advisor malfeasance or bad advice, they are sluggish to respond, loath to replace losses, and protective of the investment industry. Had any of the relevant groups—the provincial securities commissions, the Investment Dealers Association of Canada, the Ombudsman for Banking Services and Investments, the Mutual Fund Dealers Association of Canada, among others—chosen to pursue an inquiry, the advisor would claim in his defence that he could not have foreseen either the collapse of stock market prices, especially the technical sector, or the resulting drop in interest rates. Nor was he bound by rule or law to reveal how much he stood to earn from commissions paid to him as a result of selling the bonds and old mutual funds, purchasing a new stable of mutual funds, and brokering the term insurance.

The losses suffered, the couple might have been lectured, were part of the risk that all investors must assume. When you invest in markets, prices can go down as well as up; that's the risk you take. This is the common defence of ineffective advisors. The industry wants you to accept dramatic loss as a potential outcome of every investment decision associated with long-term planning for your retirement, *and it is a lie.*

There is a difference between risk and uncertainty. Risk can be measured and accounted for; uncertainty cannot. Risk can be balanced according to rules capable of being absorbed by every Canadian mature enough to open his or her own RRSP, and their mechanics can be grasped in the time it takes to sip a cup of coffee. Risk and uncertainty are very different. No one can anticipate uncertainty. Everyone can understand and account for risk.

In essence, the couple would have taken all the risk and lost. The advisor would have taken no risk and won.

The experience of this couple is not as rare as the investment industry claims. Too many trusting RRSP investors stand naked in the market while their advisors convince them they are wearing a superbly fitted and highly fashionable suit of clothes. Canadians need to be educated about methods employed by the financial and investment industry to enrich itself in an atmosphere with minimal transparency and accountability. That's my primary reason for writing this book. Here are seven others:

1. Because, in addition to losses suffered by investors through inappropriate advice, borderline-legal activities and out-and-out fraud occur with alarming frequency in the industry, destroying the life's work and dreams of Canadians while fraudsters escape with little more than a slap on the wrist.

2. Because neither the various regulatory bodies nor the industry appears to be addressing the problem effectively.

3. Because Canadian law can be construed as favouring large investment firms over individual citizens.

4. Because too many interests, including the legal profession and certain sectors of the media, support grey aspects of the financial and investment industry and overlook the concerns of small investors.

5. Because a loss of trust by citizens in the investment industry will harm Canada's economy.

6. Because prudent investment decisions made on the basis of a few simple rules, according to the investor's best interests, are still the best way to achieve long-term financial security.

7. And because the middle-aged man who sought assistance in financial planning, only to discover that the licensed, highly qualified, commission-earning advisor based every decision solely on generating benefits for himself ... was me.

You Are David,
They Are Goliath, and
You Don't Have a Slingshot

In 1987, at age 60, Armand Laflamme and his brother sold the door and window manufacturing business they had built from scratch. After almost half a century of mostly manual labour, Armand deserved a comfortable retirement, financed by his share of the $10 million selling price of the company.

Things went wrong from the start. Instead of receiving $5 million, Armand received only $2.2 million, the balance tied up and eventually lost in financial complications with the company's buyer. Still, $2.2 million represented a substantial nest egg for a man with a grade four education and, following the guidance of his son, Armand contacted securities dealer Burns Fry (now BMO Nesbitt Burns), where his account was assigned to a man named Jules Roy. Neither Armand nor his son had any investment experience, and they were persuaded by Roy to sign a number of blank documents, which Roy would complete at a later date. Armand Laflamme transferred $2 million to Roy at Burns Fry, confident that he had placed his assets in the hands of a licensed financial advisor employed by a reputable investment firm.

A year later, Roy moved to Prudential-Bache Commodities Canada Ltd. From there he sent another set of blank documents to Armand Laflamme and requested that Armand sign them—the details again to be completed by Roy—transferring his account to Prudential-Bache. Armand agreed; after all, Prudential-Bache was as large and reputable as Burns Fry.

Within a few weeks, Armand Laflamme was stunned to learn that his $2 million balance had not only declined by more than $200,000 but that Roy was managing the account on margin— that is, borrowing money from the brokerage (at a relatively high interest rate) and adding the borrowed money to Armand's assets in order to purchase larger quantities of securities, many of them outright speculative in nature. Trading larger volumes of securities generated, of course, larger commissions for the broker. Armand, through his daughter, instructed Roy to cease margin trading, limit stock market investments to $500,000, and place the balance in safe instruments such as bonds and guaranteed investment certificates (GICs).

The instructions were ignored. Losses mounted, securities were traded without Armand's knowledge or approval, and the value of his hard-earned nest egg continued to dwindle. By this time, Armand had been charged $111,000 in commissions and $272,000 on interest for money borrowed, without his knowledge or approval, to finance his margin account. On March 2, 1990, Armand Laflamme pulled what little remained of his account out of Prudential-Bache and began court action to recover at least a portion of his losses. The effort took 10 years.

The first court decision, handed down six years after Armand Laflamme launched his suit, resulted in a decision in his favour by the Superior Court of Quebec. In his ruling, Justice Lebrun found Roy and Prudential-Bache "entirely liable" and listed "quite unmistakeable and clearly proved" faults that included—

- Failure by Roy to act in accordance with the client's objectives (i.e., generate a retirement income)
- Failure by Roy to comply with the client's specific instructions

- Failure by Roy to deal with the client in good faith and in accordance with good practice
- Conducting extremely large numbers of transactions for the sole purpose of generating commissions for Roy and the brokerage
- Failure by Prudential-Bache to exercise proper supervision over Roy
- Roy being in a conflict of interest, as Roy's supervisor received a 50 percent share of the defendant's commissions

It was a devastating judgment that included instructions for Roy and Prudential-Bache to repay Armand Laflamme $1.5 million lost as a result of Roy's actions.

But Prudential-Bache was not finished. It appealed the decision and won, managing to reduce the damages payable to a paltry $70,000. To those outside the legal community, the basis of Roy and Prudential-Bache's appeal reads like an example of extreme cynicism. After a year of dealing with Roy, the appeal judge determined, Armand Laflamme would have generated enough investment knowledge to be considered experienced and qualified to assess Roy's investment tactics and should have taken responsibility for the advisor's actions. Thus, the brokerage was not responsible for any losses after that point.

While the appeal court ruling did not use the same terminology, the context and meaning appears in numerous defences launched by advisors and brokerage firms when facing client charges of malfeasance: "You are the author of your own misfortune."

Armand Laflamme might have been confounded by the ruling, but he was not yet finished. He and his legal counsel went to the Supreme Court of Canada, which agreed to hear the case on the basis that it related to the liability of a securities dealer acting as a portfolio manager. In a scathing review, the Supreme Court overturned the appeal court's judgment, restoring most (but not all) of the original amount decreed. Roy and his brokerages were ordered to pay Armand Laflamme and his family $924,374 plus interest and costs.

A substantial portion of Armand Laflamme's retirement nest egg, earned through 50 years of labour, was returned to him 13 years after it had been placed in the hands of a professional financial advisor employed by a reputable investment firm. It was May 2000. At age 74, Armand Laflamme could finally begin to enjoy his retirement without the trauma of watching his money dribble into the hands of a commission-based advisor while fighting legal battles with a giant brokerage. (Mr. Laflamme has since died.)[2]

In mid-2000, when my wife and I received the inappropriate advice from the financial advisor whose goal appeared to be to enrich himself at our expense, I had written a guide to RRSP and RRIF investing and had begun a book tracing the criminal trial of a man charged in a major investment fraud. The charges involved Bay Street broker Michael Holoday, and the story was the basis of my book *Free Rider: How a Bay Street Whiz Kid Stole and Spent $20 Million.*

Free Rider taught me much about the investment industry that I had not fully appreciated. Until details of Holoday's activities were revealed and the impact they made on his victims assessed, I had focused exclusively on the benefits of assembling and maintaining a portfolio within an RRSP in preparation for retirement. That was the bright side of investing for the future. Holoday's tale, and the flood of experiences that poured my way during and after his trial, provided a glimpse of the darker sides.

One of these sides is represented by Armand Laflamme's experience. As he discovered during more than a decade of battling egregious treatment by a qualified financial advisor and a national brokerage, the industry will fight to the last writ to protect itself from precedent-setting legal losses and any admission of culpability. Its arguments against admitting responsibility can defy logic and plumb new depths of cynicism. Consider the Prudential-Bache defence based on the idea that Armand Laflamme, with a grade four education and no investing experience, would have acquired sufficient insight in the one year of dealing with his broker to make effective assessments and decisions regarding the performance of his account entirely on his own. How does this correlate with the industry's declaration that its advisors undergo extensive education, rigorous training, and constant assessment of their professional skills, backed by years of experience? It does not, except perhaps in the brief of a win-by-any-means lawyer.

Contributing to an RRSP on a regular basis is a wise thing to do, as everyone from federal politicians to banks and brokerage firms keeps telling us. As prudent and obedient Canadians, millions of us have done so, managing by fortune, diligence, and perhaps even good advice to accumulate RRSPs with balances in the mid-six-figures. Each year, about six million Canadians dump an average of $5000 into their RRSP plans, generating $30 billion in cash looking for a place to reside for several years. The old adage about your home representing the largest asset you will acquire in your lifetime may no longer be true. Now your RRSP could outstrip your home in value, and it is liquid.

This liquidity, unfortunately, is more accessible to others than it is to you—others in this case being people within the investment industry whose careers and income depend on how much of your RRSP assets they can move first into the coffers of their firm and eventually into their own pockets. With the exception of fraud and outright theft, these earnings are obtained legally through mutual fund fees, brokerage commissions, and other avenues.

The nature of the system provides a means for the industry to generate income by acting according to its primary interests, with the interests of the investors playing a largely secondary role. In effect, hundreds of billions of dollars salted away by Canadians for their retirement represent a vein of gold to be mined for by financial advisors, mutual fund sponsors, and financial institutions in ways that most RRSP owners fail to recognize.

Too many RRSP and RRIF owners have discovered that the investment industry is designed to protect itself, which it manages to do with remarkable success; indeed, it protects itself more effectively than it protects its clients. Proving that a broker, financial advisor, or financial planner has made decisions that favour himself at the expense of the trusting client is difficult because the advisor or broker can explain and justify almost any recommendation in ways that the client can neither anticipate nor dispute. When complaints to an investment firm about inappropriate handling of an account lead nowhere, the distressed client might press on, only to find herself bounced among a half dozen or more organizations ostensibly created to protect her interests. Representatives of each might nod with empathy before suggesting that the client's case really belongs with another agency, starting a game of circle tag in which the client is always "It."

If and when a client, sufficiently motivated and probably obsessed, manages to attract legal attention to her cause, she will likely never see her claims presented in court. Instead, her case will be referred to arbitration, where she may hope for a settlement of perhaps 50 cents on the dollar. The public will never hear the terms, for such agreements invariably include the condition that no details be revealed. Should the client discuss her settlement openly, she could be required to pay a substantial penalty that usually includes the return of any money received plus punitive damages. This demand for secrecy is never made by the investor; total confidentiality is stipulated by the investment industry, and its insistence on non-disclosure represents an effective method of concealing the extent of investor dissatisfaction and investor abuse. Dig deeply enough into investor and regulator concerns and you will discover two sides to the Canadian investment industry.

One presents a benevolent face shining with trust, wisdom, and the assurance that it wants to assist Canadians in building themselves a solid financial future. Like a kindly mentor, the industry explains that individual investors are ill equipped and thus unable to make major investment decisions on their own. Only with professional assistance, investors are gently lectured, can they achieve the financial security they seek and deserve.

The other, less charitable, side is frantic in its efforts to find ways of securing ever-larger portions of client RRSPs. It strives to do so not from enhanced performance or service but through marketing efforts that prey on the insecurities, aspirations, and trust of RRSP owners. When not conceiving new ways of siphoning funds from investors, the industry keeps busy diluting demands for reform and greater accountability.

Slowly, things are beginning to change. Demands for greater transparency and accountability are even beginning to resonate among the industry's own practitioners, including proposals to elevate financial advisors to true professional status by replacing sales commissions with direct fees. In May 2005, top executives of the major regulatory bodies actually hosted a so-called Town Hall meeting in Toronto, where an estimated 500 investors gathered to vent their wrath. The meeting provided an emotional outlet for many audience members and represented the first step in what may prove to be a long journey. An equitable system will arise only when Canadian RRSP owners grow fully aware of the industry's inclination to make itself wealthy first, treating the wealth of its clients almost as an afterthought.

The purpose of this book is to shine light on the circumstances behind these events and equip you to deal with similar situations, especially if your primary interest in investing is to provide the kind of retirement income your parents counted on receiving from employers' pension plans.

Defenders of the investment industry claim that the incidents you'll encounter on the following pages are "anecdotal," as though the word were synonymous with falsehood. The industry prefers statistical data, on the basis perhaps that accounts of people pale against hard facts spat from a calculator. But statistical data will never reveal the actual number of victims, many of them senior citizens, who believe little can be done to correct errors made in their names by trusted advisors. No one knows how many investors have suffered losses due to inappropriate investment advice made primarily to enrich the advisor, because they failed to register their concerns due to embarrassment, ignorance, or outright bullying and harassment by advisors and their organizations. The industry, and sectors of the legal profession that represent investors and advisors, effectively conceal the scope of its problems.

Among the first things a lawyer specializing in charges made against an advisor or brokerage will tell you is, "Don't talk about your case with anybody." The lawyers will claim the advice is given solely to improve the prospect of obtaining a favourable settlement, a questionable assertion when made by someone who is in court this week arguing on behalf of a brokerage and advisor against a wronged investor, and back in court next week making a case on behalf of an investor against an advisor and brokerage. And among the last things you will be told when advised to sign a settlement, whether or not it meets your reasonable expectations, is the same: "Don't discuss it with anybody or you could forfeit the money you receive."

When victims draw attention to the price they paid for bad advice, inappropriate investments, altered records, fraudulent statements, and other activities that may enrich the advisor at the client's expense, they encounter a system that often either favours the sales side of the investment industry or simply refuses to get involved.

Too harsh a condemnation? Hold your judgment until after you read about—

- The realtor who returned from vacation to discover his six-figure portfolio depleted through unauthorized broker transactions and a $70,000 debt, leading to years of frustrating and fruitless efforts in civil court to obtain redress.
- The PEI woman who, when she complained about a totally inappropriate portfolio sold to her aging mother by a broker, found herself on a merry-go-round in which three industry regulators and two ombudsmen took turns directing her to everyone but themselves.
- The woman from Thunder Bay who, upon discovering that her Winnipeg broker had sold several mutual funds in her portfolio and replaced them with in-house funds generating rewards for him and his brokerage, was informed that she had authorized the trades by telephone. When she produced telephone records indicating that no such phone calls had taken place—and proved that she was out of town on days the advisor claimed he had contacted her at her home—the firm refused to accept her documents.
- The B.C. couple who, wishing to adopt a logical strategy of investing 30 percent of their portfolios in fixed income investments, were instead directed by an advisor to invest in high-risk technology-based stocks just as the tech-based bubble was about to burst. In response to their complaint, they were shown account application forms in which the advisor had altered their declared risk levels to accommodate his own strategy, one that earned him substantially higher commissions than his clients' conservative choices.
- The Toronto woman who, when she asked about steep declines in the value of her RRSP portfolio, triggered a tantrum from her

advisor, who shouted that she was ungrateful for all the work he was doing on her behalf.

- The businesswoman concerned about differences between the inflated value of her portfolio, as provided by the broker, and its shrunken value, as indicated by brokerage statements. When she did precisely what investors are advised to do in these situations and called the brokerage compliance officer for assistance, she was referred back to the broker for an explanation. Her broker turned out to be one of Canada's biggest stock fraud artists.

No matter how much it tries, the investment industry cannot claim that stories such as these are rare and anecdotal, because no one knows the precise number of such incidents. Until investors grow educated and wary, and the industry's feckless self-regulated organizations grow responsive, the situation will become worse, and the number of personal financial disasters will increase. Why? Because employers are turning from defined-benefit programs, in which the corporation assumes responsibility for managing employee pension funds, to defined-contribution programs, where responsibility for managing portfolios is assigned to the RRSP owners. The value of these RRSP accounts is measured in hundreds of billions of dollars, and the earnings from these assets, and frequently the assets themselves, are more accessible to brokers and financial advisors than to the RRSP owners.

The stories you encounter on these pages are true. Study all the statistics you wish, but until you have watched an elderly man be moved to tears over the way in which his life savings have been squandered by an accredited advisor, with neither the advisor's firm nor the investment industry demonstrating serious interest in addressing his loss, your data will remain a column of cold figures, and the scope of the situation will remain obscure.

Industry representatives, including financial planners, financial advisors, registered representatives, mutual fund salespeople, brokers, and owners of all the various designations assigned to people licensed to trade securities, insist that most of the industry's members are honest and hard working. They are correct, inasmuch as most people *everywhere* are basically honest. But they should not deride these stories nor minimize the scope of unnecessary losses suffered by RRSP and RRIF owners through mismanagement of their assets. Effective, hard-working financial planners and advisors will *welcome* this book, because the crooked members of any profession are the enemy of the honest.

The lessons on these pages are not meant to encourage you to hide your life savings under a mattress or salt them away in bank accounts where they earn miserly income. The best way to build for your future is to invest your savings, especially your RRSP assets. Doing this effectively and safely requires you to maintain the attitude of a child strolling through the forest on her way to Grandma's house. Enjoy the scenery, smell the roses, and look forward to a lovely time in a safe and cozy cottage. Just be sure to stick to the well-worn path, and never assume that everyone you meet in the woods is anxious to help you get to Grandma's safely.

With that approach, you also may succeed in surviving the same near miss that prompted this book.

Of Foxes and Hedgehogs: Learning to Do One Thing Well

When Ivor Sargent* and his wife contacted a broker/advisor to assist in managing their RRSP accounts, they defined their goals to him in clear language. In spite of this, the advisor promoted his own tactics as a means of fattening his income.

"I had been referred to this brokerage," Ivor recalls from his interior–B.C. home. "It's a large bank-owned operation. This was late 1999, and I was in my mid-50s at the time. I was following the dictum of putting a substantial portion of my retirement portfolio, and that of my wife, into fixed-income investments. This way we would avoid the effects of wild market fluctuations that could reduce the value of our investments just when we needed them."

Ivor Sargent was employing a widely acknowledged strategy of balancing higher-risk investments—stocks and mutual funds subject to unpredictable changes in their value—with investments offering lower potential returns but higher security. In the Sargents' case, they targeted 30 percent of their portfolios for fixed income investments, and were drawn to a private mortgage company as the basis for this sector.

---

*A pseudonym

"I had a close friend with a significant portion of his investments in a private mortgage company," Ivor explains. "He had been receiving a steady stream of reasonable returns for many years, so I decided to place a portion of our fixed income investments in this company."

Referred to the investment arm of a major chartered bank to handle the transaction, the Sargents were directed to an advisor who immediately challenged them on their investment strategy, telling them he knew nothing about the mortgage company but identifying it as a very high risk. Recommending that the Sargents abandon that idea, he proposed investments that would be more appropriate for them. "He said he had many of his clients invested in them, and they had been doing very well for many years," Ivor Sargent says. "He did not say they were in the technology sector, just that they would be more appropriate for us. What he did, as a means of acquiring our business, was to totally discredit our investment intentions on the basis they would be very high risk, only to recommend investments that turned out to be the highest of risks. Our wishes to have these investments in the fixed income classification were totally ignored."

The Sargents, in their own words, were "somewhat shaken" by the advisor's views, yet decided to accept his recommendations. After all, his firm was the arm of a major bank whose literature boasted that its staff employed "up-to-date market research." Within a few days the Sargents mailed their portfolio outline to the advisor, and the advisor sent them forms to complete, including an authorization for him to transfer money into his recommended investments.

The firm's "up-to-date market research" was surely flawed. Early 2000 was the worst period possible to invest in technology-based mutual funds, which had ridden an expansion bubble to heights that every professional investment advisor must have known could not be sustained; there was an enormous risk that the bubble was about to burst—which it did within a few weeks.

Why would an advisor make such a move that could hardly have been more contrary to the clients' strategy and wishes? Only one explanation fits: Because the expensive and high-risk equity-based mutual funds paid the commission-based advisor substantially more than the low-cost fixed income alternatives, such as GICs, bonds, and shares in a private mortgage company. Of course, to achieve the higher commission meant discrediting the original investment strategy proposed by the Sargents, which the advisor accomplished with time.

The Sargents' retirement portfolios began to crumble in value as the tech bubble collapsed. In late 2001 Ivor Sargent, furious at the substantial losses in his retirement portfolio directly attributable to the advisor, decided to take action. He began with a letter of complaint to the Compliance Department of the brokerage. "It took them four months to respond to my letter," Ivor says, "and their reply was literally filled with lies. Even though I supported my points with written documentation, they did not contact me once during their 'thorough investigation' of my complaints to determine their validity."

Many investors would—and have—thrown up their hands in surrender, writing off their loss to experience. Ivor Sargent did not. He carried his grievance to the Investment Dealers Association (IDA), the ombudsman of the brokerage's parent bank, and the Ombudsman for Banking Services and Investments (OBSI). Both ombudsmen refused to consider his case while the IDA was involved, although "involved" may be a doubtful description. "Seven months after I sent the IDA a complaint, I received their judgment," Ivor says. "While they claimed they found no 'major wrongdoings' by the advisor warranting discipline against the advisor, I was assured they had taken other measures, which means he received a verbal or written reprimand."

Again, no one from the IDA contacted the Sargents to clarify facts. "Someone was telling a whole bunch of lies," Ivor Sargent muses, "and it seemed the IDA did not wish to determine who was telling the truth. All of my facts were supported by written material, whereas the advisor depended on his recollection of conversations that he claimed had taken place. Those conversations never happened." This wasn't the only occasion where the Sargents had claimed that the advisor lied. Earlier, they'd discovered that information they'd provided on documents submitted to open their account had been altered to favour the advisor's choice of high-risk investments and not their own conservative strategy.

Instead of pacifying the couple, the IDA's tardy response and rejection infuriated them even further. Originally considering the advisor's actions a minor breach of rules and regulations, Ivor now felt embroiled in a web of lies and suffering as a result of the industry's failure to deal with him fairly, honestly, and in good faith. Again, he was advised to "forget about it." But he could not.

Two lawyers specializing in investment laws persuaded him that a legal challenge through the courts would be long, expensive, and likely unproductive. Only when he turned to the British Columbia Securities Commission (BCSC) did he generate a positive and meaningful response, leading to an investigation that examined both sides and reached a decision. The BCSC found sufficient evidence to support the Sargents' claim, and was instrumental in obtaining an award from the bank-owned brokerage covering 100 percent of the couple's losses due to the inappropriate advice and unacceptable actions of their broker. The entire process had taken almost two years. "We are forever indebted to the BCSC for undertaking their investigation," Ivor says, "especially after all of the other responsible and regulatory bodies either refused to do so or failed in undertaking their fiduciary responsibility."

The agreement, like most settlements of this kind, included a directive preventing the Sargents from revealing details of their case. From beginning to end, the Sargents never met the advisor personally. Nevertheless, Ivor Sargent retains a wry opinion of him.

"He refused to acknowledge the written portfolio outline I sent to him, which clearly showed the investment recommendations he gave us were totally contrary to our wishes. And upon my complaint to his brokerage company, he stated nothing but lies in support of his recommendations.

"Other than this, the investment advisor may have been a person of some quality."

To fully appreciate the manner in which the financial and investment industry taps into your retirement savings, you need to recognize how the industry functions, and weigh some unpleasant facts.

In spite of efforts to position themselves as wise and contemplative professionals, brokers and financial advisors are essentially middlemen. Like all middlemen, they don't actually create anything. Rather, they provide a service, earning an income by moving products from source to end user. Dress it up with graphs and jargon, but the description still applies: When you deal with a broker, financial planner, or mutual fund salesperson, you're dealing with a middleman.

Here's another down-to-earth way of seeing things: When public corporations and bond issuers deliver profits to the investment industry in the form of stocks and bonds, the industry immediately takes its share. Small investors, including those trying desperately to build a nest egg for their retirement or their children's education, divide whatever is left over.

Taking things a step farther, your interests and the interests of Bay Street and its spin-offs are diametrically opposed, because the bigger the slice of the pie you take, the less remains for the investment industry. When it comes to paying you through potential investment gains, the industry shouts over the sound of brass bands and dancing cheerleaders. When it comes to paying themselves, they tend to whisper or change the subject.

A second fact to file: Almost every organization dedicated to providing investment counsel is involved, to some extent, in a conflict of interest. This salient truth, which the industry would prefer also not to discuss, was recognized in the United States when the Securities and Exchange Commission (SEC) dropped the hammer on half a dozen of the world's largest investment firms. These firms, the SEC determined, were beholden both to public companies seeking cash from investors and to investors seeking returns on their money. The brokerage firms underwrite the issues of private shares, committing to purchase sizeable blocks of the securities before adding a sales commission and selling the shares to investors. So far so good. But SEC evidence showed that the firms were promoting shares in companies whose prospects were so unpromising that they were described by brokerage personnel as "dogs." Supposedly objective analysts within the brokerage firms would "assess" these same shares as an excellent investment, hang a "Buy" sign on them, then watch brokers and financial advisors promote the securities to their clients— at which point the mutts were transmogrified into pedigreed Best of Show winners. This process carried the role of middleman to new highs, or lows if you prefer.

Brokerages in Canada function under the same conflict cloud, as do self-regulating organizations created to protect investor interests. Provincial securities commissions such as the Ontario Securities Commission claim their goals are *to foster fair and efficient capital markets and to provide protection for investors from unfair, improper, or fraudulent practices.*[3] Fostering fair and efficient capital markets means nothing less than attracting outside capital from corporations and organizations that seek cash from investors to finance their operations. This kind of capital, especially given the current globalization environment, is remarkably fluid and more than a trifle skittish about excess regulation. If Sam Zillionaire decides that a sector in Canada is imposing too many rules on the way he can sell his shares or bonds, and on the way he can treat his minority shareholders, he'll take his money where the laws are less stringent, the regulations are more flexible, and the enforcers are quick to wink at the odd non-compliance issue. In such an environment, no securities commission or regulatory organization can claim it puts investor concerns first, since any perceived imbalance may frighten off capital. How well is equilibrium maintained between capital sources and the interests of small investors? According to a growing number of small investors and industry critics, not well at all.

Another fact to consider: Much of the investment industry holds you and every other retail investor in contempt. If you truly value your RRSP as the primary source of retirement income, the industry trumpets, you must actively invest the funds and not salt them away in a low-paying bank savings account or a batch of lethargic GICs. Most Canadians grasp this concept and agree. Then, dropping the other shoe, the industry stops patting your head and begins slapping your hand, insisting that you are not competent to manage your own RRSP portfolio. You don't have enough time to make your own investment decisions, it suggests. And if you have, you will inevitably make nothing but bad choices, it scolds. Do you know any other business where it is *de rigueur* to insult the customer?

Consider the Sargents' case. An advisor strongly criticizes their initial strategy, rejects their proposals based on his expertise, and insists that his recommendations are the more preferable alternative. After his choice proves disastrous, both his firm and the dominant regulatory agency shrug off the client losses, claiming that's the risk investors must accept. Note, however, that the advisor and his firm did not risk any of the commissions earned through the clients' purchase of the recommended products. Not a penny of it.

The financial and investment industry proclaims love and concern for small investors at the drop of a Dow Jones Average, yet almost every service institution at its disposal favours the industry's interests over those of small investors. These include mammoth associations and organizations representing chartered banks, mutual fund companies, dealers, brokerages, investment counsellors, insurance agents, and financial planners. All pay lip service to investor protection, but their actions too often appear directed toward maintaining the status quo. No association comparable to the industry's own self-regulated, self-serving organizations plays a similar role on behalf of investors. Beyond the sluggish pace of the civil law courts and industry regulators, only a few lone voices are shouting into the wind, railing against unfairness and abuse.

Small investors need the investment industry every bit as much as it needs them. This book is not about how to destroy the industry's effectiveness, minimize its benefits, or maximize its operating complexity. It is about the need to introduce openness into the relationship.

Whom Do You Trust? Maybe Only Yourself

Up to this point, the focus in this book has been on brokers, financial advisors, and financial planners because they are investors' primary source of contact, and because the vast majority earn their income from sales commissions. As you will discover as you continue reading, brokers are not the only drain on your investment growth. In some cases, they're not even the most critical. There are other wolves in the forest, some less benign perhaps but all basing their livelihood on that large portion of money that follows a serpentine route from the creators of investment wealth into your account and out again. They include—

- Mutual fund operators who prove that the best way to get rich is not to invest in a mutual fund—it's to own one
- Fraud artists in Armani suits who equate a licence to trade securities with authorization to steal

- Securities analysts who tout shares in corporations that they themselves wouldn't touch with a 10-foot pole
- The Investment Dealers Association, provincial securities commissions, and other self-regulating organizations whose structure and indolence could teach the federal bureaucracy a thing or two about avoiding decisions
- Canada's chartered banks, which treat retail investors the same way the proverbial slaughterhouse treats hogs—harvesting everything but the *oink*
- Packaging experts who add little more than glitz to an existing product, charge you for the extra packaging, reduce your potential earnings with high fees, call it a "wrap account," and convince you it's a bargain

One way or another, they are all middlemen. Their products are created by others who need your money to finance their operations, and who promise to reward you with dividends and potential capital growth. The middlemen bring both sides together and handle the cash transactions. That's a reasonable service. The problem arises because Canadian investors generally have no idea how extensive the middleman system is. They do not realize how many hands slip into the pockets of their RRSPs to withdraw a little money here and a little money there until, over the long run—and what other savings plan runs longer than retirement preparation?—untold thousands of dollars have seeped from their nest eggs.

Wherever substantial amounts of cash begin to flow, the shorelines of the money river grow crowded with people ready to scoop out a portion for their own benefit or, in the case of more outrageous fraud artists and embezzlers, divert the entire stream into their ponds. This appears obvious to almost everyone except the average investor. Two reasons for this are obscurity and trust, and the investment industry nurtures both.

Of the hundreds of billions of dollars invested in their RRSPs, most Canadians have little idea about the nature and structure of these investments—the ones not ensconced in sleepy bank savings accounts—or their performance levels. Amid internet access and extensive media coverage of investment markets, this is inexcusable. The average investor's knowledge is moving in the opposite direction from the amount of cash the average Canadian is investing. *We're putting more money in places we understand less.* A 1980 investment industry study indicated that just 10 percent of adults in the United States had direct contact with securities markets; barely 20 years later, the estimate had risen to 50 percent because more and more Americans were relying on their own investment programs, fuelled by federal government tax incentives, to generate retirement income.[4] Given the cultural and economic similarities between the United States and Canada, and the determination of Canadians to generate a self-sufficient retirement income, the figures in Canada are likely identical. No evidence exists, however, to indicate that the awareness of either Americans or Canadians of the investment industry's operations has risen by nearly the same degree.

You Don't Have to Know How to Drive the Bus. But You Should Know the Route.

The investment industry will publicly dispute but privately admit the following statement: When seeking reasonable long-term growth from your RRSP and assurances that the assets will remain available when you retire, you need to grasp a few logical rules that are unassailable in their effectiveness and will guide you in your relationship with a broker and financial advisor. These rules are proven, they are simple, and they are included in Chapter 12 as part of the rather basic but effective analogy of a road trip. Other people can drive the bus, as it were, but only you should determine the destination, and know the route beforehand.

The investment industry seeks to convince you that you are ignorant of basic investing guidelines, and it is often correct, although it
neglects to add that you don't need an MBA to be able to comprehend
the primary rules of good investing. As a result, you depend on
"professional" guidance for decisions.

Whatever definition of the term "professional" you may
harbour, it probably relates to a person performing a specialized
function in an objective manner. Objectivity, or the lack of it, lies
at the heart of many complaints about the actions of commission-
paid "professional" financial advisors. If your advisor's investment
recommendations influence both the growth of your RRSP and the
income of the advisor, what happens when one conflicts with the
other? How do you suppose the broker resolves that conflict? In
your favour or his?

Or consider this analogy: The vast majority of us have no idea
how a television set works beyond our use of basic controls such as
the on-off switch and volume level. It doesn't matter. We don't need
to understand digital comb filters, magnetic quadra poles, vertical
aperture compensation, or other internal complexities. We just
need to know that a clear picture and sound will arrive when we
turn it on. This ignorance of internal operations would not prevent
us from complaining if the TV set blew up after a few months of
use and no one accepted responsibility for our loss. At the very
least, we would demand a refund and avoid purchasing that brand
of TV in the future. We might also shun the dealer who recommended the set to us.

During the tech market collapse of 2000 and the bear market that
followed, most Canadians watched the value of their RRSP assets
shrink like a TV image when power is lost. Few abandoned their
brokers and financial advisors. Instead, most accepted without question the argument that investment losses are inevitable from time to
time. This is not necessarily a true statement, nor did the losses need

to be as deep and disturbing as they proved to be. RRSP and RRIF owners who silently accepted deep reductions in the value of their investments in common stocks, either directly or within mutual funds, were basically hoodwinked. How? By being convinced that they did not see the entire picture, by permitting their investments to include greater risk than necessary, and by having their trust exploited.

Read the promotional material provided by any full-service brokerage firm or mutual fund company and ask yourself what the underlying message is. *The message is always trust*—trust us to know what is happening in the stock market, trust us to manage your money wisely, trust us to make decisions that you are unqualified to make, and trust the various self-regulatory organizations to look out for your interests. But can you? Too many Canadians have discovered their trust misplaced in everything from their financial advisor to the Canadian legal system. It's time to correct things.

Let's Hear It for Capitalism!

For all of its warts, capitalism, like democracy, remains the best of the available systems. By definition, investors believe in the system and reject, as do I, any treatise for controlled markets. Socialists we are not.

Committed capitalists preach the benefits of a free market, one that exists to make the pursuit of self-interest economically efficient. They neglect to point out that free markets work best when both sides of a deal know the score, and this is where the bright and shiny armour of the investment industry grows rusty. To be blunt, much of the industry does not want you to possess more information than needed to make a sale to you. Remember the adage, "A little knowledge is a dangerous thing"? The investment industry seems to believe that substantial knowledge is even more dangerous—not to you, but to them. Wider knowledge provides wider choices. This may be helpful to you, but it is not generally helpful to much of the investment industry, which prefers to limit your choices.

You may choose to believe that the investment industry exists to make you wealthy. It does not. It exists to build its own wealth.

You may choose to believe that organizations established to monitor the capital markets are dedicated to serving the interests of the small investor. They are not. They are equally concerned about encouraging the entry of corporations into the capital markets and protecting the interests of the various members making up the organization.

You may choose to believe that enforcers of federal and provincial laws will respond to claims of larcenous behaviour such as forgery and the misstatement of personal information with the full weight of the law. They will not. Canada's investment terrain is strewn with the wreckage of clients whose losses due to broker malfeasance were never totally replaced (nor were the brokers themselves punished beyond fines they could, in most cases, easily afford to pay).

Many questionable actions in Canada's investment industry have grown more outrageous and widespread in the years since 1980 as a result of the mounting value of RRSPs, which represent an unprecedented level of investment value in the hands of an extraordinary number of Canadians. The larger the RRSP pot grows, the greater the number of hands dipping into it.

Over 6 million Canadians owned RRSPs or RRIFs in 2005, representing a total value well in excess of $500 billion. In an asset base that large, mistakes are bound to happen. When the assets are entrusted to third parties whose income is dependent on where and how often the assets are directed, rather than how well they perform, the boundary between honest errors and conscious misdeeds grows murky.

"The fox knows many things," the Greek poet Archilochus taught long ago, "but the hedgehog knows one great thing." Archilochus describes the fox as a cunning creature, fleet of foot and mind. The hedgehog, in contrast, is slow and ambling, preferring to mind its own business. The fox knows many ways to ambush the hedgehog, and often tries. The hedgehog knows only how to roll itself into a ball with spikes protruding outward, protecting itself until the fox departs—and it knows how to do this perfectly.

In an industry populated with brilliant, sly, and ambitious investment advisor-foxes, it is essential that RRSP/RRIF owners know how to assemble a diversified portfolio of high-quality stocks, bonds, and mutual funds; why and when to trade them when necessary; and who might be claiming a portion of their investment assets, and by how much. With this much knowledge and a reasonable degree of awareness, you need not fear the foxes.

Without it you are unclothed and unprotected, lacking both the hedgehog's spikes and its talent for using them.

BROKERS AND ADVISORS:
WHOSE MONEY IS IT ANYWAY?

When Sandra Gibson[5] was 25 years old, her father persuaded her to begin investing her money, a policy she followed for the next 35 years. Her father was seeking to teach her financial independence, and he succeeded. Her experience with two brokerage firms produced another lesson.

In the afternoon light of her mid-Toronto living room, the divorcee tells her story with a shifting blend of outrage and humour. Having built an impressive portfolio from an inheritance and earnings during her career in real estate, Sandra Gibson relies on income generated by her investments to support herself. She structured her portfolio to safeguard a sizeable share of her assets during economic downturns, generate cash to cover her living expenses, and provide some degree of growth to account for inflation. There is nothing complex about this recipe—it's Investment 101 stuff.

In 2000, Sandra grew concerned about the private investment counsel she was receiving from the brokerage firm, associated with a large European bank, that was handling her account. "They didn't seem to have any focus to their strategy," she recalls. "At one point they suggested I start investing in German banks, which were doing terribly at the time. When they couldn't provide a rationale, I decided to move on."

A friend suggested she transfer her portfolio to a division of a major bank as a temporary measure while she sought the services of another discretionary portfolio manager. This proved more complex and costly than she expected. "When I informed my previous broker that I was moving my account, they began applying all kinds of fees I had never heard of before, including a thousand-dollar 'closing of relationship' fee. In total they took about $5000 out of my account, just because I chose to move it to another place."

Sandra Gibson's new financial advisor handed her a blank Know Your Client form to record her personal investment goals, level of investment knowledge, and other details. "I signed it on his assurance that he would complete it later," she says ruefully. "I told him I had good, but not sophisticated, investment knowledge. I had never dealt in futures or options, for example. I also stated that my investment goals were preservation of capital and income production, with some growth opportunities."

She grew comfortable with her advisor's warm assurances that he would be looking after her account according to her needs—so comfortable that it was several months before she realized the advisor had moved a substantial portion of her account into call options based on a short-selling strategy.[6] This was not only contrary to her directives but represented the opposite end of the preserve capital/generate income risk spectrum. "I had no experience in short selling," she points out. "It's not something I understand or that I want to be invested in."

Then disaster. "In October 2002, I saw that a substantial number of call options had expired and that I was short a large number of stocks," Sandra says. "The stocks had rallied [risen in price], which meant that I had to buy them at a higher price, and I called the advisor immediately. 'I didn't see the rally coming,' he told me, 'and I wasn't able to get all of my clients out of the market in time.' I said, 'You mean it wasn't physically possible for you to

push all the buttons?' and he said, 'That's right, I couldn't do it.'
He admitted that some buttons had been 'pushed,' but none of
mine were. Then I learned that I could be responsible for covering
all the potential losses in my account—and it came to $700,000.
I went into shock!"

Sandra Gibson's first inclination was to move her account out of
the brokerage as quickly as possible. "But what brokerage would
accept my account with so many bad short positions and such a
large potential shortfall? When the advisor tried to calm me down
by saying the market would soon drop and the short positions
could be covered then, I decided to stay. I didn't have much choice."

Stay she did, but soon after, when the brokerage made a
trading error costing her $4000, she wrote instructions to the
branch manager demanding that the company replace her loss
and instructing the firm that no trades were to take place without
her direct and explicit instructions. This was especially important
because she would be on holiday in Mexico for all of February
2003 at a location without a telephone. "I mentioned that I would
be visiting a nearby internet café every day," Sandra says, "and
provided an email address where I could be reached if any
problem arose."

No contact was made between her and the broker during her
vacation, but when she returned in early March, a stack of
envelopes bearing the brokerage's return address stood waiting for
her. "My heart sank when I saw them because I knew what they
were. They were receipts for transactions I had never requested—
over 20 of them."

Sandra hoped for either an explanation or an apology for the
trades made in direct contradiction to her instructions. She received
neither. "When I called to ask why they had done these trades
after I instructed that none was to be made, the advisor almost
shouted at me. 'I've been busting my ass to put money in your
account, and you can't even understand what I'm doing for you!'

I asked about the short positions I still had, and if I would have to cover them with my own money if the market didn't drop. He told me to forget about it because whatever we lost on one group of trades we would more than make up in another." She shakes her head. "He intimidated me until I finally gave in. I'm sure he wouldn't have spoken to a man that way."

Through several weeks of haggling, Sandra Gibson finally moved her account to a smaller brokerage, where a representative immediately covered her short positions and converted the balance of her account to income trusts and preferred shares in blue-chip stocks—"exactly where I should have been from the beginning."

She sought legal counsel to recover at least a portion of her losses and filed a complaint against the advisor with the Investment Dealers Association. An investigator reported that the advisor claimed Sandra had made several long-distance telephone calls to him while on vacation in Mexico, each instructing him to make the trades she was objecting to. This assertion was easy to prove, or refute, from telephone records, although nothing more was made of it.

Sandra Gibson's experience with lawyers specializing in investment matters has not been any more encouraging. "The first lawyer, a high-profile attorney in these matters, insisted on communicating with me via emails exclusively. When one of my emails went astray he accused me of causing delays. He refused to meet with me and discuss legal procedures, so I decided to move on. I found another lawyer who refused to file a statement of claim, insisting he could negotiate an informal settlement." After more than a year of inaction, she went in search of a third lawyer, which also produced nothing.

Her current lawyer was, in Sandra Gibson's words, "blind-sided" by the brokerage's legal counsel. "She was the first of the lawyers to request and be granted an examination of the brokerage's documents," Sandra explains. "When she studied the facts and made her case to the brokerage based on this new information, the other side agreed to discuss a settlement. They said they were prepared to accept my claimed losses, but they disputed my opportunity losses, which represented money I might have made if my instructions had been followed. A meeting was scheduled to discuss the matter, one that the brokerage insisted I not attend." Nothing was settled at that session.

Sandra refuses to admit defeat. She continues to seek about $400,000 in lost assets due to the broker's actions taken in direct contradiction to her instructions. Her current lawyer, like previous counsel she has retained, is convinced that she has an iron-clad case of advisor negligence (supported by the Investment Dealers Association—see below). The investment firm in question continues to fight a rear-guard action in the expectation that she will simply give up and go away.

Perhaps the most startling aspect of Sandra Gibson's tale concerns the advisor whom she accuses of mishandling her funds and rejecting her instructions in favour of pursuing his own strategies. In mid-2006, following a three-year investigation, the Investment Dealers Association (IDA) agreed with Sandra. So did the advisor himself when he "admitted that during 2003 he engaged in conduct unbecoming ... by conducting his business consistent with the registration of a Portfolio Manager without being registered as such and engaged in discretionary trading in six clients' accounts."[7]

In addition to his mishandling of Sandra Gibson's account, the advisor dickered with other accounts without the clients' knowledge and to his advantage. This would appear to strengthen Sandra's case against the advisor's firm, a funding member of the IDA. Apparently it does not; their own regulating agency declared their guy guilty, but they continue to fight the aggrieved investor tooth and nail.

The advisor, after admitting his wrongdoing, was assessed five penalties by the IDA: a six-month suspension; strict supervision for

12 months following re-registration; an order to rewrite and pass the industry's Conduct and Practices Handbook exam; a $30,000 fine; and "disgorgement" of $28,000 accrued from his clients as a result of his actions.

When Sandra learned of the $28,000 disgorgement she contacted the IDA, pointing out that a portion of that money was hers and asking when it would be returned to her. She was informed that the IDA does not reimburse investors. The ill-gotten $28,000 would flow into IDA coffers and remain there.

"Where there is no possibility of restitution," Paul Bourque, IDA's Senior Vice-President, Member Regulation, points out, "fines and disgorgements are placed in the IDA's discretionary trust fund and are used to offset costs incurred by the Discretionary Hearing Panels or ... for projects that are deemed to be in the public interest."[8] (For more information on IDA rules and policies, including the organization's inability to provide restitution except under extraordinary circumstances, see Chapter 9: SRO or SOL?)

It's a Matter of Who Gets Paid ... and How

Driving much of the changing attitudes of investors toward the brokerage industry is growing concern over the folly and unfairness of the industry's commission-based remuneration system. Stockbrokers, whatever description they might hang on themselves (the industry prefers *registered representatives,* or *RR*), delight in calling themselves professionals. The word suggests more than it defines (the *Oxford English Dictionary* identifies *profession* as "any calling or occupation by which a person habitually makes a living"). Those engaged in helping clients meet a goal or set an investment strategy want us to equate their activities with highly skilled activities such as those practised in the medical profession. But the analogy isn't a good one. How much trust would you place in a physician who earned his or her income from commissions paid by pharmaceutical companies whose medication the physician prescribed? How confident would you be that the doctor's recommendations were directed toward your physical well-being rather than his or her own financial health? Yet this is how the brokerage system works.

The commission-based brokerage industry does everything it can to conceal its means of making money, both during and for years after the transaction. Search any full-service brokerage website and explore the library of promotional material it distributes, looking for information on the commission the brokerage will charge to purchase or sell securities on your behalf. There is none, although the commission you paid will appear on your statement *after* the fact. Nor is a full-service stockbroker likely to discuss competitive management expense ratios (MERs), the fees that mutual funds charge for handling your investment, much of which is returned to your broker for steering you into the fund. (I'll deal with that mess in the next chapter.)

"Salespeople in other industries earn a living from commissions," brokers may mutter in defence. Buy a car, a refrigerator, or a stereo system and a portion of the purchase price will likely be kicked back to the person who sold it to you. Brokers, of course, don't like being compared to car salespeople, and it may be unfair—to the person selling the car. Cars come with warranties, and if the salesperson talks you into spending a few thousand bucks on a new Whizzmobile with all-power equipment, you have some assurance that the thing will function at least until its warranty expires. Three weeks after a commissioned broker talks you into dropping a major portion of your RRSP into the *Standback & Duck* Emerging Markets Venture Fund, promising it will generate long-term growth for your retirement, and it sinks like an anchor, will you have the same opportunity to set things straight? You may think you have, through organizations such as the Investment Dealers Association, your provincial securities commission, or the civil courts. But plan on taking precious little hope with you if you go, as I'll examine later.

Simply put, the system works in favour of brokers and against unsophisticated investors. Here's how.

Imagine you're buying paint for your living room. You enter a paint dealer or hardware store and ask for semi-gloss white latex paint. Pretty specific. Assume that the paint salesperson turns to the shelf where the paints are displayed and finds two brands of paint that fit your description, both similarly priced. One, however, earns the store $10 in profit, the other, $15 in profit. Can you expect the salesperson to choose the $15-profit brand? Of course you can. Can you blame him? Hardly.

Brokers will claim that a good paint salesperson asks questions about the customer's needs before choosing the brand of paint, and that may be so. Substantial evidence exists, however, that many brokers follow the biggest-margin rule in choosing investments for their clients. How else to explain that the largest mutual funds, in terms of assets, offer the largest returns for brokers who recommend and sell them, and rarely the best returns for the clients who buy them? Or to put it another way: *Why are the most effective mutual funds, as measured by long-term returns to their investors, often the smallest in total assets under management?*

Industry defenders will say that it's easier for a small fund to generate profits, which is not true at all—a lot of small funds are dogs. The truth is that successful funds often pay no commissions to brokers, so the brokers never recommend them. Mutual funds managed by companies such as McLean Budden, Saxon, and Phillips, Hager & North consistently score above-average in long-term returns for investors, yet are rarely, if ever, recommended by brokers, *because these funds are focused on making the investor wealthier, rather than the advisor.*

Brokers also argue that they have a responsibility to assist clients in avoiding inappropriate high-risk investments. They have, and the best ones do. But within the industry, broker performance is measured less by the smiles on the faces of clients and more by the size of the sales commissions generated. Like it or not, full-service commissioned brokers are salespeople, and salespeople are pressured to meet ever-higher sales targets, generating more commissions for themselves and more income for the brokerage.

The problems with this approach multiply with every success. Once a broker or advisor achieves recognition as a Big Producer, she is cut a good deal of slack when it comes to discipline and supervision. You don't quickly fire a broker pulling in a million dollars in commissions each year, and too much wrist slapping for problems such as sloppy paperwork may drive her out of the firm and into the arms of another brokerage. In case after case, high-production brokers and advisors charged with malfeasance ranging from recommending inappropriate investments to out-and-out theft from a client's account were treated with such partiality by management that complaints and concerns regarding their actions were often deflected or minimized.

Losers Have No Friends in the Investment Industry

Michael Holoday, one of the most infamous of Canadian scam artists in the industry, rose to membership in the Chairman's Club of his large brokerage within three years of obtaining his trading licence and several years before his 30th birthday. Only the top 5 percent of all brokers at Midland Walwyn, Holoday's employer at the time, earned this recognition, yet no one seriously questioned how Holoday achieved so much so soon. When questions about his methods of building client assets and relationships were asked from time to time, at least one member of the company's board of directors shrugged his shoulders and admitted that he did not understand Holoday's system. No one chose to dig farther, because no one wanted to upset a million-dollar-a-year producer, and Holoday was permitted to continue dipping his fingers into his clients' assets. By the time the industry stumbled onto his tricks, over $20 million had passed through his hands and vanished.[9]

Brokers argue that Holoday and others are anomalies—exceptions that prove the rule about investors needing the wisdom and resources of honest brokers. Admittedly, the honest brokers easily outnumber Michael Holoday and his ilk. Unfortunately, the brokerage industry's definition of honesty is more dependent on what the broker fails to tell the client than on information provided to the client.

Should clients demand straight answers to tough questions when a broker makes an investment recommendation? The brokerage industry agrees they should. But this effectively negates the trust between broker and client. *If the broker's role is to assist in building the client's assets in a manner that reflects the client's objectives and tolerance for risk, why should it be necessary to grill the broker about suitability and alternatives?* Second opinions may be advisable where major surgery is proposed or a serious disease has been diagnosed, but rarely does the outcome affect the income of the physician or surgeon. Seeking a second opinion on a personal medical matter may be considered prudent, but any attempt to obtain an opinion of one advisor's recommendations from another broker is likely to infuriate the first broker and delight the source of the second opinion (who will almost always criticize the first broker's strategy).

The other factor at play here is the exasperated response of advisors to tough questions from clients, described in classic fashion by Sandra Gibson. Clients are often caught in a no man's land between being blamed for not digging far enough into broker actions when they fail to ask questions, and being accused of not appreciating the hard work of their broker when the same questions are posed. Too many advisors are guilty of bullying their clients whenever the advisor's recommendations are seriously questioned.

Do not expect the industry to provide satisfactory and timely support as a result of inappropriate investment advice provided by your licensed financial advisor/broker/registered representative. Investigations are slow, decisions are slower, penalties are light, and any replacement of the losses suffered will be both rare and stingy. The lesson is clear: The best way to protect your investment assets is to take charge of their care and assume limited reliance on the systems and measures provided by the industry.

At the brokerage level, several devices exist as evidence of the industry's concern for investor protection. They may be well meaning, but their effectiveness is determined more by the individual investor's diligence than by their mechanics. If your RRSP or RRIF is held at a brokerage, you may believe that various means, including those below, are in place to protect your investment. In reality, they offer more protection for the brokerage than for you.

The Know Your Client Form: Not Exactly Show and Tell All investments can be categorized as suitable or unsuitable, supplemented by some absolute dogs. The measure of each investment's suitability depends on the investor's economic status, long-term needs, expectations of return, and investment knowledge. A wealthy person with several thousand disposable dollars may choose to spend it on a weekend at a casino or on shares in a high-risk gold mine venture. Either action would be suitable. But the gold mine should never represent a major portion of the average Canadian's RRSP investment, especially if the plan's owner is 40 years of age or older.

Penny mining stocks are an obvious example of an unsuitable RRSP investment. Others are more difficult to determine for inexperienced investors but are readily apparent to licensed brokers—or should be. The Know Your Client (KYC) form is designed to establish your suitability for various investment options and confirm that the investments your broker recommends to you are in fact appropriate.

Investors may be required to complete and sign a KYC form provided by the broker or advisor. Brokerage staff can read KYCs like a road map, evaluating net worth, gross annual income, investment objectives, risk tolerance, and investment knowledge, which all function as guideposts toward suitable investments. In theory, this evaluation process is true. In practice, it is not always applied.

Opening a brokerage account involves signing a multitude of documents, most drafted in dense legalese. The KYC document may be portrayed as just another piece of paperwork, with the new client cajoled to sign a blank form, leaving the advisor to fill in the details. Since the KYC form does not commit the client to an obvious financial obligation, many clients add their signatures as instructed. In a legal sense, it is foolish to sign any document without reading and understanding it. Practically, it is a perfectly reasonable act, and thousands of KYCs in brokerage files contain information that bears little resemblance to the client's real situation. It's all a matter of trust, remember?

While fudged data on a KYC form does not represent a financial obligation by the client to the broker, it provides the broker with the investment equivalent of a get-out-of-jail-free card. Financial advisors with visions of Ferrari in their eyes may be tempted to insert a fictitious description on a blank KYC form bearing the investor's signature, indicating the investor claimed to be sophisticated and to have substantial wealth and other qualities justifying high-risk investments. If a client discovers her savings have been stripped almost bare through unsuitable investments justified by such claims on the form, cries of "I expected someone else to fill in the details" will not carry a great deal of weight or sympathy among regulators or judges.

In recent years, brokerages have instigated the practice of forwarding copies of KYC forms to investors after they were reviewed by someone in a position of responsibility, such as the branch manager or the brokerage's compliance officer. In this manner, investors have an opportunity to sound an alarm when the information bears little resemblance to their actual status. An investor receiving a copy of a KYC form in this manner owes it to herself to set aside the trust factor and review the information. Anything at odds with her situation, especially information relating to net worth, gross income, risk tolerance, and investment objectives, should be reported and corrected before investment decisions are made.

The Prospectus, Also Known as How I Cured My Insomnia Law dictates that you cannot purchase new securities without being provided with a prospectus (unless the securities are exempt from this requirement). Reading a prospectus means absorbing several pages of dense language printed in small type. Or, as former fund salesman and current critic of the investment industry Cyril Fleming put it, "It's like handing me a document in Greek and when I complain that I can't read it, telling me to consult a Greek/English dictionary." About the only message you'll absorb from a prospectus is that investing is hopelessly complex and should be attempted only by a professional or in the presence of one—that is, a licensed broker or advisor.

You have 48 hours after receiving a prospectus to change your mind and ask for your money back. There are people in this world who have amputated their own limbs when necessary. There are also people without a law degree who can fathom the meaning of every phrase and intent in a mutual fund prospectus with one reading. I suspect the numbers of each are about equal.

From a practical standpoint, you need address only two key elements in any mutual fund prospectus.

What are the investment objectives of the fund? Is it to invest in Tibetan microbiological ventures when you agreed to purchase units in a conservative Canadian blue-chip value fund? Is it to generate income when you thought you were investing in long-term capital growth? If the description does not match the investment strategy you understood your advisor to have recommended, call within 48 hours of receiving the prospectus and ask for clarification.

What are the fund's charges and fees? Is a sales commission being paid to your advisor? If so, how much is it, and was it negotiable? Does the fund waive a front-end commission for a back-end deferred sales charge (DSC)? Were you aware of this? Do you agree to it? How much is the management expense ratio (MER), the amount of your investment that is withdrawn by the mutual fund management firm each year? Both DSCs and MERs represent money out of your RRSP, and are detailed in the next chapter.

Discretionary Trading: Close Your Eyes, Cover Your Ears, and Hang On Never relinquish the right to approve decisions on buying and selling assets in your RRSP except under extraordinary circumstances. The decision should remain yours alone, and you should agree to transactions only after your advisor provides sufficient rationale and reveals any costs involved. Brokers and advisors who perform transactions without consultation or approval are engaging in discretionary trading, a practice that is illegal unless a signed agreement is provided by the client.

The opportunity for a broker or advisor to trade in a client's account without prior consultation opens the door to the possibility of churning an account—buying and selling common shares, mutual fund units, bonds, and other investments over and over for the sole purpose of generating income for the broker through the commissions earned from each transaction. Evidence that trades in your account have been conducted without consultation and approval should be presented to the branch manager of the firm handling your account, along with a demand that the practice cease and any losses incurred as a result of the trading be reimbursed. If the brokerage refuses to do so, seek legal counsel. Even if the brokerage replaces your losses, consider changing firms. Churning is theft, and why should you trust anyone who has stolen from you?

Compliance Officers: They're Either With You or Against You (Hint: They're Not Always With You)

Every investment firm boasts a compliance officer or, if the firm is substantial enough, several of them, dedicated to ensuring that certain rules of investment policy are followed. This may be reassuring to investors who like the idea of someone watching over their accounts and the actions of their broker or advisor. It should not be. The primary role of compliance officers in a brokerage or securities trading firm is to protect the firm, not the assets of clients.

The Investment Dealers Association (IDA), the industry's self-regulating organization, defines the role of a compliance officer as "a support function, much like a legal department, and not a business line function. In the normal course, the Compliance Department does not have direct authority over line personnel such as those in Sales and Trading." And later: "Investigations which include a review of the supervision of business functions may not directly involve Compliance Officers, whose role is to advise and support the Executives responsible for those functions."[10] Nothing in the description addresses the need to protect individual investors.

Obviously, if a compliance officer is made aware of actions that appear to conflict with the client's needs or directions, he will—or should—investigate, applying cease-and-desist rules if necessary. On the knife-edge of decision making, however, the compliance officer's actions will be directed toward avoiding damage to the firm rather than damage to the client's interests. Often, of course, these amount to the same thing. But not always.

When clients of Michael Holoday called the compliance officer at Holoday's brokerage firm to complain about problems in their account statements, their queries were directed back to the broker. In retrospect, this was like complaining about a fox in the henhouse and being told the fox would fix things. The same compliance officer, once Holoday's actions became apparent, eventually alerted the police to his discoveries, and justice began its slow and agonizing process.

Had the compliance officer acted on the clients' behalf rather than that of the brokerage firm when questions were first raised, Holoday's scams would have ended months earlier.

Things have changed since then, the industry assures us. Perhaps. But the principal role of the compliance officer remains to protect the firm's interests first.

Monthly Statements: They Are Not Junk Mail Think of each RRSP statement as a weather vane, revealing in which direction the wind is blowing, and how strongly. You are looking for confirmation of any transactions that occurred, evidence of transactions you do not recall approving, fees or charges against your account you do not understand, and the general status of your plan, indicating either reassuring growth or disturbing losses. Losses should not necessarily trigger a call to your broker or advisor. During the extended bear market of 1999–2003, even clients of the brightest, most dedicated advisors suffered losses in equity-based mutual funds and individual stocks. In situations such as this, the key is not whether you lose but how much the losses stack up against your personal investment strategy and the general investment environment. A quick glance at the financial pages of a newspaper will provide a basic benchmark. Has the Toronto Stock Exchange dropped by 5 percent over the past month? If so, a 3 percent loss in your Canadian equities is not something to fret about.

You don't need to scan your statement like a beady-eyed tax collector studying a corporate balance sheet. You do need to take it seriously, check for any surprises, and file it away at least until your next review with your broker or advisor.

Comfort Letters: Do Not Take Comfort in Receiving One Unsolicited communication from your broker should be welcome from time to time, with the exception of a happiness, or comfort, letter. Such a letter may appear on the letterhead of your broker or advisor, the brokerage branch manager, or the compliance officer, and its wording will change according to the purpose of the person sending it. Somewhere in the body of the letter, however, you will discover one or more of these queries:

- Are you satisfied with the performance of your account and the service provided by your broker or advisor?
- Do you understand that risk is associated with all investing activities?
- Do you review your financial statements on a regular basis?
- If you had a question or comment about your account, would you contact your broker directly?
- Are you aware that certain charges may be applied to your account according to the trading activity, "etc."?

The letter may request you to acknowledge its contents, sign your name at the bottom, and return it to the brokerage as soon as possible. The brokerage will likely pay the postage.

Such a letter should bring neither comfort nor happiness to you. Instead, it should set red lights flashing and sirens screaming. Happiness/comfort letters might better be termed trouser letters, because they are designed to cover the advisor's ass. Their arrival is an almost certain indicator that something may be awry in your account, and your acknowledgment of the account's status, confirmed with your signature, could enable the firm and its staff to successfully defend itself against charges of malfeasance should the value of your RRSP drop through the floor.

What kinds of things might prompt a brokerage to issue such a letter? Any of the following:

- Excessive trading in your account, suggesting churning
- Substantial losses, beyond those suffered by the market in general

- The presence of unsuitable high-risk investments
- A dramatic change in investment strategy
- The opening of a margin account or other activities suggesting unprecedented levels of risk
- High commissions and fees withdrawn from your account balance

Your best response to a happiness/comfort letter is a refusal to sign it. Instead, telephone the sender and ask the following questions, noting his or her response:

- What prompted you to send me this letter?
- What is there about my account that is causing concern?
- Have I suffered unusual losses?
- Am I trading too much?
- Are the commissions too high for my account?
- Is either the brokerage or my broker/advisor being investigated?
- Did you send this letter to other clients?
- Is the activity in my account consistent with my investment objectives?
- By the way—what are my investment objectives according to your records?

Once again: Never sign any document relating to your account without fully understanding its meaning and implications, because such a document is almost certainly designed to provide the brokerage with protection somewhere down the road. In one of the most egregious examples of employing documents as weapons, Michael Holoday asked a client to sign a letter praising Holoday's performance, then used the letter to allay concerns at a brokerage where he sought employment. A year later, when Holoday's fraudulent activities were revealed, that brokerage sued the client for $10 million, arguing that the letter bearing the client's signature represented 50 percent of its decision to hire Holoday. Since the brokerage was claiming a potential

$20 million loss, the brokerage claimed that its client owed the firm $10 million. Welcome to the investment industry.

If you should encounter a situation in which you believe you have a strong case for legal action, be aware of Armand Laflamme and Sandra Gibson, Michael Holoday's aggrieved clients, and several others yet to be encountered in this book. Their experience suggests that the tactics employed by brokers/advisors and their firms, via their legal counsel, are as relentless and unyielding as any prosecutor/defender encounter in a first-degree murder trial. If you believe that unauthorized actions by your broker/advisor have cost you substantial assets, and that you have a strong legal case to seek replacement of those losses, understand this going in: While you, as an ill-treated investor, may be playing for a tie—the return of your claimed losses—the investment firm will be playing for a kill. For the most part, the goal of investment firms is not only to avoid making restitution but also to effectively silence the voice of aggrieved clients and maintain the firms' own lily-white virginal image. How else, after all, could they dare attract new clients with the entreaty "Trust us"?

The Gospel According to John De Goey

How can clients believe that their best interests are being addressed once they understand that the primary role of the compliance officer is to protect the brokerage, and a major goal of management is to motivate the advisors to generate income via commissions from trades within client accounts?

A solution may be at hand, encroaching into the industry with all the speed of a glacier and none of its power. Among its more vocal proponents is an articulate financial advisor named John J. De Goey. De Goey boasts the familiar alphabet of professional qualifications behind his name, but that's where the similarity with the majority of brokers and advisors ends. For one thing, his resumé includes a stint with Consumer and Corporate Affairs Canada rather than the banking or accounting background most advisors bring to the job. This experience undoubtedly influenced an even more remarkable difference between him and other financial advisors: He wants to see the commission-based system replaced with direct fees charged separately to clients, and the sooner the better.

"Financial advisors call themselves professionals," De Goey says in his enthusiastic and articulate manner, "but they are not. Most are commission-based sales agents masquerading as professionals. Name one true profession that depends entirely on commissions paid by the products or services they recommend. There is none, and the industry has to start admitting it."[11]

"The current system is inherently unfair to the investor," he explains. "Consider mutual funds. Some pay no commissions, but good luck getting a commission-based advisor to recommend one, no matter how well it fits your needs. Others pay varying rates of commissions and incentives. How can an advisor claim to be unbiased in his or her recommendations when their decision has a direct and substantial impact on their income?" In that situation, De Goey suggests, who can blame advisors and brokers for making recommendations that benefit them most?

The motivation for an advisor to recommend investments that suit the advisor's needs rather than the client's is strengthened by the lack of any legal recourse for the investor. An advisor who recommends high-risk investments, such as derivatives, risks being accused of providing inappropriate advice, and both the advisor and the firm management could be subjected to fines (but not always—see Chapters 9 and 10). An advisor who proposes a Canadian equity-based mutual fund that charges high management fees and kicks back a large proportion to the advisor, rather than another fund with superior performance but no kickbacks, risks nothing and gains substantially.

While De Goey hoped to stir up a hornet's nest of industry controversy with his 2003 book, *The Professional Financial Advisor*, a year after his book's appearance there was still no stampede by advisors toward the new investment Jerusalem. Why not? "It's like Christianity," De Goey smiles, picking up on the analogy. "Everybody wants to go to heaven but nobody wants to die first."

Say, Just Where *Are* Those Customers' Yachts?

It remains to be seen whether or not De Goey will succeed in dragging his colleagues toward genuine professional status. He may be riding a wave after all. As long as New York State Attorney-General Eliot Spitzer grabs headlines with his crusade against Wall Street malefactors, and millions of Canadians grow aware of the manner in which the investment odds are stacked against them, the problem will not vanish beneath cries of anguish from some brokers and advisors that their financial future is being threatened.

More than 60 years ago, Fred Schwed authored a critical look at Wall Street in a book titled *Where Are the Customers' Yachts?* The book has remained in print since, and until the answer is provided by brokers and advisors whose dreams of financing their yacht purchases are driven by hidden fees and commissions paid for by their clients, neither the book nor scepticism about their "profession" is likely to vanish.

Mutual Funds:
You Win, They Win;
You Lose, They Still Win

Beth Green* personifies many of the clichéd qualities people
attribute to residents of Prince Edward Island—close family ties,
a sense of trust, and an independent nature. When her 20-year
marriage collapsed some time ago, she moved from Quebec
back to PEI where she operated a bed-and-breakfast and
remained near her mother. In the mid-1990s, she began assuming
responsibility for her mother's modest investment portfolio,
working with a financial advisor at the brokerage arm of a
major chartered bank.

Upon the departure of this advisor in 2000, a new advisor
based in Charlottetown assumed responsibility for the portfolio. By
this time, Beth's mother was approaching 90 years of age, and
both she and her daughter determined that net monthly payments
of $800 were to be withdrawn from the remaining asset base of a
little more than $70,000.

The new advisor suggested the entire amount be invested in
three mutual funds: CI Global GIF (Guaranteed Investment Fund);
CI International GIF; and BPI Global Equity GIF, whose assets were

---

*A pseudonym

merged with the CI Global fund in November 2005. All are categorized as DSC (deferred sales charge) and segregated funds.

"She explained that these were segregated funds," Beth Green recalls. "According to her, they offered 'full downside protection and a return on the total investment less withdrawals after a set period of time'. When I asked what this meant, I was told that after 10 years the value of the funds would be at least $70,000 less the value of any withdrawals. So, if my mother withdrew $35,000 during that period, at least $35,000 would remain in the account."

It soon became apparent, however, that the account's value was depleting far faster than could be explained by the withdrawals. Beth noted that $2,326 had been withdrawn from the account to pay deferred sales charges on funds previously held in the portfolio—a fee that the new advisor had not disclosed. Statements from Transamerica Life Canada—not the brokerage with whom Beth believed she had been dealing—indicated substantial reductions in the value of the account, well beyond the amount represented by the cash withdrawals. Instead of growing in value, the new funds were rapidly shrinking.

"I began questioning the wisdom of the funds," she recalls, "and the only response the advisor could give was 'I share your concern.' She never offered a solution. Finally, in the summer of 2005 when the account's guaranteed value had dropped to barely $18,000, I became openly angry with her. That's when the advisor suggested that the poorly performing funds could be exchanged for other CI funds without penalty. I directed her to do so, but it took another three months for this to happen, and all the while the funds kept losing money! That's when I decided to launch a complaint."

The complaint began with a call to the Toronto head office of the brokerage, where a representative in the client relations department suggested Beth express her concerns in a letter, assuring her that the matter would be resolved "within two or three weeks." On November 2, 2005, Beth mailed an articulate and concise letter to the Manager, Client Relations, as directed. "About four weeks later I received a telephone call and spent two hours in an interview—I thought of it more like the grilling of a police witness—asking me every possible detail of the situation," she says. "Then I waited a further two months for a reply."

The firm's reply, reflecting only the views of the broker who had proposed the three CI funds, was replete with rejections of Beth's complaint and riddled with outright errors. Among its claims:

- *Beth Green and her mother selected the CI funds.* "Neither my mother nor I have enough knowledge to do that," Beth says. "They were not 'selected' by us. [The advisor] is the one who recommended these highly volatile funds for an elderly person. We trusted her professional expertise, but they [the funds] were not suitable at all."

- *The CI funds recommended by the advisor were segregated "because they offered the additional security of principal guarantees ..."* Of all the investment vehicles available, none is less suited for making periodic withdrawals than segregated funds, which are essentially an insurance product costing substantially more than identical non-segregated funds. (For details on segregated funds and their inappropriateness for RRSP investments, see Chapter 7, "A Guide to Investment Divorce.") These were also deferred sales charge (DSC) funds, which exert penalties for withdrawals over a five- to seven-year period. "Knowing we planned to make withdrawals," Beth notes, "it's obvious that the advisor did not perform due diligence in ensuring my understanding of the issues involved. Surely the Client Relations Manager could see that."

- *Fees, based on the DSC nature of the CI mutual funds, appeared in the account statements.* Since no objection to these charges was raised at the time, the brokerage claimed, the advisor assumed that Ms. Green and her elderly mother understood and approved them.

In every instance where Beth's concerns conflicted with the claims of the firm's advisor, the advisor's recollections were given full weight and Beth's statements were discounted. Repeatedly, the brokerage's response notes, "According to [advisor's name]'s notes ...," "[advisor's name] recalls ...," and "According to her...." Nowhere in the letter was the question of the appropriateness of segregated DSC funds for a 90-year-old woman evaluated. "So much for an impartial appraisal," Beth notes dryly.

"We believe [the advisor's] recommendations were suitable based on the financial goals you expressed to her," the letter concluded. "We thank you for the opportunity to investigate and respond to your concerns."

Beth refused to concede. She wrote to the Attorney General of PEI, who replied that they were forwarding the material to the Investment Dealers Association (IDA).

She also contacted the Ontario Securities Commission (OSC), because the brokerage head office is in Ontario and the OSC is considered the prime regulatory authority. The OSC directed her to the IDA, to the Ombudsman for Banking Services and Investments (OBSI) and—surprise!—to the PEI Securities Commission (PEISC).

The IDA suggested that she contact the OBSI.

OBSI stated they would not investigate the matter until all of the other regulators—IDA, OSC, and PEISC—had completed their evaluation.

Standing defiantly at the centre of the circle of finger-pointing, Beth kept applying pressure on the brokerage. On March 13, 2006, she was informed that her complaint had "entered the queue" to be assessed by the parent bank's ombudsman, and she should expect to hear from them within 30 days. More than 60 days later, she was informed, "... our office has now commenced our investigation and review of your file. We will forward our findings and a decision to you as soon as possible."

During the last week of June 2006, two events occurred: A letter from the ombudsman arrived, rejecting Beth Green's claim again; and an advertisement appeared in PEI newspapers announcing the appointment of her mother's investment advisor, the same woman who had recommended the disastrous portfolio, to the position of Vice-President. The ombudsman's lengthy letter continued to assign all responsibility for any inappropriateness of the investments to Beth and her mother. In the ombudsman's letter, the advisor's role is depicted as little more than a stenographer's ("She discussed ...," "She went over ...") and the principal decision-making task is assigned to Beth Green ("You completed the contract ...," "... you requested ...," "... you chose ...," "It was your decision ...").

In July 2006, Beth turned to the last resort, the Ombudsman for Banking Services and Investments (OBSI). On the basis of the advisor's recommendation of segregated funds—considered an insurance and not an investment product—OBSI first referred her to Canadian Life and Health Insurance Ombudservice (CLHIO). Only when investor advocate Ken Kivenko intervened on her behalf did OBSI agree, with some reluctance, to evaluate the case.

"I don't expect the losses in my mother's account to be replaced," Beth Green concedes. "I at least want the advisor to be reprimanded for providing totally inappropriate advice, and for the brokerage to concede her error. But that may be too much to hope for."

Regrettably, the experience of Beth Green and her mother is repeated time and again within the investment industry, usually following a six-step progression:

1. Client states objectives to the investment professional.
2. Investment professional proposes specific vehicles to meet these goals.
3. The vehicles are instruments such as segregated mutual funds with a deferred sales charge, investing in high-risk sectors (technology, emerging markets, and similar fringe areas).
4. When volatile investments begin losing money at a substantial rate, the client's concerns are minimized ("I share your concern ..." or "Just be patient ...").
5. The value of the investor's portfolio shrinks to the point where the client questions the wisdom of the advisor's recommendations and the appropriateness of the chosen investments.
6. The client's complaints are rejected because he or she approved the professional's recommendations.

Is that the case here? Clearly it is, based on an examination of the funds proposed for Beth Green's mother who, remember, was approaching 90 years of age and wanted to make systematic withdrawals from her small portfolio.

All three funds proposed by the advisor have similar characteristics:

- Their stated investment objectives are "to obtain maximum long term capital growth."[12] Long-term capital growth is a questionable objective for a 90-year-old woman, especially one seeking regular cash withdrawals.
- The managers of these funds favour volatile technology-based companies, a curious mix for someone whose risk level and investment horizon are understandably restricted.
- They are segregated, making them suitable in some instances as an insurance instrument but totally inappropriate as a means of generating cash flow.

- They include a deferred sales charge (DSC), meaning that money withdrawn from the funds before the expiry of a fixed period is subject to penalty.
- Their shoddy performance explains their unpopularity and resultant small size (CI International GIF had barely $7 million in assets). Over five years between May 31, 2001, and May 31, 2006, the CI Global GIF averaged an *annual loss* of 3.63 percent. CI International GIF averaged an *annual loss* of 4.07 percent during the same period.
- Fees and expenses withdrawn from fund assets to cover CI's operating costs and profit explain at least part of the funds' poor level of returns. In 2003, for example, CI withdrew 4.99 percent from the BPI Global Equity GIF to cover the fund manager's costs and the company's profit. As a result, the fund generated gross returns of 8.3 percent but investors were left with barely 3 percent of that amount.

Ken Kivenko, an investor advocate and publisher of a mutual funds newsletter, scoffs at the suggestion that this portfolio was suitable for an elderly woman desiring substantial monthly withdrawals. "This is not a well-structured portfolio for a senior," he points out, "since the allocation is 100 percent equity with no cash or fixed income securities. This 100 percent segregated-fund portfolio is designed for high risk and volatility. And why was $2,326 withdrawn from the account? Was it to cover DSC costs on old funds before the new ones were purchased? Wouldn't it have been more beneficial to the client for the advisor to move funds within the same family, which can normally be done without paying a penalty?"

The False Mystery of Mutual Funds

For 60 years after their introduction, mutual funds were mysterious playthings of the investment-savvy and the idle rich. Most people understood that common stocks were shares in a public corporation; owning one share out of a million available meant you owned a similar portion of the actual company (or, more correctly, of the company's publicly available capitalization), as well as a portion of profits declared as dividends. Investing money in the right company at the right time promised better opportunities for real wealth in the long term than salting pennies away in a bank account. It still does. But for the sometime-investor focusing on her RRSP as the principal investment opportunity in her life, stocks in public companies carry the aura of roulette tables and shell games.

The challenge for small investors was deciding what companies' shares to buy, how much to pay for them, and when to sell them. Most people lack the time, inclination, and knowledge to perform these tasks effectively, and mutual funds solve the problem by pooling money from thousands of investors into one professionally managed operation. For a fee, known as the management expense ratio, or MER, a fund manager makes these decisions and his success is measured by the growth or decline of the fund's value over time. The MER is applied to the total amount of all money invested in the fund and subtracted on a daily basis over the calendar year. A MER of 2.5 percent applied to a $100 million fund—a rather small fund today—yields $2.5 million to the fund manager annually.

When you invest in a mutual fund, you purchase a number of units at the current market price. A $10,000 investment in a fund whose units are valued at $10 buys you 1000 units. As the total value of the fund increases or decreases, the value of each individual unit rises and falls accordingly. At each year-end, funds distribute profits as extra units. The profits are generated by a rise in the market value of the companies that the fund has invested in, by the dividends paid to the shareholders (mutual funds that own stocks are shareholders), or both. Instead of increasing the value of individual units, distributions increase the number of units in the same proportion. Thus, should the mutual fund described above yield a 10 percent profit in one year, your $10,000 investment might now represent 1100 units valued at $10 each, not 1000 units valued at $11.[13]

Mutual funds remained exotic to traditionally conservative Canadians for years, in part because they were sold by the same brokers who traded stocks. Most Canadians, especially those with RRSPs, chose to save rather than invest, treating stocks and bonds as mysterious alien devices requiring special skills, inside information, and perhaps even a degree of larceny. The vaults of the chartered banks bulged with cash deposits in savings accounts that paid a fixed interest rate, were at least partially guaranteed, and could be accessed with the stroke of a pen on a withdrawal form, all because mutual funds made people uncomfortable.

Even with growing participation in RRSPs through the 1970s and into the 1980s, Canadians still preferred the dull certainty of daily interest savings accounts and guaranteed investment certificates (GICs) over the baffling vagueness of mutual funds. In 1987, Canadians invested barely $20 billion, less than $850 per capita, in mutual funds. Yet 13 years later, well over $400 billion was sitting in Canadian mutual funds, representing $15,525 for every man, woman, and child in the country.[14] What happened?

The original $20 billion grew as a result of an increase in the value of equity markets over the years, but this growth was nowhere near the 2000 percent increase represented by mutual fund values. Instead, four loosely connected occurrences in 1987 boosted the natural spirit of free enterprise to produce what some observers describe as a boon to retirement-bound Canadians, and what others consider an investment device worthy of a Frankenstein.

Four Horsemen of the Mutual Fund Invasion

The infamous stock market crash of October 19, 1987, represents a watershed point in the story. Black Monday, as it was tagged, marked history's largest single-day drop in North American stock market values, when prices fell 22 percent. The resulting chaos and paper-based carnage generated headlines and commentary that echoed long after market prices began recovering their previous levels. Canadians who had not invested in equities to that point grew aware that substantial money had been lost in one day, but they could not ignore that the same losers appeared to be recovering their losses rather quickly.

It was no great distance from there to the concept of earning similar levels of wealth while reducing the chance of losing it in a repeat of Black Monday. The idea gained strength when pundits began mouthing assurances that there would be no repeat of that event, blamed for the most part on pre-programmed computer trading. Changing the computer programs would reduce the chance of such catastrophic losses in the future without limiting opportunities for growth, an industry statement that novices heeded with great interest.

The year 1987 also marked the 40th birthday of the first wave of baby boomers. Many things happen to people when they turn 40, and not all of them are necessarily bad. The idea of retiring while retaining your health, both mental and physical, grows more appealing with every day beyond the age of 40. One of the most successful marketing campaigns in Canadian history, London Life's Freedom 55 theme, launched in the late 1980s, consisted of two messages to the early boomers: You are just 15 years away from early retirement, and, How are you going to accumulate the money to enjoy it? Not with GICs and savings accounts, that's for sure. There had to be a better way, and so the boomers began studying alternatives more closely.

Event number three in 1987 was marked by the deregulation in Canada of four interlinked services: banks, trust companies, insurance companies, and stockbrokers. Until then, each industry had been effectively isolated from the others, with the scope of the services it could offer restricted by regulations. Banks did not deal in equity investments; trust companies could not make personal loans; only licensed brokers could sell insurance; and stockbrokers were the financial equivalent of the neighbourhood drugstore, trading investment products for cash. Deregulation of banking, insurance, and investments produced many changes to the face of the country, but in a dollars and cents measure none had a greater impact than the opportunity for chartered banks and trust companies to provide and promote equity investment opportunities, sold as mutual funds first through their own branches and later through their own brokerage companies.

Banking deregulation altered the public's perception of mutual funds almost overnight. One day they were considered mysterious playthings of the wealthy, the next day they were being discussed by the same smiling folks you met when you made a deposit in your chequing account, or paid your telephone bill, or shyly inquired about a loan to buy a new car. The structure of mutual funds hadn't changed, for the most part, but the method of marketing them had. By the late 1980s, every chartered bank in Canada was promoting its own family of funds, encouraging clients to move their money out of GICs and savings accounts and into the funds. It was tempting, promising, and painless.

Mutual funds were no longer intimidating. Were there any more solid, secure, and trustworthy institutions in the world than Canadian chartered banks, which retained at least a vestige of the same prudent and conservative philosophies of the dour Scots who founded most of them? If banks were offering mutual funds, could they be that risky? And since mutual funds are favoured by the rich, can there be any better way to retire at 55 and spend the winter walking a beach in Florida? Not bloody likely!

With the banks marketing their own house brands of funds, independent fund managers such as Trimark, Mackenzie, Templeton,

AGF, and others stepped up their sales promotion programs, all aimed at RRSP owners. The banks might have the consumers' confidence, but the independent fund managers had the performance figures and the marketing savvy to grab the attention of investors. Banks not only were new to the mutual fund game, they were also conservative. This made consumers feel rather more comfortable with the bank funds, but comfort eventually was edged aside by greed. Where the banks were promoting annual returns of 10 to 12 percent, the stronger independent funds were boasting returns of 15 to 20 percent. Bigger returns meant faster RRSP growth, and faster growth meant edging closer to the beach walked by those smug and satisfied retirees in the Freedom 55 TV commercials.

The Marketing Gimmick That Spawned a Monster

One downside was apparent for mutual funds operated by independent managers. Novice Canadian investors had difficulty getting around it, and the independent funds looked on it as an anchor holding back a roaring speedboat.

Banks did not apply sales commissions to their mutual funds, promoting them as no load, which meant, in the promotion vernacular, *Every Penny of Your Investment Goes to Work from Day One.* The banks' funds were sold by salaried employees who, once licensed and qualified to carry out the transaction, handled mutual fund sales the same way they opened savings accounts, sold GICs, and accepted loan applications.

Independent mutual funds, however, were sold through financial advisors and brokers who earned their income from commissions on the stocks, bonds, and mutual funds traded on behalf of their clients. Sales commissions for mutual funds came off the top of the investor's nest egg and could reach as high as 9 percent. Unsophisticated investors naturally balked at this idea. If an RRSP investor had

$10,000 to plunk into a savings account or a bank-sponsored mutual fund, all 10 grand began earning interest from the first day. Handing $10,000 to an independent mutual fund could mean that as little as $9100 made it into the fund. Practically, it made sense—somebody had to be paid for doing the work of connecting you with the mutual fund. Psychologically, it was a poke in the eye, and many Canadians investing in mutual funds chose the comfort and economies of bank-sponsored funds.

In truth, the upfront sales commissions were negotiable, although polite Canadians either chose to go along with whatever amount their advisor proposed or simply walked away. Some brokers and advisors used the high front-end load as leverage to close a deal by offering, without being asked, to reduce their "usual" 9 percent commission to half that amount. Even then, it hurt to see 4 or 5 percent of your hard-earned money go into someone else's pocket right off the top. The truly wealthy, who had been purchasing mutual funds for years, never paid anywhere near that level of sales commissions. With $1 million and more to invest in a fund, a tiny percentage of the total was more than adequate compensation to the salesperson. Half of 1 percent in a $1 million investment meant $5000 in the salesperson's pocket, an amount that could be recovered by the investor in one day. Only the little guys, who could least afford it, saw front-end commissions take a major bite out of their savings. Life was unfair.

And then Mackenzie changed everything.

Of all the independent mutual fund companies in Canada, none was more aggressive or savvy at marketing its products than Mackenzie Financial Corporation. Borrowing from industries as varied as beer and tobacco, Mackenzie literally roared ahead of the pack in the 1980s when it sponsored a racing car emblazoned with its logo. While enticing customers with racetrack glamour, the company was rewarding brokerage salespeople in a similar jet-setting manner. The company's annual sales promotion programs for advisors and mutual fund salespeople grew infamous for the scope of the rewards offered. Place enough clients and, more importantly, enough clients' money with Mackenzie mutual funds and you were jetted off to a five-star hotel in Hawaii, Barbados, Las Vegas, and similar destinations at Mackenzie's expense. Well, not really—every penny in a mutual fund originates with clients, but who wants to dwell on that while sipping mai tais in Maui?

Mackenzie, and the advisors and salespeople who promoted its funds, were doing well in 1987, but Mackenzie introduced a way they could all do even better. That was the year Mackenzie launched the Industrial Horizon Fund, sold without a front-end load. When you put money into the Industrial Horizon Fund, not a dime was skimmed off for the salesperson or financial advisor who sold you the fund. Advisors loved pushing the Industrial Horizon Fund to whomever they might encounter because it was easy to seal the deal. Other independent funds took money off the top of your investment to pay your broker, but now, with the Industrial Horizon Fund, neither Mackenzie nor the broker took a penny. Was this evidence of unprecedented generosity? Not in the least. It was the effect of a deferred sales charge, or DSC. Brokers and advisors called it a gold mine, because they still earned about 5 percent commission up front, just as before. Small investors called it a godsend. Over the years, critics began calling it a monster. The DSC works like this.

While none of your initial investment is deducted to cover sales commissions when you purchase units in the fund, a sales ("redemption") charge is applied if you sell them within a fixed period. (DSC mutual funds are referred to as "back-end load" funds for this reason.) When first introduced, this period extended nine years, but it has since been cut to seven years for most funds. The amount of the redemption charge is reduced each year the fund is held. Hold the fund long enough and you pay no sales charge when you sell it. A typical redemption schedule looks like this:

REDEEM YOUR ASSETS DURING …	AND YOU PAY
Year 1	5.5%
Year 2	5.0%
Year 3	4.5%
Year 4	4.0%
Year 5	3.5%
Year 6	2.5%
Year 7	1.5%
Year 8 and beyond	0%

Since equity-based mutual funds—funds that invest primarily in publicly traded shares of corporations—were touted as ideal for long-term investors, this feature sounded like a good fit. It became an even better fit when advisors actively encouraged clients to hold on to the fund even when the earnings were disappointing, a brilliant tactic that put a positive spin on a negative feature. If your mutual fund was losing money instead of making money, why dispose of it in the first few years and pay a DSC for the privilege, ensuring that you'll lose even more money?

Consider this scenario: You invest $10,000 in the *Standback & Duck* funds and discover to your horror, two years later, that the value of your investment has declined to $8000. Hey, markets go up and markets go down, and nothing about mutual funds is guaranteed, right? Still, you begin to question the financial acumen of the people running the fund and decide to get your money out and cut your losses—until your financial advisor points out that a 5 percent redemption charge will be applied against the original investment in the fund, representing another $500 loss to you. Wouldn't it be better to hang on and wait for the fund to recover? Many people do.

The marketing appeal to investors who failed to foresee this scenario was phenomenal, and within months of its introduction virtually every mutual fund sponsor was beating the drum about its own back-end load fund. Like other aspects of the mutual fund industry created to attract and retain clients, the DSC was a song-and-dance act produced by fund sponsors, directed by brokers and advisors, and acted out by their trusting clients. It was also more proof, if proof were still needed, that there is no free lunch.[15]

Return of the No Free Lunch Rule

Everyone in the investment industry bragged about the benefits of back-end load funds to investors, but no one discussed costs and incentives, except in the deepest, darkest paragraphs of the fund's prospectus. Mutual fund salespeople—advisors, brokers, insurance sales staff, and anyone else with a licence to trade securities—continued to earn fat upfront commissions from their sales, just as before. The funds could afford to pay the sales commission up front *because they skimmed a larger amount off the top of the client's investment year after year* through a higher MER.

As noted earlier, the MER is drawn out of client assets to cover the fund's operating expenses. For the majority of funds, the MER does not cover the cost of trading shares held within the fund. Mutual fund managers buy and sell shares and bonds according to the fund's objectives. Just as you would pay a fee or commission when trading shares in the stock market, fund managers have to pay similar charges. Well, actually, they don't—as a fund unit holder, you pay for the trades, but you don't know it. Nor do you see it, because the cost is hidden from both you and the MER. If the fund manager decides to purchase 1000 shares of Acme Widgets, priced at $10 per share, to be included in the fund portfolio, and the trading commission to be paid is $100, the price per share will actually be $1.10 per share. You didn't expect the fund to dip into its MER, did you? So in addition to the MER deducted from the fund's performance, trading costs are subtracted as well. In many mutual funds, this can be considerable. Some funds actually buy and sell as much as 60 percent or more of their portfolio each year. Every trade can cost you money in higher costs and lower returns.

In theory, the MER is related to the degree of effort and expertise needed to manage the fund on behalf of the investors, or unit holders. In practice, they tend to be determined by whatever the market will bear and, in Canada, the market bears too much.

Most Canadians pay little attention to the MER because they have no idea what it is, how it is paid, and how much it costs. The awareness is growing, but it remains appallingly low, and during the late 1980s it was essentially non-existent.

This made it easy to increase the MERs of DSC-based funds high enough to accommodate the now-hidden sales commissions. Once upfront and deducted from the original investment, the commissions were now concealed and paid for over time by the mutual fund investors through a higher MER. Clients were encouraged or induced to retain the DSC funds long enough for the commission to be recovered through the increased MER. No Las Vegas magic act made better use of smoke and mirrors.

Among the many pros and cons of investing your RRSP or RRIF in mutual funds, one fact is acknowledged by just about everyone outside the mutual fund industry (and perhaps surreptitiously by some within the industry): *Excessive mutual fund MERs represent a serious drain on the financial resources of people who purchase the fund units.* A superb illustration of this view is provided by Barclays Global Investors, a maverick fund company distributing exchange traded funds, or ETFs. (For more about ETFs, see Chapter 6.)

In the spring of 2005, the cheeky folk at Barclays estimated that April 26 would be Fee Freedom Day for Canadian mutual fund investors that year. This was the point where mutual fund investors stopped paying their mutual fund managers, through the MER rates, and started paying themselves.[16] Mid-April was actually a substantial improvement over the previous year. In 2003, Fee Freedom Day arrived on July 28, meaning that more than half the earnings from mutual fund investments were paid to mutual fund managers and not to the investors.

Another illustration of the unfairness of the Canadian securities industry concerns U.S. mutual funds and their availability to Canadians. Or, more accurately, their unavailability. The North American Free Trade Agreement (NAFTA) was created to open the door for a flood of goods and services across The World's Longest Undefended Line on a Map. Originally, this was to include stocks and mutual funds. Today, you can purchase shares in American companies such as Microsoft, Exxon, and General Electric, but do not attempt to buy units in well-managed U.S. mutual funds with low MERs. In spite of NAFTA, they remain unavailable on this side of the border, and Bay Street has made no effort to remove the barrier. Why should it? The average Canadian mutual fund charges a MER of 2.62 percent, while the average U.S. fund applies half that amount. Would lower MERs help Canadians build their RRSPs and manage their RRIFs more effectively? Bet on it. Will our mutual fund mavens block the availability in Canada of low-MER U.S.-managed funds such as Vanguard, with its enviable track record of generating returns for investors? Same bet.

Many mutual fund sponsors seem to view their MERs as an unlimited source of income to be tapped whenever they choose. How else to explain these statistics garnered by one of the leading research firms serving the Canadian investment industry?

1. The average MER of all mutual funds in Canada rose from 2.02 percent in 1995 to more than 2.7 percent as of June 30,

2006. No evidence of a correlation between these increased MERs and higher mutual fund expenses is apparent.

2. Almost 8 out of 10 mutual funds increased their MER levels between 1998 and 2004, a period when sharp drops in mutual fund returns were recorded virtually across the board.

3. Investors paid sponsors of Canadian mutual funds $2.8 billion via MERs in 1995. By 2005, this amount had quadrupled to more than $12 billion.[17]

Do not expect your financial advisor or mutual fund salesperson to discuss MERs unless challenged, at which point she will likely reply that the level of total return—the money you hope to make—is more important than the MER amount, which is the money the fund is certain to make. You might pause here for a moment to ponder who the winner might be in this business.

MER charges have been compared with a death by a thousand cuts, leaving you (or in this case, your RRSP portfolio) bleeding almost unnoticed. Prime examples: the original Trimark Fund, launched in 1981 and one of the most successful global equity funds (investing in companies around the world), and its DSC sibling, the Trimark Select Growth Fund, introduced in 1988, the year after Mackenzie shook up the industry with the DSC. Duplicating the front-end load Trimark Fund in every aspect but one, the Select Growth Fund replaced the front-end load with a DSC, using the standard seven-year declining redemption charge. The original Trimark Fund boasted a MER of 1.62 percent, which was eminently reasonable for a fund of its scope and calibre. The Select Growth Fund applied a MER of 2.40, an increase of 50 percent. How much impact does the larger MER have on the fund's performance— or more specifically, on the money the fund generates for you and your RRSP? Compare the figures (as of January 31, 2004):

DSC VERSUS NO DSC–TRIMARK FUND RETURNS				
FUND	3 YEARS	5 YEARS	10 YEARS	SINCE INCEPTION (MONTH/YEAR)
Trimark Fund	5.11	9.41	10.57	15.22 (9/81)
Select Growth Fund	4.52	8.79	9.45	11.57 (5/89)

SOURCE: GLOBEFUND.COM, FEBRUARY 10, 2004. REPRODUCED WITH PERMISSION.

Those are decent returns, especially over the long term, proving that Trimark's fund managers were earning their keep. (It also proves the point that mutual funds, carefully selected, continue to represent an essential element in any well-managed RRSP portfolio.) Apply the no free lunch rule, however, and the price of the no-load arrangement becomes clear—a reduction of almost 3.5 percent annually over the life of each fund, *despite the fact that the investments in both funds are identical.*[18]

Higher MERs resulting from back-load funds are not the only price paid by investors who trust their advisors for guidance. The binding contractual agreement between the fund company and the investor in a DSC fund means a substantial penalty will be paid if the investor tries to act according to his or her own interests. If you were sold units in the AGF International Value Fund on a DSC basis sometime in 2000 or 2001, you learned this expensive lesson.

The International Value Fund was a star in AGF's stable through the late 1990s and into 2002. Its net sales of $1.6 billion in 2001—hardly a banner year for mutual funds—exceeded those of every other fund in Canada and, with total assets under management of over $7 billion, the fund was the second-largest of its kind in the country. Everyone acknowledged that the fund's success was the product of one man's genius. His name was Charles Brandes, and he managed over a third of all of AGF's mutual fund assets out of his San Diego–based company, Brandes Investment Partners. In the year 2000, Brandes managed to squeeze 27.78 percent return out of the fund for unit holders of the AGF fund, and even through the snarling bear market of 2001 he produced a profit while similar funds were sliding into a crevasse. Everyone was happy—unit holders who watched their RRSP values grow, financial advisors who were earning healthy sales commissions, and AGF, which boasted the largest, most successful foreign equity mutual fund in Canada. The only person unhappy, or at least not as happy as he might have been, was Brandes himself, and in early 2002 he announced that he was jumping ship from AGF to launch his own line of funds in Canada.

The news shook the Canadian mutual fund industry, and while AGF management made reassuring noises to the folks who owned the $7 billion in fund assets, recent investors who purchased units on a DSC basis were faced with a difficult choice: remain with an unproven and probably inferior manager of their assets, or pay as much as 5.5 percent to jump ship and follow the guy whose performance they had sought in the first place. Most DSC funds permit you to switch within the family of funds—in this case, to another AGF fund—without paying a redemption charge. You can also redeem 10 percent of the value of your funds each year without incurring this charge. Neither option, of course, enables you to drop a fund without penalty if the fund proves either unsuccessful or unsuitable for your investment needs or, as in this case, when the attraction that drew you to the fund walks out the door.

Here is how the AGF International Value Fund performed from July 2002, after Brandes jumped ship, to the end of June 2006, plotted against the Globe International Equity Peer Index. Compare it with Brandes' own fund over the same period, versus the Globe Index.

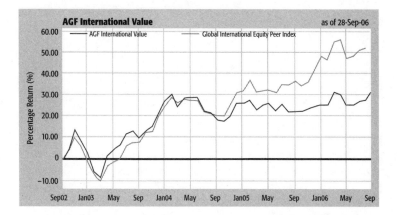

If you purchased units in the AGF International Value Fund on a DSC basis in September 2002, just before the fund's highly regarded manager departed, you would have watched the fund underperform the Globe International Equity Peer Index for the next four years, or you would have paid a penalty to bail out.

Many investors purchased the AGF fund on a DSC basis just before Brandes departed, and watched their fund underperform the index by 20 percent while the new Brandes funds exceeded the same measure of 10 percent, a 30 percent aggregate difference. They could sell their AGF units and purchase the Brandes fund, but only after paying a substantial DSC.

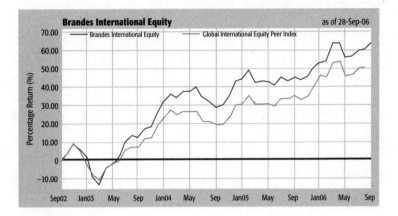

Owners of the AGF fund, especially those who chose it for the expertise of its manager, Charles Brandes, and did not choose a DSC option, could have followed him to his own fund in September 2002 and watched their money outperform the Brandes-less AGF. Over the next four years, owners of the Brandes International Equity Fund saw their investment outperform the AGF fund by more than 30 percent and the benchmark Globe International Equity Peer Index by 10 percent.

CHARTS SOURCED FROM WWW.GLOBEFUND.COM. USED WITH PERMISSION.

Trailer Fees: You're Hitched and You Don't Know It

Much of the investment industry loves to trumpet the phrase "Buy, hold, and prosper!" like a mantra, suggesting that these three actions are all that's needed to ensure growth in your RRSP. In fact, mutual fund operator AIC Ltd. has trademarked the core expression as its corporate slogan: "Buy. Hold. And Prosper." The phrase originated with multi-billionaire investor Warren Buffet, who used it to summarize his investment philosophy of carefully choosing well-managed companies, buying shares in them at an attractive price, and building on that investment over time. This is far more complex and demanding than the three-verb inculcation employed to condense Buffet's strategy.[19]

"Buy, hold, and prosper," as created and practised by Buffet, has merit because it defers the taxes applicable when an investment is sold for a profit, enhancing long-term growth. It also works best for closed-end funds or corporations like Buffet's Berkshire Hathaway operation, and not nearly as well for open funds like the vast majority marketed to Canadians for RRSP purposes. Finally, it assumes that the "buy" portion of the recipe occurs only when the price of shares in a blue-chip corporation such as Petro-Canada or TD Bank is low enough to represent a bargain. Buying shares in companies when the price reflects or exceeds their true value rarely ensures prosperity. Overpay for any investment and you can "buy and hold" forever without making a penny.

In fact, "Buy, hold, and prosper" has greater meaning to the commission-based salespeople who foist DSC-based funds on their clients than to investors. Over the long term, fund salespeople prosper as long as their clients hold these funds, regardless of the fund's performance. *While the clients watch the value of their mutual fund (and RRSP investment) dribble away as a result of a bear market or substandard performance by the fund manager, the person who talked you into that turkey is growing wealthy from your original investment.*

How? With trailer fees, used by mutual fund companies to influence your financial advisor with your money. Trailer fees ensure prosperity for fund companies and advisors and, from time to time, even you. The difference is that your future prosperity is uncertain, while theirs is guaranteed.

A trailer fee is a sales commission paid to the person who sold you the mutual fund for as long as you own the units. Like every expense incurred by mutual funds, you get the bill. Once again, the bill is never presented to you, and mutual fund companies would prefer that, like Aunt Edith's drinking problem or Uncle Eddie's criminal past, you just not talk about it. (Why are they called trailer *fees* and not trailer *commissions*? Because you and I would balk at a commission paid where no transaction has been made to generate it. It's another example of mutual fund window dressing.)

As long as you retain ownership of the mutual fund units sold to you, the person who made the initial sale receives, every year, a portion of the assets you hold in that fund. The amount varies by fund company and fund type; it is as high as 1 percent for front-end load funds, and 0.5 percent for DSC funds.

Not every mutual fund pays trailer fees, nor does every fund carry a load, either front-end or back-end (DSC). Commission-based salespeople rarely if ever discuss no-load funds or acknowledge their existence. To commissioned-based advisors and brokers, no-load funds are like a drunk at a formal reception—everybody pretends he's not there.

If $100,000 of your RRSP is invested in *Standback & Duck* funds paying a trailer fee, as much as $1000 will be removed each year via the MER and forwarded to whoever sold you the fund, whether its value grows or not. Imagine if your advisor talked 100 clients into purchasing $10,000 worth of *Standback & Duck* funds each year. Who is really getting wealthy from these funds?

Trailer fees are a carry-over from the life insurance industry. The investment industry would prefer that you not know about them, and that people like me not talk about them. This was made clear in February 2004 when AIC, the "Buy. Hold. And Prosper" company, announced a new schedule of trailer fees payable to brokers and others selling high-MER/DSC funds managed by AIC. Here's how AIC promised to pay their commissioned "professionals" who sold the qualifying funds to their clients and encouraged the clients to Buy. Hold. And Prosper.

AIC FUNDS		
DSC YEAR	**ANNUAL TRAILER FEE (%)**	**DSC REDEMPTION FEE (%)**
1	0.500	6.0
2	0.525	5.5
3	0.550	5.0
4	0.575	4.5
5	0.600	4.0
6	0.625	3.5
7 and beyond	0.750	Nil

SOURCE: AIC FORM 03-1560-E (12/03).

Note that the trailer fee increases each year a client retains the AIC mutual fund in his or her portfolio. Imagine a client approaching the commissioned broker or advisor, three years after purchasing an AIC fund, to ask about the wisdom of selling the fund and transferring the investment to a different fund company in pursuit of better returns. Regardless of the fund's returns—and AIC funds by and large have not been stellar performers—the advisor must explain that it will cost the client 5 percent of her initial investment to withdraw from the fund as a result of the DSC—not a pleasant prospect if the fund's value has declined in the interim. In addition, moving out of an AIC fund will mean lost income to the advisor of as much as 0.75 percent of the client's investment every year. Do you honestly think all brokers and advisors will respond to the client's request for guidance with an unbiased opinion? Do you believe in the tooth fairy?

In the same February 2004 revised trailer fee schedule noted above, AIC made an extra effort to paint a rich and rosy future for advisors selling AIC funds, by converting the trailer fees from cold percentages to hot dollars (the Year 1 revenue includes the initial sales commission).

COMMISSIONS AND TRAILER FEES FOR SELECTED AIC FUNDS ($)								
CASH FLOW*	YEAR 1	YEAR 2	YEAR 3	YEAR 4	YEAR 5	YEAR 6	YEAR 7	TOTAL REVENUE
AIC Regular	5500	500	500	500	500	500	500	8500
AIC Pools	5750	750	750	750	750	750	750	10,250
AIC Funds	5500	525	550	575	600	625	750	9125

* Initial investment of $100,000; zero market appreciation

SOURCE: AIC FORM 03-1560-E (12/03).

Assuming no growth in the client's investment over seven years— a daunting thought, but not unheard of—the salesperson would have pocketed as much as $10,000 in sales commissions and trailer fees over that period, with the prospect of continuing future returns.

Meanwhile, the client's investment hasn't shifted a penny. If the investment is worth less than the initial $100,000, the salesperson still collects, albeit not as much in actual dollars. If the client's investment increases, so does the annual trailer commission. If the client wins, the salesperson wins; if the client loses, the salesperson still wins. Just who is taking the risk here?

The iceberg of deception beneath this visible tip is revealed on the same AIC document listing these revised trailer commissions and DSC redemptions, for prominently displayed in the upper right-hand corner is the AIC admonition: *For Advisor Use Only— Not to be distributed to investors.*

AIC does not want current or potential investors to be aware of the amount of money withdrawn from their accounts to reward the "professional" commission-paid advisors. Indeed, it does not want investors to know of the very existence of trailers, or any other revelation illustrating how AIC drains money from the clients' asset base. This lack of transparency, and the intense effort of most mutual fund sponsors to keep their clients in the dark about such matters, drives people such as Glorianne Stromberg mad. Stromberg is the author of two scathing critiques of mutual fund sales and management policies. Referring to AIC's "not to be distributed to investors" chart and its "upwardly creeping trailer fee," Stromberg notes that "everything that comes out [of the clients' assets] is slightly more outrageous. We need to improve the disclosure system in the mutual fund industry, but every time a proposal is made to improve transparency, the industry either drags its feet or fights it directly."[20]

Nor was AIC the only fund sponsor eagerly looking for ways to fill its cash drawer at the expense of RRSP/RRIF owners. Investors Group, the country's largest mutual fund sponsor, jacked its DSC schedule up by as much as 200 percent in mid-2003, as the table below shows.

INVESTORS GROUP REDEMPTION FEES			
WHEN REDEEMED	**OLD RATE**	**NEW RATE**	**INCREASE (%)**
Years 1–2	3.0	5.5	83.3
Year 3	2.5	5.0	100.0
Year 4	2.0	4.5	125.0
Year 5	1.5	4.0	166.7
Year 6	1.0	3.0	200.0
Year 7	None	1.5!!!!	150.0
Year 8 and beyond	None	None	Unchanged

SOURCE: *THE GLOBE AND MAIL*, "HOW TO AVOID FEES," MAY 20, 2003.
REPRODUCED WITH PERMISSION.

Did Investors Group raise its DSC schedule because the company needed more revenue to stave off financial disaster? Hardly. The previous year (2002), its parent company reported gross income from fees alone exceeding $1.8 billion, leaving a net income before interest, taxes, and dividends of almost $512 million, representing a 28 percent profit margin. Over the same year, Investors Group recorded sales of almost $5 billion and boasted total managed assets—the sum of all portfolios owned by its clients—of more than $37.5 billion.[21]

Was Investors Group planning to improve the quality of its service to clients, or perhaps reduce its MER, or add value to justify the higher DSC schedule? Apparently not. In fact, the company slipped in yet another squeeze play on its clients by adding to the new DSC schedule a note that it retained the right to apply redemption fees to clients who switched between Investors Group funds. By accepting your Investors Group advisor's recommendation to transfer your RRSP dollars into one of its DSC mutual funds, you agreed to pay a penalty to redeem the units even if the fund proved to be the biggest dog since Rin Tin Tin.

By the way, do not assume that shunning a fund with a DSC is one method of avoiding trailer fees. AGF, for example, offers both DSC and non-DSC options on many of its funds. With an AGF fund carrying a DSC, the advisor receives an upfront commission of 4.9 percent, reduced to 3 percent or less for a fund with no DSC. Why would an advisor propose purchasing a fund with no DSC? Would it be to free you from the penalty of selling the fund within a few years if you were unsatisfied with its performance? Perhaps. More likely, however, it is because most AGF equity funds pay an annual trailer fee on front-end loaded funds that is double that of DSC funds.

If you pay an upfront commission of 2.5 percent for a non-DSC fund from AGF, after five years your advisor has collected 7.5 percent of your original investment in commissions versus 7.4 percent (4.9 + [0.5 × 5]) with a DSC fund. For every year past the fifth, the front-end load sale puts your advisor ahead of the game. And if the fund increases in value year by year—hey, wasn't that the original idea?—the trailer fee grows accordingly, increasing the advisor's gain.

Brokers and advisors argue that trailer fees compensate them for services that do not involve trades and thus present no opportunity to earn commissions. There is undoubted value in the wise counsel of an advisor who recommends that you ignore transient hiccups in the market and economy and remain fixed to your established strategy, if this is indeed appropriate. Trusting that this advice is valid becomes a matter of faith on your part once you are aware of the trailer fees. The underlying concern here is not whether financial advisors deserve to be paid for their counsel. Of course they do, and fairly. A clear rationale exists for the use of trailer fees to replace other, more costly methods of remuneration for the industry (see below). The larger question addresses the lack of transparency and the effect of a commission-based system on advisor objectivity.

Is the Writing on the Wall (or the Prospectus) for DSC Funds?

Canadian investors are not nearly as gullible as many fund sponsors might have believed. Since the true nature of DSC funds was highlighted in this book and elsewhere, they have begun to vanish as rapidly as Don Cherry's hair. During the year 2000, 74.2 percent of mutual funds sold in Canada were based on a DSC. In 2005, this had plummeted to 56.5 percent.[22] (These figures do not include no-load funds sold by banks and by direct-seller companies such as Saxon and Phillips, Hager & North.)

In April 2006, Royal Mutual Funds announced it was eliminating all sales charges on third-party funds—i.e., all funds not managed by Royal—sold by the firm's in-house financial planners at RBC retail branches. The licensed staff at these branches are salaried, and earn bonuses when their sales exceed established thresholds, a system that avoids encouraging them to promote one product over another according to the bank's benefit. In fact, there is no incentive to favour mutual funds over other instruments such as bonds or GICs, which the bank markets as well.

With no front-end or DSC loads, how does Royal profit from the sale of these funds? Through trailer fees, usually 1 percent on equity funds and 0.5 percent on bond funds. This is one place where trailer fees make sense; no one expects the middleman to work for nothing, even when the middleman is Canada's largest chartered bank. Assuming the funds are performing well, 1 percent a year to the source of the advice is a reasonable price.

Financial advisors aiming for longer-term wealth growth for their clients, instead of short-term wham-bam upfront earnings, will profit from this arrangement. Here's how:

A DSC fund may pay the salesperson 3.5 percent up front and 0.5 percent in annual trailing fees for seven years (the typical term of a DSC fund before penalties no longer apply), providing 8.5 percent remuneration. With a 1 percent annual trailer fee and no up-front commission, a non-DSC fund pays 7 percent over the same period, but this applies—expectedly—on rising asset levels and will extend beyond the seven-year period of the DSC.

If annual trailer fees provide the exclusive returns for advisors, and they operate in an environment where client earnings are the prime criterion, investors are certain to benefit.

How Do You Like Your Obfuscation?

It's unlikely that anyone in Canada is more tuned to the need for reform in the country's mutual fund industry than Glorianne Stromberg. Nor is anyone more outraged, in her quiet, measured manner, at the industry's antics. Stromberg practised corporate and securities law for several years before being appointed to the Ontario Securities Commission in 1991. While filling this role in February 1994, Stromberg was directed to review the regulation of mutual funds in Canada. Her report, *Regulatory Strategies for the Mid-'90s: Recommendations for Regulating Investment Funds in Canada,* was issued in 1995. Three years later, she was asked by the federal government's Office of Consumer Affairs to conduct a similar study to outline how Canadians making mutual fund investments within their RRSPs might obtain reasonable protection when dealing with salespeople, advisors, and the industry generally. This produced *Investment Funds in Canada and Consumer Protection: Strategies for the Millennium* in January 1999.

Both reports and their recommendations were received with great enthusiasm by consumer watchdog groups, and with nods of approval by industry representatives (individual advisors tended to react with shrugs or sneers). Stromberg was feted and congratulated in much of the media. Her hard work and perception were evident in every aspect of the study, and her proposals were acknowledged in many quarters (but by few brokerages) as both practical and effective. So what happened?

Stromberg smiles and shakes her head. "Not much," she says. "We made some small steps forward, and I'm pleased about them. But the resistance to keeping investors informed continues as strong as ever. Look what the industry wants to do with the prospectus. They say they want to simplify it, but this just means they want to remove much of the relevant information. Now the CSA [Canadian Securities Administrators] is going further by suggesting that clients do not have to receive a prospectus before making an investment decision, and the advisor needn't supply one unless asked for it."[23]

Like swallowing bitter medicine, reading a prospectus is supposed to be good for you, but few people absorb it. The laws of every provincial and territorial securities commission in Canada state that a prospectus must be prepared whenever an issuer (company, limited partnership, trust, or mutual fund) promotes securities to the public. It must provide full, true, and plain disclosure of important facts relating to the securities being issued and be delivered to every person who invests in the securities. The prospectus includes details of fund performance, management guidelines, fees and commissions, and various other minutiae, buried in text that appears to be written by legal scholars for whom English is a second language and Chaucer is a near contemporary.

"Nobody ever reads a prospectus," many mutual fund sponsors mutter. Observers such as Glorianne Stromberg point out that a prospectus is rarely made to be read—it's made to fulfil a legal requirement. Many prospectus samples appear designed to reduce the likelihood of *anyone* reading it, and since most mutual fund sponsors agree with Stromberg on this point, suspicion remains that fund sponsors are ensuring a self-fulfilling prophecy. The prospectus does, however, establish ground rules for management of the fund and, in theory at least, provides assurance to the investor that her assets are managed according to her expectations.

In recent years, fund sponsors have begun proposing that the rule requiring them to distribute a prospectus with every purchase be waived in favour of simply telling the investor that a prospectus is available. If you want one, ask for it. Otherwise, who cares? Wary minds might suggest that fund sponsors would prefer a complete elimination of the prospectus lest investors begin discovering why so many people in the investment industry sail yachts and drive BMWs, while not enough clients do either.

From time to time, some enlightened fund company decides to make its operations more transparent, assuming that candour and clarity might generate greater trust and, ultimately, more investors in the fund. The most recent company to try this tact was Fidelity, who actually made an effort to simplify their prospectus, making it more accessible and easier to absorb. Nice idea, except that other mutual funds grew antsy about the idea of clients having an opportunity to learn all they should know about their funds' operations, and certain quarters of the industry reportedly applied pressure to maintain a standardized approach to prospectus design and content. The result has been wall-to-wall obfuscation. Score another one for the mutual fund industry.

Finally, when it comes to defending itself against charges of setting its priorities well ahead of investors, the mutual fund industry slips into a defensive mode that makes a cornered grizzly bear appear cuddly. This is not a business that takes criticism lightly. Ken Kivenko, an investment advocate who publishes *The Fund Observer* (formerly *The Fund Monitor*), a newsletter critical of industry practices, compiled some "marginalization" approaches to the industry's critics.

FUND INDUSTRY MARGINALIZATION APPROACHES TO CRITICS

CRITIC	APPROACH
Academia	Obscure professors just trying to get attention.
Newspapers/Media	They're just trying to sell more papers.
Investor advocates	A bunch of cynics with too much time on their hands.
Former regulatory commission staff	That's why they're called "former"!
Deposit insurance commissions	All they want to do is move fund assets to bank accounts.
Consumer groups and organizations	A perpetual bunch of gripers that don't understand the business.
Securities regulators	A bunch of do-gooders with a theoretical cost-insensitive approach to regulation.
Low-cost fund companies	They'll stay small.
Independent fund industry analysts	They're all on the take with hidden agendas.
Abused investors	People who should never have invested in mutual funds—a bunch of whining Canada Savings Bonds/GIC refugees.
Attorneys General	They're seeking publicity as a route to the premier's office.

IT SHOULDN'T BE COMPLEX—
IT SHOULD BE OPEN

Barbara Benson* prefers to meet in a midtown restaurant instead of her rental apartment. She should not even be living in an apartment, she believes; she should be living in a condominium.

At age 75, Barbara remains an exceptionally attractive woman. She arrives impeccably groomed, in a sleek black dress and wearing subtle silver jewellery, looking every bit the society doyenne. In fact, during the last 15 of her working years, she was an office secretary. A single mother since her marriage dissolved when she was 40, Barbara managed to raise her two children without financial assistance and is proud of her daughter's obtaining a medical degree and her son's establishment of a successful contracting business in her native Winnipeg.

Those were reasons enough to take pride in her achievements, but there was more. "I worked full time until I was 68 years old," Barbara says in her gentle voice, which carries no hint of bitterness or resentment. "I was always determined never to be a burden to my children, especially when I retired. I scrimped and saved, and did without a lot of things. I never bought a

---

*A pseudonym

home, but I contributed to my RRSP every year and invested outside my RRSP."

Thanks to her long-term contributions and some wise counsel, by 2000 Barbara managed to accumulate $440,000 in her RRSP (converted to a RRIF when she turned 69) and her non-registered portfolio. At age 70, with substantial assets in hand, her primary focus should have been on preserving capital—holding on to what she had, rather than seeking growth, which invites elevated risk.

"I paid attention to everything I heard and read about investing," she recalls with a wry smile, "caught up in the hype about where the market was going and how to take advantage of it." She attended seminars, including those featuring a local financial advisor who hosted a Saturday afternoon phone-in radio show dealing with financial and investment matters. The advisor promoted investments described by him as "fabulous mutual funds" and "fantastic opportunities."

"He was well known throughout the city," Barbara says. "A real promoter, and he invited listeners to call him on his cell phone after the show to discuss their portfolio. He kept emphasizing that there would be no charge or obligation for a consultation, and no charge for financial planning. So I thought, 'Why not?'"

The broker–cum–radio personality balanced his aggressive, sometimes haranguing attitude on the radio with impressive qualifications. Both a certified financial planner (CFP) and registered financial planner (RFP),[24] he was vice-president and regional manager of a national investment firm.

Barbara Benson stirs her soft drink with her straw as she recalls her decision to obtain a free opinion of her portfolio from the broker. "When I visited him at his office, he went to his computer and showed me the 'dogs,' as he put it, in my account. According to him, they were all dogs, and if I really wanted to ensure my financial security in the future, I should transfer both of my accounts to him. So I did."

It was April 2000, on the cusp of the collapse of the North American equity markets, led by the fall of tech stocks such as Nortel. Transferring her accounts required Barbara to sign a number of documents, and among them was one authorizing her new broker to sell her current investments and purchase other ones on her behalf.

"When I moved my accounts to him, he sold everything in both portfolios—everything!—including all the investments I had outside my RRIF," Barbara recalls, and her until now smiling exterior shows its first sign of crumbling. "It was disastrous!"

The first hint of calamity arrived in a letter from Canada Customs and Revenue, noting that the sale of mutual funds and stocks held outside her RRIF had produced a tax liability based on the capital gains generated when her portfolio assets were sold. She had never faced a capital gains tax in her life, and she had to cover the tax bill out of her savings.

If Barbara's advisor had set out to coordinate her new portfolio expressly to produce maximum losses, he could not have done a better job than the assortment of mutual funds assembled for her.

First, he spread her assets among 43 mutual funds, almost all in the technical growth sector that reached its zenith in mid-2000, around the time he purchased them. Tech funds (industries based on computer products and services, wireless and cell phone equipment manufacturers, biochemical developments, and so on) are risky investments that generate extreme price volatility and exceptionally high MERs and, coincidentally, large commissions for the salesperson. Barbara's lifetime investment was now in the worst place at the worst time. Incredibly, the celebrity broker–broadcaster found a third way to ensure that her investments shrank even further.

Of the 43 funds purchased for her accounts (all with DSCs), 22 were priced in U.S. dollars, a tactic explained by the advisor as a means of obtaining diversification. "He told me Canadian stocks made up only 2 percent of all the world's investment markets," she says. "'You must diversify your investments,' he kept saying, 'and get a lot of them out of the country,' Naturally, I went along with him."

In reality, Barbara's investments were more crucified than diversified. Geographical diversification represents a wise investment strategy, but truly effective diversification involves spreading your investments over a broad range of countries, economies, and industries, yet Barbara's mutual funds were valued in U.S. dollars exclusively. The downside of geographical diversity is a heightened risk of currency fluctuation. When the Canadian dollar falls against foreign currencies, investments in countries with a currency of a higher value will rise in proportion. That's the good news. Any rise in the loonie's value against another country's currency, however, decreases the value of investments priced in that currency.

From 2000 onward, Barbara's foreign-based mutual funds fell not only because they were in high-risk sectors but because they were priced in U.S. dollars, which began a long slide against the Canadian dollar. While anyone with Canadian-priced high-risk investments saw their portfolios erode by 30 to 40 percent, Barbara's dropped by a further 20 percent based on the decline in the U.S. dollar against the loonie.

Barbara's losses were beyond distressing and crippling—they were criminal. Consider the following list showing the changed value of each fund between April 2000 and March 2003.

BARBARA'S RRSP – BEFORE AND AFTER[25]			
FUND	APRIL 2000 ($)	MARCH 2003 ($)	GAIN/LOSS (%)
AGF American Growth	9370	2570	−72
AIM European Growth	14,630	5430	−63
AIM Global Health Sciences	2770	1585	−43
AIM Global Technology	5600	1400	−75
CI Global Tech Sector	5710	1420	−75
CI Global Telecom	8140	3550	−56
CI Global Telecom Sector	3950	720	−82
Fidelity Focus Technology	4930	1285	−74
Fidelity Global Asset Allocation	38,695	23,190	−40
Fidelity Growth America	9935	5015	−50

During the three years that Barbara entrusted her savings to the broker, only 1 of the 43 back-loaded funds purchased for her by the broker showed a profit. This was Fidelity Focus Financial Services, purchased at $1265 in April 2000 and valued at $1365 three years later, producing $100 in profit for annual earnings of less than 3 percent, about the same as a bank's daily interest savings account.

"I had so many tearful meetings with [the advisor] about these losses," Barbara explains. "He would tell me to be patient, to trust him. If I suggested selling some of the bad mutual funds, he said it would cost too much money to sell them because they had a deferred sales charge, and the only way to get my money back was to hold on to them. But they kept falling and falling, and by the spring of 2003 I had lost over $200,000. I was devastated and terrified. I had to do something!"

In early 2003, Barbara took her statement, showing the myriad mutual funds and steep losses, to another advisor in the same brokerage firm, who was appalled. The second advisor, convinced that Barbara's portfolio had been designed to make her advisor wealthy rather than Barbara, raised the matter with the company's compliance officer and pointed out how her accounts had been mishandled. In response, the compliance officer shrugged and noted that Barbara's accounts dated before [the compliance officer's] arrival at the brokerage and claimed he therefore could do nothing.

Things are looking up for Barbara Benson, if only somewhat. The new advisor totally restructured her portfolio, selling or transferring all of her fund holdings into more suitable investments, and by 2006 she had recovered about half of the losses she suffered under the previous advisor's guidance. As you read this, she may even be back to the asset value level she had in 2000, but she will, of course, have lost more than six years of potential growth.

The advisor who directed Barbara Benson's money into the disastrous mix continues to maintain his reputation as an investment genius with a phone-in show on a local radio station, imploring listeners to contact him for an assessment and restructuring of their portfolios. How many of his clients have suffered the same devastation, but are too embarrassed or too intimidated to express their concerns publicly?

While investment "professionals" may construct a portfolio that appears designed to enrich themselves through sales commissions, trailing fees, and hidden incentives, rarely are they called to account for their misdeeds. Whenever they are, their defence is consistent and widely accepted by regulators: Equities by nature rise and fall over an extended period, and clients must assume that the long-term trend will be upward while accepting the downside risk. If challenged, Benson's advisor would no doubt use this defence, bolstered by claims that she was an experienced investor and by assurances that the market would likely recover, eventually allowing her to recoup her losses.

Nothing in any investment guideline would justify creating a port-folio for a 70-year-old woman consisting almost exclusively of high-risk, back-loaded mutual funds, with a majority of them set in U.S. currency. The concept defies every tenet of astute investing. Barbara Benson's highly regarded financial planner likely reaped about $20,000 in upfront sales commissions plus perhaps $5000 in trailer fees over the three years that her portfolio was under his management. The firm's compliance officer fulfilled his role as sentry on behalf of the brokerage—not the clients—by noting that he had assumed his position after the account had been opened and thus could do nothing. Should the client have launched action to recover her losses on the basis of mismanagement of her account? Perhaps. A number of regulatory bodies exist to address this kind of malfeasance, but the record of their effectiveness in cases such as this one is abysmally low, as you shall see.

Nor is the legal system sufficiently equipped or dedicated to deal with the matter. The civil courts are crowded, banks and brokerages insist on closed-door arbitration, and lawyers are expensive. A plain-tiff may be required to pay a retainer of several thousand dollars at the outset of legal action, plus monthly charges for a year or more, with little assurance that legal costs will be recovered. Meanwhile, the defendants boast an almost impregnable defence. Bolstered by the alphabet of degrees and certificates trailing their name, advisors and brokers will claim that their investment guidance was appropriate at the time it was given. Every financial advisor with a calendar and calculator might concur that stocks listed on the Toronto Stock Exchange will rise by 10 percent next month, but this is no guarantee that they will not fall by a similar amount instead. Every investment involves risk, and clients should know this going in. Why blame the advisor for unforeseen events beyond his or her control? The basis of the industry's defence can be summed up in this manner: When a broker's prescience is accurate, his actions are justified; when it is faulty, the client must accept the risk.

Investors who manage to pursue their claims to arbitration may encounter a sceptical, unsympathetic response. One client at an arbitration session explained to the judge that she had sought only relatively secure investments, had never expected more than a 10 percent annual return, and had insisted on minimizing any risk to her capital, accumulated over several years of patient growth. Yet within a year of a new advisor restructuring her account after her previous advisor retired, she saw an erosion of over 30 percent in her RRSP account, all of it based on the new advisor's guidance. Wasn't this evidence of account mismanagement? The judge simply shrugged. "Not necessarily," he said. "I lose money in the stock market myself from time to time." A decision was handed down in favour of the advisor, leaving the client to dip into the remainder of her savings to cover her legal fees.

Age Must Be a Factor in Determining Strategy

The investment industry tries to shrug off complaints about undue losses, especially in RRSP/RRIF accounts owned by members of the over-60 crowd, by noting that clients must accept the risk of loss when investing, and much of the regulatory and legal apparatus appears to support this argument. The claim is so much hogwash.

Once again: *There is a difference between risk and uncertainty.* Risk can be assessed and accounted for. Uncertainty cannot be. Risk is interest rates rising and the stock market dropping. Uncertainty is September 11, 2001. It is the duty of every financial advisor to address the question of risk in each client portfolio, and it need not be the client's duty to help in determining this factor, because *when it comes to RRSP and RRIF accounts, the overriding determination of risk is the client's age.* The calculation is, or should be, automatic.

Working from the client's age, the path toward prudent account design becomes open and accessible. The submitted strategy may (and perhaps should) vary according to aspects of a client's knowledge and lifestyle, but age is the primary determinant. The most common method of applying this reasoning is to match the percentage of guaranteed investments—GICs, government bonds, and cash—to the client's age. At 35, you need only have about one-third of the value of your RRSP in guaranteed investments; at age 75, guaranteed investments should represent three-quarters of the total. (For more details on this formula, see Chapter 12.)

Guaranteed instruments do not totally eliminate risk but, as with other risks, this one can be managed. Long-term bonds and GICs carry the risk that rising interest rates and inflation will reduce their value over time. A five-year GIC paying 4 percent annual interest may look reasonable today, but if the same investment is paying 7 or 8 percent next year and you're locked into the lower rate, you lose ground. The risk can be managed by laddering fixed-interest instruments such as GICs and bonds. An investment of $10,000, for example, can be divided into fifths, with one-fifth maturing in one year, another fifth maturing in two years, and so on. Each year the maturing investment is rolled over—reinvested at the current interest rate—for five years. In this manner, when interest rates rise you take advantage of the higher interest paid by investing a portion of your fixed-interest assets in the new rate, and when they fall you already have a majority of the investment growing at the old rate.

Once the age-percentage rule for fixed-interest investments is understood, it may be manipulated according to individual needs and expectations, but the rule still holds. I know of one 70-year-old man, for example, who has flipped the rule—he holds 70 percent of his RRIF portfolio in equity and resource-based mutual funds, primarily gold and precious metals in mid-2004, and only 30 percent in fixed-interest vehicles. He is also an experienced, astute, and gifted investor with no dependent children, no mortgage on his luxury home, and an in-home business that generates a substantial annual income. He understands and preaches the rule. But he also qualifies as an ideal exception to it.

The Fiction of "Inevitable Losses"

Advisors, planners, and brokers tend to discuss risk only after the fact. In this sense, they are like the elevator mechanic who points out, as you plummet down the open shaft, that you can't expect the elevator to be there all the time. "Be prepared to take losses," they admonish.

It is not unrealistic to expect that losses can be avoided with your RRSP/RRIF investments. This expectation may be difficult to realize, but isn't that why you rely on a professional advisor in the first place—to achieve goals and levels of growth that you are unable to accomplish yourself? As investors, we have to start discarding the notion of accepting periodic losses from mutual funds even while the fund managers and commissioned salespeople reap profits from them. There is a precedent for such thinking. His name is Warren Buffet.

Over 39 calendar years stretching from 1965 to 2003, Buffet's company lost money for investors only once, in 2001, when the value of shares in his Berkshire Hathaway firm dropped 6.2 percent. For the record, the S&P 500, a standard index of stock performance, fell almost twice as far that year and slipped a further 22 percent in 2002, yet Buffet regained his 2001 loss plus an additional 4 percent. Perhaps losses are inevitable only if you expect them to be.

There are few Warren Buffets in the world, and even fewer of them are advising Canadians on their RRSP/RRIF portfolios. Yet Buffet can teach us some things that provide enlightenment, if not enormous wealth. As both an investor and a realist, his success was built by following two cardinal rules:

RULE NO. 1: Never lose money.
RULE NO. 2: Never forget Rule No. 1.

Buffet managed to fulfil Rule No. 1 for 38 out of 39 consecutive years by applying diligence, focus, and hard work to the project—hardly a unique recipe, but one unfamiliar to many commission-based brokers and financial advisors. I anticipate their objection to this comment will be based on practicalities. Buffet has just one account to manage—his own, on behalf of shareholders in Berkshire Hathaway. Brokers and advisors may deal with hundreds of portfolios, with each client expecting individual attention to his or her special needs. That's a valid point, but it falls apart under close examination.

Putting it simply, too many advisors are handling too many accounts. Seeking to maximize one's income is understandable, but going beyond the point where service quality slips below an acceptable standard is inexcusable. One of the most common complaints made by RRSP investors is that they hear from their advisor once a year, usually just before the deadline for RRSP contributions. If advisors can find time in February to make blanket calls to everyone on their client lists, they should be able to schedule quarterly or at least semi-annual portfolio reviews of every portfolio whose assets are six figures in dollar value. Dedicated advisors will provide consultation as required at a level well below this figure, helping to build the client's assets even when the assets barely justify the advisor's time, with the expectation of future benefits when the client prospers. This is a form of investing, after all.

The alternative pursued by some advisors is to rely on computer programs when making investment decisions for clients. This has the benefit of producing reams of peripheral information in order to impress clients with enough data to divert their attention from the fact that their goals are not being met.

Year by year these reports, based on off-the-rack computer programs, expand in content and shrink in relevance. Along with a year-end statement revealing that Barbara Benson had seen 40 percent of the value of her investments vanish after three years with her radio-celebrity broker, she received a 16-page personal financial plan, the substance of which was primarily boilerplate and the value worthless. No full-colour pie chart or graphs could conceal the fact that few if any of the investments were appropriate for her age and status.

Among the report was a page titled Goals and Priorities, noting that at age 73 (in 2002), her life expectancy was 85. Yet the asset mix assembled for her (including both RRIF and non-registered accounts) by the advisor consisted of—

Cash	0%
Income	20%
Growth and income	20%
Canadian growth	10%
Global growth	33%
Aggressive growth	17%

Equity-based mutual funds are generally categorized according to two measures: value and growth. Value-based funds invest in established companies that are underpriced at the time of purchase; growth-based funds purchase shares on the promise of what they might become, rather than on actual profits. As a result, growth-based funds tend to be far more speculative than value-based funds and harbour much higher MERs. So why were none of Barbara Benson's funds based on value? She sought income and security. What she received was speculation and risk. (For more details on value versus growth funds, see Chapter 12.)

Whenever advisors scramble for quick answers to meet an expanding client list, they follow a herd mentality. Instead of pondering the full range of investment alternatives, they note the general direction of thinking in the marketplace and follow the crowd. Are other advisors recommending a particular mutual fund or fund sector this month? There must be something to it, so why not propose it? There is safety in numbers—if the investment tanks, an advisor's defence can be that scores of others were making the same decision, so there must have been some perceived benefit. The herd mentality remains as prevalent among financial advisors as it does among investors, and when the herd breaks into a stampede, only the wise advisors suggest you step aside and let it pass. *When everybody thinks the same, nobody is thinking at all.*

Examples of exceptional long-term performance may not be common, which makes them exceptional. But neither are they non-existent. It's not difficult to locate funds that score consistently below average over the long term, although it's difficult to understand why advisors continue recommending them to clients. This does not mean that consistent long-term growth *exceeding* the average is impossible. Our own Warren Buffet may be a man named Eric Sprott. In 1982, had you entrusted a mere $1000 to his Sprott Managed Accounts, it would be worth—hold on to your calculator—$339,454 in April 2006. Over 20 years ending April 30, 2006, the accounts generated an average annual return of 26.18 percent.[26] Before you leap for the telephone to call your broker or advisor, note that Sprott no longer accepts investors in this particular account.

Exceptional? Yes, it is. But this fund's success proves the folly of believing that no one can beat market averages over the long term. It can be done. And while you should not expect your advisor to locate a Sprott Managed Account behind every calculator, he or she should spend more time searching for ideally suited investment alternatives, something that few advisors appear to be doing.

The prospect of advisors reducing their client list to a manageable size is unlikely to occur as long as their income remains commission-based. Call it greed, call it business acumen, call it human nature, but while advisors rely on the steady receipt of commission cheques and trailer fees—in other words, as long as they function primarily as salespeople and only incidentally as investment counsellors—the financial disaster suffered by Barbara Benson and thousands of other Canadians whose trust exceeds their comprehension will continue unabated, unchallenged, and uncontrolled.

Why Won't They Tell You How You Are Doing?

Except for the legal profession, no group holds its cards closer to its vest than the financial investment industry—brokerages, financial planning firms, or fund companies. Of course, they don't own the cards. You do.

Only a handful of rebels such as Hans Merkelbach (see next chapter) choose to disclose the annualized rate of return or losses to clients. Yet, as financial services columnist Rob Carrick points out, only with an average annual rate of return can investors truly see if their results are sufficient to meet their planning objectives.[27] Imagine driving to a far-off destination with a fixed arrival time and not being able to learn your average speed from start to finish. That's retirement planning without knowing your average annual return on the investments in your RRSP.

The data would not be difficult for investment firms to calculate and reveal on their regular statements, yet the industry continues to resist providing such knowledge to its clients. Why? One source claimed that providing returns would motivate investors to think strictly short term, leading them to make rash decisions chasing after an extra percentage or two. The irrationality of many investors is well established, but this rationale fails against the astonishing volume of advertising and promotion that fund companies generate whenever their products deliver relatively high—and invariably short-term—returns. "Leave us free to tempt investors to a hot fund-of-the-month," seems to be the industry's position, "but don't ask us to reveal an annualized rate of return."

At least part of the industry's concern is expressed in that statement, however. Clients indeed would take their business elsewhere if the annualized performance consistently and dramatically underperformed an earnings target agreed upon by the investor and the advisor.

This bulwark that keeps investors in the dark about the RRSP performance may yet crumble. In early 2006 a group of fee-only advisors, people independent of sales commissions and trailing fees, launched a petition to the Ontario Securities Commission (OSC) on the group's website, showmethereturn.com. The petition asks the OSC to require investment firms to reveal the annual rate of return on client statements. To its credit, the OSC included the proposal in its Fair Dealing Model (FDM), floated in early 2004 and still being evaluated by a committee of regulators and investment industry representatives. It took the OSC four years to prepare the FDM and it has taken the evaluation group three years to study it. How long will it take to implement its ideas? Hint: Don't hang by your thumbs.

The Seduction Factor: Do We Become Angry or Chagrined?

Canadians with RRSP and RRIF portfolios pay MER rates considered excessive in other markets, and the gap continues to widen. Between 1980 and 2005, average MERs on mutual funds sold in the U.S.A. fell from 2.32 percent to 1.13 percent, a reduction of more than half.[28] Yet, during the same period, the average MER paid by Canadians *rose* a similar amount. Why do Canadians put up with such an inequitable situation? For two reasons: lack of knowledge on our part, and lack of transparency on the part of the industry and its marketers.

Consider money market funds, which are suitable as a place to park your RRSP contribution while you decide on a long-term investment strategy, or as the cash portion of your RRSP. Money market funds invest in government treasury bills, which means they are about as difficult to manage as a sidewalk lemonade stand. Check the financial pages of your local newspaper for the interest that federal and provincial governments are paying on 90-day T-bills and you have performed all the research required to run a money market fund. Everything else is mechanical. You buy the T-bills, sell them after 90 days to earn accrued interest, use the cash to buy more, wait another 90 days, and so on. That's how to manage a money market fund. It's not only a no-brainer, it's risk-free.

MERs for money market funds are admittedly much lower than any other type of mutual fund, but many have excessively high MERs in relation to the returns they generate. The difference in *gross* earnings between mutual funds is essentially infinitesimal. After all, every fund dips into the same pool. But the difference in your net earnings is phenomenal.

For a true evaluation of money market fund costs, add the MER to the latest total annual return, divide the sum by the latest annual return the fund generated, and multiply by 100. The result represents the percentage return of money earned from your dollars but retained by the fund manager. A reasonable figure might be 30 percent; the average is 40 percent, and many are higher—far higher. Here's a sampling of the amount of money various Canadian money market funds pocketed, based on the above formula.[29]

SELECTED MONEY MARKET FUNDS: % RETURNS AND PROFITS RETAINED BY FUND

FUND	MER	RETURN*	TOTAL	RETAINED
Acuity Money Market	1.85	1.2	3.05	60
AGF Canadian Money Market	1.58	1.5	3.08	52
AIM Short-Term Income B	2.20	0.6	2.8	78
Investors Money Market	1.14	2.1	3.24	35
Maritime Life Money Market C	2.14	1.0	3.14	68
TD Premium Money Market	0.32	2.9	3.12	10
Altamira T-Bill	0.42	2.8	3.12	14

* As of May 31, 2006

The AIM fund paid itself 78 percent of the profit earned by its unit holders' money for performing the same function as the other funds. Why? Because it can. If you like the TD Premium Money Market fund with its relatively healthy return and low 10 percent retention of earnings … feggitaboutit—unless you have $250,000 to invest. That's the ante needed to join this fund's party, and it's one reason for the rock-bottom MER. File this under The Rich Get Richer. The Altamira fund is just as good and requires a much lower ante, but lots of luck having a commission-based advisor recommend it to you—it's no-load, like all Altamira funds, and pays no commissions or trailer fees.

Since the cash portion of most RRSPs and RRIFs should not exceed 15 or 20 percent of the portfolio's total, these low yields won't seriously depress your portfolio's performance in the long run. In essence, low returns are the price you pay for liquidity and security. But why pay one fund manager eight times as much to hold your money as another, since both are investing in identical instruments?

If you would drive several blocks to save a nickel a litre on the gasoline you put in your car—and most people will—why wouldn't you make a decision to pay one-eighth as much in management fees for several thousand dollars of your RRSP investment? *Because you were not aware of the alternative.* Gas stations post their prices prominently. Mutual fund companies do not.

Market Timing: A Great Way to Ensure a Profit from Your Mutual Funds

Legal and borderline-legal activities of mutual fund sponsors in the United States were highlighted in 2003 through the headline-grabbing efforts of New York State Attorney General Eliot Spitzer. Spitzer attacked a number of abuses that had gone unnoticed and uncorrected for years and that lined the pockets of mutual fund executives at the expense of investors.

Among the activities identified by Spitzer and his crew was late trading, which is similar to placing a bet on a horse race after the winner has been declared. Late traders use the six-hour time difference between the closing of European stock markets and the closing of markets in New York to make profits unavailable to retail investors. When the London market closes, the gain or loss for that day is fixed, but North American mutual funds investing in European stocks are still priced according to the previous day's close. A sharp rise in European stock markets would trigger a late trader to purchase units that day in a mutual fund holding these stocks. The fund's unit value would rise overnight and be sold for a certain profit the following day when new valuations were posted.

It sounds like a sure way to make money, except for a couple of obstacles. One is a question of law—late trading is illegal in the United States. The other is a question of practicality—no one except mutual fund insiders could even attempt to get away with it, because investors cannot buy and sell mutual fund units that way, thanks to high penalties for trading funds within 60 days of purchase. Yet several dozen people in the United States managed to practise late trading and make a bundle of money in the process. Spitzer's investigation proved that top management in many mutual fund companies knew or should have known that their own people were conducting late trading, but they declined to take action until threatened with criminal charges.

A variation on late trading is market timing, which takes advantage of stale prices created by differences in time zones while the markets remain open. Market timing is not illegal although, like late trading, it requires extraordinary access to securities that is unavailable to ordinary investors. Taking advantage of market timing requires the means to buy and sell within a short period of time often measured in hours, an opportunity that is unthinkable for mutual fund unit holders like you and me. Is this merely a matter of membership having its privileges—in this case, membership in the financial/investment community with access to overnight trading? No, because that attitude suggests that everyone on the inside wins and no one on the outside loses.

Market timing enables a small group of people to enjoy opportunities the rest of us envy. They earn a profit without actually spending money on the investments within the fund—the ones that people like you and me make possible. And the profits they take home come directly out of our pockets, one way or another. Money rushing in and out of a fund means the fund manager must keep substantial cash on hand, perhaps more than she wants, to handle the late trades. This is cash that cannot be invested the way you and I expect it to be; one qualified source estimates market timing can cost legitimate fund investors between 1 and 2 percent annually in lost earnings.[30]

Responding to a spate of revelations regarding late trading and market timing among U.S. funds, in November 2003 the Ontario

Securities Commission (OSC) leapt into action in defence of Canadian mutual fund investors. It wrote a letter.

The letter, sent by OSC chairman David Brown* to all publicly traded mutual funds under OSC jurisdiction, politely requested fund managers to provide evidence the managers had of late trading in their funds, along with the results of any investigations launched. The matter was of questionable urgency, since it gave the fund managers almost six weeks to respond. Here is what the OSC promised to do with its findings:

> *Your responses will be kept confidential to the extent permitted by law. Note however that it is our intention to summarize the feedback we receive on an overall basis and to report back to you on those results at a later date.*

And the letter concludes:

> *As is our normal practice, we ask that you provide a copy of this letter to your funds' auditors and to your funds' and/or the manager's Board of Directors, or to the funds' trustees, as the case may be.*
>
> *We look forward to working with you to reaffirm investors' confidence in the mutual fund industry. Thank you in advance for your cooperation.*[31]

If the OSC were seeking to "reaffirm investors' confidence in the mutual fund industry," why did it promise to report its results only to the mutual fund managers? Who is looking after the interests of the retail investors, whose $400-plus billions are funding the industry?

---

*Mr. Brown has since retired as OSC chairman.

Well, perhaps the media. Six months later, *The Globe and Mail*'s Report on Business section ran a series of articles on the Canadian mutual fund industry, kicking off with a detailed examination of the churn rate for more than 100 international and global funds. The conclusion? Late trading might not have been carried out by insiders, but evidence arose that its slightly less nefarious cousin, market timing, had been lining the pockets of various insiders.

The churn rate measured how often units within the fund changed hands over the four-year period from 2000 to 2003; a churn rate of 100 percent was the equivalent of every unit in the fund being bought and sold within one year. The results, in many cases, did not require an affable letter from the OSC to generate some suspicions.

SELECTED CANADIAN MUTUAL FUNDS, 2000–2003

| | CHURN RATE (%) | | | |
FUND	2000	2001	2002	2003
AGF Asian Growth Class	383	1185	599	364
AIC Global Advantage	908	1627	1046	431
AIC Global Diversified	898	1619	900	270
CI International Balanced	292	–	1300	764
Clarington Global Equity	286	400	457	292
RBC Asian Equity	246	325	522	115

SOURCE: *THE GLOBE AND MAIL*, JUNE 21, 2004. REPRODUCED WITH PERMISSION.

Note that units in AIC's Global Advantage fund—managed by the "Buy. Hold. And Prosper" company—changed hands more than 10 times annually in two consecutive years. During 2001, the equivalent of each unit in both AIC funds was bought and sold about every three weeks. If we assume that a substantial number of fund holders held their units, the rest must have been traded far more often than every three weeks to produce this figure. Why? Market timing, *The Globe and Mail* report suggested.

Admittedly, these are not gigantic funds in terms of asset value. The CI International Balanced is the largest, with assets just under $500 million, and the AIC Global Diversified is the smallest, at less than $40 million. Even so, how could units valued at almost half a billion dollars change hands 13 times in 12 months, as the CI fund appears to have done during 2002? There may be a logical explanation for this phenomenon, but if the OSC discovers it, we may have to wait a very long time for its mandarins to share the data with investors.

Canada not only lacks an Eliot Spitzer to chase down evidence of this activity and lay charges where appropriate, it lacks both the structure and determination needed to aggressively root out abuses throughout the financial and investment industry. Nothing like the U.S. Securities and Exchange Commission, with all its powers to protect the small investor, exists in Canada. Nor can we expect one in the foreseeable future. (For details on this lack of investor protection, see Chapter 9.)

No one likes to be reminded of his or her ignorance, but most people who invest in mutual funds must face the reality that *they don't know what they don't know.* They trust "professionals" whose obligation toward their own well-being often dominates any comparable concern for the clients' well-being. In investment, as in romance, trust and ignorance produce a willingness to be seduced, and Canadians have been seduced by the mutual fund industry specifically, and the investment industry generally, for decades.

Soft Dollars—They're Paid for with Your Hard Cash

Little by little, the blackout material is being peeled from windows in the mutual fund industry to reveal how it manages to skim money out of the hundreds of billions held in trust. One of the more arcane methods relates to soft dollars.

Soft dollars does not refer to rubber loonies. It's a backdoor method used by mutual funds to retain a larger portion of the MER charged against the funds in your portfolio—or maybe pay for a junket or two to Phoenix in February. Here's how it works.

Mutual funds buy and sell shares in the companies making up the funds in the same way everyone else does—through brokers. A fund trading $100 million in stocks every year represents a major account to brokerages that charge a commission on every trade. Persuading fund managers to place trades with their brokerage takes more than a smile and a shoeshine on the part of brokers. One of the things it may take is a rebate on commissions. This is neither new nor exclusive to the investment industry. But it's the manner in which these rebates are handled that raises concerns.

Suppose the brokerage charges the mutual fund five cents for every trade handled—a nickel for every share purchased and every share sold. The hard-dollar cost to the mutual fund might be just two cents per share; the remaining three cents becomes either a cash rebate (which should go directly into the fund assets and thus into the hands of investors—an unlikely event) or a credit to be exchanged for specialized services. The credits are labelled soft dollars.

Is it worth getting excited about a lousy three-cent rebate? Yes it is, because of the scale of things. Trade enough shares and those three-cent rebates start adding up to real money—like $100 million annually, or about 20 percent of the industry's total trading commissions, according to one source.[32] The total may be even higher, because one qualified critic of soft dollars suggests the rebate portion could represent as much as 80 percent of the transaction commissions paid from fund assets.

Soft dollar rebates can be spent by mutual funds on a variety of items, such as research reports, financial analysis software and the computers to run it, trips for fund managers and staff to attend investment conferences in Switzerland or seminars in Arizona, and rent on VIP boxes in arenas and stadiums where advisors and brokers, not fund investors, can nibble smoked salmon and sip Chardonnay high above the ice or turf. Some of these perks can be justified in terms of assisting fund managers and staff to do their jobs, but that's what the MER is for—management expense ratio, remember? Spending the hidden commissions on these items means the fund gets to retain a larger portion of the MER for itself.

Canadian regulators are several steps behind those in the home of laissez-faire capitalism when it comes to protecting retail investors from this contrivance. In 1998, the U.S. Securities and Exchange Commission discovered that soft dollars were used to purchase fund-management "necessities" such as Broadway theatre tickets, limousine rides, and interior design services. The SEC brought its hammer down on a number of investment industry giants, including Massachusetts Financial Services, Morgan Stanley, Janus Capital Group, and Bank One, persuading them to abolish the use of soft dollars.

When this news broke, the supposed pacesetter among Canadian securities watchdogs, the Ontario Securities Commission (OSC), claimed it would take action. The subject, said a spokesperson for the OSC, "is definitely on our radar screen … and we are definitely keeping abreast of all the developments in the U.S. and the U.K."[33] As we shall see, statements like this suggest we should "definitely" not expect anything of substance to emerge from the OSC for some time.

Meanwhile, people with more clout than individual investors and more perspicacity than the OSC, such as those managing the Ontario Teachers' Pension Plan Board (total 2004 assets: $76 billion), refuse to use soft dollars offered by brokerage firms, claiming, "They are so rife with conflict of interest [they] shouldn't be touched with a ten-foot pole."[34]

Soft dollars are yet another symptom of the way your RRSP assets, if invested in a mutual fund, become accessible in various ways to those we entrust with our money. Unjustifiable high MERs, punitive DSCs, hidden trailer fees, soft dollars, and a prevailing lack of transparency all warrant serious investigation by appropriate regulatory bodies.

Perhaps because we are Canadians and typically unresponsive to rabble-rousers, or simply because it's more soothing to be chagrined at our innocence than angry at our persecutors, we have done little or nothing in response to the misdeeds of people we entrust to help us build a secure financial future. It's time we defended ourselves with knowledge and armed ourselves with a determination to trust ourselves first. In this manner, we can remind the investment industry just who is working for whom.

The mutual fund industry will claim that investors never comment on MER levels and DSCs as long as the funds are producing 15 percent or more interest, as many (but certainly not all) achieved during the late 1990s. That's like saying that everyone has a reliable car when it's running well. The test of quality arises when conditions are less than ideal, for both driving and investing. (Nor is the industry's self-serving claim necessarily true. From 1996 to 1999, the Toronto Stock Exchange 300 composite index delivered outstanding returns—more than 17 percent annually—yet the number of complaints rose more than 150 percent.)[35]

The industry's comment avoids the issue of transparency. It is not far-fetched to suggest that a clearer vision of its operations might provide Canadian investors with more realistic expectations and greater confidence in the abilities of their advisors.

On a wider scale, Canadians need to understand how the mutual fund industry earns income from the assets of its unit holders and how its structure invites abuses that would be intolerable in any other business. Consider Power Corporation of Canada, controlled by the

Desmarais family. Among its holdings are five companies, each promoting its own line-up of mutual funds. In mid-2004, these tallied as follows.

THE INFLUENCE OF POWER CORPORATION AND ITS SUBSIDIARIES	
POWER CORPORATION DIVISION	MUTUAL FUNDS MARKETED
Canada Life Assurance	70
Great-West Lifeco	116
Investors Group	345
London Life	56
Mackenzie Financial Corporation	226
Total	813

On that basis, about one of every four mutual funds marketed to Canadians is controlled by one company which, in turn, is controlled by one family: the Desmarais family. This kind of concentration of power is not unusual in Canada—the print and broadcast media industry is similar—but this does not make it any less intolerable or dangerous.

You Own the Shares, So Why Not the Power?

Investors who purchase units of mutual funds investing in publicly traded companies own portions of these firms, just as they would if they bought shares in the corporations on the stock market. With one difference: Mutual fund unit holders lack the voting power that direct-purchase shareholders enjoy.

To be sure, granting mutual fund unit holders similar powers to those of direct-purchase shareholders complicates the process, but it's basically a matter of crunching computerized data that already exists. Of course, this would also require unit holders to become involved and make appropriate decisions—an attitude that Canadian investors have rarely demonstrated in the past. Without the considerable shareholder power of unit holders, however, questionable treatment of majority shareholders becomes possible, such as the one conducted by the notorious Conrad Black, or Lord Black of Crossharbour as he prefers to be known.

In 1996, Black manoeuvred five independent members off the board of the large and influential Canadian newspaper corporation Southam Inc., essentially giving Black total control over the corporation and providing him with the opportunity to tighten his grip on the print media in Canada. He achieved this demonstration of corporate power despite owning only a 41 percent stake in Southam, substantially less than the majority of outstanding shares needed to stage such a coup, because several mutual fund managers and pension fund administrators chose not to vote on the matter. At least one mutual fund, Trimark, opposed the move, but its votes, representing about 10 percent of the outstanding shares, were not counted due to an "administrative error." Black described the ousted directors as "an obdurate rump."[36] Before you reach for your dictionary, here are the definitions of *obdurate: hardened in wrongdoing; stubbornly wicked; hardened in feelings; resistant to persuasion; unyielding.*

No one knows how many unit holders in mutual funds investing in Southam shared this opinion; they were never offered an opportunity to comment. Nor were they permitted an opinion regarding the concentration of so much media power in the hands of one individual. And so, despite the presence of securities administrators who profess concern about the rights of minority shareholders, Black streamrollered over them thanks to the acquiescence of various fund managers. Or, as the thesaurus-loving Lord Black might choose to put it, but probably will not: *Their prepotency was inestimably attenuated by unfettered hegemony.*

Let's just say they got screwed.

Where Is the Quid Pro Quo for Investors?

Investor advocates have long called for greater transparency in all dealings between mutual fund sponsors and corporations, with little success. Such disclosures could be easily implemented in the various communications distributed by the fund companies to their unit holders, but none seem interested—primarily because the unit holders are not aware of the situation and thus are themselves uninterested. But given the illegal activities uncovered by Eliot Spitzer and his attack dogs in the United States, and the much weaker enforcement machinery and atmosphere in Canada, are we to assume that the Canadian industry is substantially more trustworthy? Only at our peril.

Anyone who doubts the power of the country's mutual fund industry and the strength of its resistance to greater oversight should reflect on periodic attempts by securities administrators to monitor its actions.

In early 2002 the Canadian Securities Administrators (CSA), the closest entity Canada has to a national securities commission, began examining ways to ensure that the mutual fund industry in this country is behaving itself. Among the goals addressed by the CSA were avoidance of conflicts of interest and assurance that the industry is acting according to the welfare of investors. Mutual fund companies owe more than a fiduciary obligation to the people who entrust the firms with their assets; they owe a wider responsibility to act according to the same general guidelines applied to other industries.

The CSA chewed over recommendations from mutual fund representatives and, after almost two years, it burped up a Pablum-like formula that had everyone criticizing its blandness—everyone, that is, except the mutual fund industry.

The proposal unveiled by the CSA in January 2004 suggested, rather innocuously, that mutual fund companies be required to set up independent review committees (IRCs) to monitor potential conflicts of interest that arise. In most industries, a board of directors is assigned the role of overseeing operations, but guess what? Canadian mutual funds are not required to have boards. So the idea of each fund employing an IRC (some already do) sounded both wise and tenuous. The industry was being asked, in effect, to once again regulate itself[37]—hardly a draconian proposition. In fact, the proposed rule permitted a fund company to ignore the proposals of its own IRC, if it chose to do so.

Even this restrained idea was too much for the industry to accept, and it responded to the idea of compulsory IRCs by demanding a quid pro quo. If mutual fund companies were to be required to establish IRCs to monitor potential conflicts of interest, they insisted on the right to free managers from previously restricted transactions, even if these transactions might conflict with investor interests. And they got it.

Among the transactions that the industry wanted more freedom to conduct was self-dealing, which occurs when the parent company of a mutual fund instructs the fund to purchase shares in a third company to benefit the parent corporation. The practice is strictly prohibited in the United States and the United Kingdom; in Canada, the industry wants flexibility to engage in it.

The IRCs, by the way, will have the right to publish their findings in the funds' annual reports. But guess what? The industry also wants to repeal the need to issue annual reports to every unit holder. First it fights the establishment of IRCs, and then it proposes a method of keeping IRC findings from investors.

Investor groups were outraged at the gutting of the original plan. Managers of mutual fund companies simply nodded and smiled. One commentator noted that Canada and the United States were moving in opposite directions when it came to protecting investor interests. "We see ... the continued divergence of the paths being taken [by the SEC] in trying to bolster its already extensive mutual fund governance regime," said industry critic Stephen Erlichman, "and by the CSA's made-in-Canada solution proposing a more narrow independent review committee model without any requirement for mandatory compliance plans."[38]

Erlichman is referring to a U.S. mutual fund governance system, in place since 1940, which calls for mutual fund companies to maintain a board of directors, among other directives. When scandals of mismanagement and self-serving policies began brewing in the fund industry, the SEC tightened its control by demanding stricter compliance procedures and dictating that at least three-quarters of all mutual fund directors must be independent of management.

Glorianne Stromberg, whose qualifications for commenting on industry practices are as stalwart as her reputation for speaking her mind, was furious at the proposals. She declared them "outrageous," adding, "They fly in the face of common sense" and are "akin to revoking the rules of the road and leaving it to individual users of the road to set their own rules. The resulting chaos and injuries could be catastrophic." In case anyone doubted her emotional state of mind, Stromberg declared, "The CSA's stated expectation that fund managers and their independent review committees [IRCs] will start with the existing rules and build on them is pathetic in its naïveté."[39]

The mutual fund industry remained smugly silent—"except for the sound of champagne corks popping," commented one wag.

INVESTMENT PORNOGRAPHY
AND RED SUITS

Larry Elford hardly presents the appearance of an angry man, even when his words grow bitter in their attack on a business that once provided him with an annual income exceeding the dreams of most Canadians. He smiles and laughs easily, and delights in his newly assumed role as one of Canada's most outspoken investor advocates. As he recounts his experience in the investment industry, his passion and demeanour suggest a reformed sinner seizing the pulpit of an evangelistic church to preach warnings of fire and brimstone.

"The industry likes to say it's no better or worse than other professions when it comes to its share of bad apples," Larry says. "They'll claim maybe 5 percent of advisors break the rules to line their own pockets." He pauses for effect, holding a smile. "Well, I say it's more like 80 percent."[40]

Really? Four out of five advisors are not to be trusted?

"This is not a business of trust," he continues. "It's a business of misleading people. I was a part of it for 20 years, and the longer I was there, the harder it became to stay among the 20 percent who were practising what they were preaching, which involved looking after other people's money by putting their clients' interests ahead of their own."

One early example of the industry's efforts to mislead people, according to Larry Elford, occurred in 1988 when the business cards of every broker at his firm's office in Lethbridge, Alberta, were replaced with new cards. "The old ones identified us as brokers," Larry grins as he speaks, "which is what we thought we were. But this happened just after the fall of the stock markets in October, 1987. The term 'broker' had a negative definition, so overnight we became 'investment advisors.' Nothing had changed in our training or our work. We were still salespeople. But the industry didn't want the public to hear that. 'Salespeople' suggests putting up your guard. 'Advisor' means handing them your trust."

Some might term this a marketing decision rather than an effort to mislead the public. Larry disagrees, claiming it's symptomatic of an industry refusing to accept any controls over its operations that could hinder its opportunity to squeeze as much profit as possible from trusting investors.

"Instead of practising the trade of the industry," he comments, "most advisors practise the tricks of the trade. Don't forget that this is a self-regulating industry, which means it gets to choose the rules it enforces and the rules it ignores. It can—and does—look the other way when some rules are broken, and punishes people for breaking other rules. That's not an environment conducive to ensuring honesty."

When it's proposed that the commission-based system may encourage advisors to make decisions in their interests over the interests of clients, and that a fee system would alleviate that problem, Larry scoffs at the idea. "Bad advisors want it both ways," he claims. "They want a fee structure that says they're professional, and a commission system that earns them extra money. Then they can double-dip."

According to him, advisors "double-dip" by promoting the fee system as a means of eliminating investor concerns associated with commission-based service. "They'll tell the client, 'My compensation is linked to my success at growing your portfolio. When it goes up, we both win.' That sounds very nice, but as soon as the client is on the fee system, the advisor loads up the portfolio with every new issue that comes through the door, and each one pays the advisor an underwriting fee that the client never hears about."

He spent his 20-year career with three large brokerage firms—Midland Walwyn, ScotiaMcLeod, and RBC Dominion. All lectured their brokers/advisors on the wisdom of creating a profile to set themselves apart from others. "It was like branding," Larry explains. "So I looked for my own brand. Would I be the community-minded advisor? The symphony sponsor? The sports and athletics guy? I decided I would be known by my unyielding ethics. Really. That was my brand. Total honesty."

His brand proved successful. After Larry had worked for 20 years as a broker/advisor, the portfolios of his book of clients exceeded $100 million, which is impressive anywhere but especially in a smaller community like Lethbridge. In 2003, the *Lethbridge Herald* published a column written and submitted by him. Titled "To Fee or Not to Fee," it discussed the definition and implications of mutual funds with deferred sales charges, front-end loads, trailer fees, and so on. "I wrote it as an investor education piece," Larry says, "talking about things that everybody in the business knows about but few investors understand. Nowhere did I promote any product, nor did I mention the name of my brokerage. It was simply a means of educating consumers."

His employers didn't see it that way. Citing an Investment Dealers Association (IDA) rule that prohibits licensed brokers/advisors from publishing unauthorized and unapproved marketing material, Larry's firm threatened him with an array of penalties ranging from a fine to demanding that he rewrite his qualifying examination to outright dismissal. He saw the company's reaction as an extension of the industry's hypocritical policies and resigned. "I got tired of other people pissing in my pool," he says.

Larry Elford now owns a helicopter service in Lethbridge along with a coffee shop, wine bar, and other investments, and spent much of the summer of 2006 traversing Canada with a film crew, interviewing clients and industry critics for a planned documentary on the state of the industry.

What of his claim that 80 percent of brokers/advisors in Canada break the rules in dealing with their clients? How can he justify it?

"Imagine you have a police force in which 80 percent are good cops, dedicated to protecting the public and doing things strictly by the book," he responds. "Don't you think they would put pressure on the 20 percent of bad cops who were giving everyone else a bad name? Sure they would. Now turn it around—80 percent are crooked and only 20 percent are clean. How many of the clean guys could risk blowing whistles on the majority? And if they did, what are their chances of being heard? That is what's happening in the investment business. The bad cops are silencing the good cops." He grows uncharacteristically glum for a moment. "I left a business that I enjoyed because I had to, and I resent it. Now I'm trying to change it from the only place I can—from the outside."

Before leaving, he hands his business card across the table. On the reverse side from his name and business logo, the card bears this quotation from Reverend Martin Luther King: *Our lives begin to end the day we become silent about things that matter.*

Many financial advisors and brokers view unsophisticated investors as sheep. Sheep are passive, dutiful animals to be shorn of their wool, generating income for shepherds while leaving themselves naked. Sheep are easily intimidated and can be herded by an animal no more clever than a border collie. The biggest difference between sheep and most people who invest their RRSP and RRIF money is that the shepherd feeds the sheep. When it comes to mutual funds, the sheep feed the shepherd.

Elford's opinion of advisors notwithstanding, the vast majority of RRSP investors need qualified advice if only to counter their own irrational approach to investing. What are the roots of this irrationality? Financial advisors, brokers, mutual fund salespeople, and mutual fund sponsors claim that they are genetic, like a predisposition of some people to gamble, take drugs, or smoke cigarettes. Investor advocates suggest the more likely causes of irrationality are misplaced trust, fear, and manipulation.

Here's a classic example of investment irrationality. Suppose, during your weekly grocery shopping, you discover your favourite canned tuna on sale. Last week it cost $2 a can. This week it's only $1 a can. That's a deal, so you sweep a dozen cans into your shopping cart and stack them in your pantry. You have made a rational buying decision.

If the price had doubled, and instead of $2 a can the tuna was selling for $4 a can, would you stock up in the same manner? Of course not. That would be irrational. Yet this is the same way most people choose mutual funds. When the price of mutual funds and stocks shoots skyward, we allow ourselves to be convinced that it's time to board the bandwagon. We pay inflated prices for mutual fund units and stocks that others bought at half the price not long ago. When the funds and stock prices topple from the high price we paid for them, we grow even more irrational and sell the devils to ... well, usually to the clever (and wealthy) folks we bought them from when the price was high.

Everyone who absorbed the lessons of grade two arithmetic can comprehend the wisdom of "Buy low, sell high." Why do so many Canadians, intent on maximizing the earnings from their RRSPs and RRIFs, insist on buying high and, when the price inevitably collapses, selling low? Are we that irrational? Are we that genetically disposed to failure?

To a degree, these actions are a result of the manner in which mutual funds are sold and the way the salespeople are rewarded.

Investment markets, including stocks, bonds, mutual funds, resources, and commodities, are priced according to two emotions: fear and greed. Or, if you prefer, depression and euphoria. Nightmares and dreams.

Fear drives people to sell in the face of threats ranging from terrorism to an oversupply of pork bellies. Greed persuades them that everyone else is getting rich, so they should join in.

Marketers of mutual funds know this axiom and have become expert at exploiting it to a remarkable degree. When things are going well, they feed our greed. When times get tough, they nurture our fears. There's nothing personal about it. It's strictly business.

Purveyors of Investment Pornography

During the last half of the 1990s, when mutual funds everywhere began generating substantial earnings in a market driven by abnormally low interest rates and a hyped tech market, mutual fund marketers engaged in investment pornography. The pornography description applies, financial advisor John J. De Goey explains, because "it gets you all hot and excited, but ultimately doesn't lead to anything productive." Mutual fund returns, trumpeted in newspaper advertisements with the same large type once reserved for declarations of war, qualify for the most egregious class of investment pornography when blasted from financial sections of our newspapers and financial commentators on radio and TV. The statistics and opinions must be important, or else why are they receiving so much attention? But to those with a time horizon extending 10 years and beyond—which includes anyone under 70 years of age with an RRSP—investment pornography is, or should be, as insubstantial as tomorrow's weather forecast. It will be hot or cold, sunny or cloudy, calm or windy, wet or dry. And the next day, it will be different. Same with financial news. "In the short run," De Goey advises, "returns are unknowable. In the long run, they are inevitable."[41]

In the late 1990s, when almost every mutual fund was crowing over annual returns of 15, 20, 25 percent and more while bonds were paying barely 5 or 6 percent, it was irrational to ignore returns that high. So millions of Canadians slid billions of RRSP dollars into funds at the top of the earnings curve. The higher the curve went, the more people clambered aboard, as though bandwagons roll on forever. They do not.

The ride was paralleled by the Bre-X phenomenon, which gave mutual fund companies an opportunity to create a new and exciting investment opportunity—or at least the illusion of it.

Bre-X Minerals Ltd. proved to be one of the great scams of all time, but while its worthless stock was rising ever upward, mutual fund companies saw an opportunity rising with it. Bre-X was the product of exploration for gold. So why not create a mutual fund based on exploration stocks, connected to natural resource funds? Well, why not bet the bundle on today's daily double while you are at it? Many exploration stocks are as likely to pay off as nags at a racetrack. This became a classic example of *funds du jour*.

When Bre-X and its resource cousins collapsed, telecom and internet companies took their place as new daily specials. Soon their high double- and even triple-digit returns made up much of the investment pornography. Encouraged by commissioned advisors, RRSP owners clambered aboard at the top of a new roller-coaster ride.

One of the most colourful guys in Canadian investment history was a stock promoter named Murray Pezim. One month he might be pushing a gold mine in Peru, the next month a textile company in Sudan. Pezim didn't promote stocks according to their value. He promoted what sold best. "If they want red suits," Pezim would say, "give 'em red suits." Murray Pezim died several years ago, and little has changed since.

Mutual Funds Bury Their Dead

Few of the hot exploration and resource mutual funds that set pulses racing back in the good ol' days of Bre-X and 25 percent annual returns are still around today, because the mutual fund industry keeps itself busy during bear markets by burying its dead, claiming the funds have been resurrected as winners. Perhaps no other industry in the world has the gall, the ability, and the dedication to conceal its failures by dressing them in the garb of success.

When every chicken shack operator could score a success by launching a mutual fund based on tech and internet stocks, AIM Trimark followed Murray Pezim's red suit rule and introduced several new funds investing in the tech bubble. They included the AIM Global Telecommunications Class, AIM Canadian Leaders, and, in June 2000, AIM RSP Dent Demographics Fund, all marketed with much fanfare and healthy MERs.

None of these new funds had any rationale for their existence beyond an attempt to take advantage of a marketing opportunity. In the bull market that dominated the late 1990s, fund companies expanded their line-up as a means of multiplying the potential number of funds that might prove winners. In effect, this was using someone else's money to bet more numbers at the roulette table— it increases your odds of winning and, if you lose, it's money out of someone else's pocket.

In a bear market, when few funds are able to post advances, the marketing strategy dictates that poor performers be hidden behind the skirts of more successful products.

The AIM RSP Dent Demographics Fund was a classic marketing example. The "Dent" had nothing to do with the risks of leaving your car in supermarket parking lots. It referred to the fund's inspiration, a man named Harry S. Dent, whose qualifications include a Harvard MBA, a degree in economics, and a book he authored in

2000 declaring North American stock markets would climb inexorably through to 2008, thrusting the Dow Jones Index to 40,000 or more, fuelled by baby boomer wealth and acquisitions. In mid-2000, the bandwagon was moving. Huzzah! Hop aboard and ride with us to wealth, or be left behind to wallow in poverty and squalor! That's as a good a reason as any to launch a mutual fund, right?

When its U.S. parent created a fund carrying Dent's name and based on his fearless predictions, AIM Trimark followed the lead in Canada, dressing Dent in a red suit. Perhaps it should have been a hair shirt, because here's how the fund performed over the next three years.

AIM DENT DEMOGRAPHIC TRENDS FUND	
2000	−32.68%
2001	−32.06%
2002	−17.22%

SOURCE: CONTRATHEHEARD.COM, JANUARY 2003. REPRODUCED WITH PERMISSION.

Anyone who bought $10,000 of Dent's red suit at the beginning of 2000 had a mere $3790 in his or her account three years later. The bandwagon hadn't just broken down—it had rolled backward into a ditch. AIM eventually buried the wreck in its Global Theme Fund. While at it, the company disposed of two other former stars, now ailing dogs, tucking its Global Telecommunications Class into the AIM Global Technology Class, and dumping its AIM Canadian Leaders fund down the gullet of the Trimark Canadian Endeavour fund.

Glorianne Stromberg calls this technique "survivorship bias," designed to mislead investors into believing the fund sponsor is more successful than it appears. "It's a marvellously effective and efficient way," she suggests, "to fool most of the people all of the time."

"Buy and Hold." But When, and for How Long?

In fairness to mutual fund sponsors, their marketing efforts are questionable and outrageous because they are permitted to be. Permission is granted from two groups: investors, who buy canned tuna/mutual funds with confidence when the price is high and sell with panic when the price is low; and regulators, who are unequipped or unwilling to demand more responsible actions. *The tactics of mutual fund marketers are used because they work, and they work because investors enable them to work*—through fear, through greed, and, unfortunately, through ignorance.

Consider the marketing program favoured by AIC, the "Buy. Hold. And Prosper" company, in the spring of 2003. In its publication titled *History Rewards Excellence,* AIC employed a variation on the device known in mutual fund marketing circles as a mountain chart, so called because, in tracing a fund's growth value over several years, the line appears like the north slope of Mount Everest— constantly rising past crevasses here and there on its way to an apparently infinite summit. With the bear market in 2000, mountain charts grew unfavourable because they were now showing the other side of the mountain, leaving the peak high above and far behind.

AIC's adaptation of a mountain chart is brilliant in its concept and doubtful in its credibility. Instead of using a line graph, it measured the growth in value of five sample companies over a 15-year period, thus justifying the firm's theme of "Buy, Hold," and so on. Here's what the chart showed (prepare to be impressed):

AIC'S FIVE EXAMPLES OF SPECTACULAR RETURNS	
COMPANY	GROWTH IN VALUE (%)*
American Express	+429
Johnson & Johnson Inc.	+1048
Loblaw Co. Ltd.	+1359
Nike Inc.	+1724
Pfizer Inc.	+1474

* December 1987 to December 2002

SOURCE: AIC LTD. PRESENTATION: "HISTORY TENDS TO REWARD EXCELLENCE"/*TORONTO STAR*, MARCH 30, 2003.

Are you reaching for your wallet yet? Wait for some key facts.

First, only five companies are listed. It is not difficult to search out five companies at any point in time that have delivered impressive, even spectacular, returns. The trick is to identify them *before* growth is achieved, not after. It is also important to note that an equity-based mutual fund may hold shares in 100 or more companies; again, it is not surprising that a handful might deliver extraordinary results.

Next, note that four of the five companies are U.S.–based. Three of these—Johnson & Johnson, American Express, and Nike—were held in AIC's Value Fund, but only two—American Express and Johnson & Johnson—were among the fund's Top 10 holdings. Taken together, all five represented less than 10 percent of the fund's total holdings. How well did the other 90 percent fare?

Finally, and most importantly, consider the time frame being analyzed. In the investment game, 1987 is remembered as the year of the October Black Monday crash, when stocks tumbled through the biggest single-day collapse in history. Had you purchased American Express in early October 1987, before Black Monday's collapse, it would have taken seven long years to recover the pre–Black Monday price. In December 1987, American Express was a once-in-a-lifetime bargain. Were you wise enough to purchase it then? Were AIC's fund managers? Who knows? Nor did AIC identify the recent performance of these Big Five stocks, perhaps because after October 1999, American Express, Pfizer, and Nike all dropped in value—Nike by 20 percent.

What, in the end, did AIC's figures reveal? Only that the primary marketing tactic employed by mutual fund sponsors is the same one used by people fishing for trout: Dangle something fleshy on a sharp hook, yank at the right moment, and keep the net handy.

The fleshy bait in this case is a history of impressive returns, the hook is the whispered legally required escape-clause/mantra "Past performance is no indication of future earnings," and the net consists of DSCs and sage advice about buying, holding, and prospering. Guess who the fish is.

Choosing Funds Strictly on Past Performance Is a Mug's Game

Fund performance over 1, 3, 5, and 10 years (if applicable) represents the core of investment pornography. The figures are used by RRSP/RRIF investors, as well as by advisors, brokers, and salespeople, as the basis for choosing a mutual fund. But how much can you rely on them?

Suppose it is 1999 and you are faced with choosing between two funds—the *Standback & Duck (S&D)* Canadian Equity Fund, and the *Fear & Greed (F&G)* Canadian Growth Fund. Both invest primarily in Canadian companies and both sport similar MERs. You start by examining the returns each has generated for its unit holders over the past five years, and they look like this:

S&D vs. F&G AVERAGE ANNUAL RETURNS (%)*					
FUND	1 YEAR	2 YEARS	3 YEARS	4 YEARS	5 YEARS
S&D	5.7	11.5	15.9	16.2	13.6
F&G	11.4	9.9	12.6	12.5	8.7
* January 1994 to January 1999					

Over the previous five years, the *S&D* fund produced average earnings each year of 13.6 percent for its unit holders. The *F&G* fund,
while respectable at 8.7 percent earnings each year, looks weak in
comparison. Which do you trust to make the most of your RRSP
assets over the next five years? Most would choose the *S&D* fund,
which explains the strong correlation between the best-performing
mutual funds of last year and the bestselling funds of this year.

Small problem: *It doesn't work.* Buying last year's winners on the
basis of that measure alone is as foolish as using last year's calendar.
Here's proof.

Standback & Duck and *Fear & Greed* are pseudonyms for two
actual Canadian equity-based mutual funds. If you had plunked
10 Big Ones down on the *S&D* fund back in 1999, see how you
would have done five years later.

S&D vs. F&G AVERAGE ANNUAL RETURNS (%)*					
FUND	1 YEAR	2 YEARS	3 YEARS	4 YEARS	5 YEARS
S&D	20.4	15.2	10.3	14.1	14.3
F&G	81.4	57.7	31.9	28.2	25.5
* January 1999 to January 2004					

Your $10,000 investment in the *S&D* fund back in 1999 grew to $17,150 over the five-year period (14.3 annualized average × 5 years = 71.5 percent growth of $10,000). Hey, not bad. Had you chosen the *F&G* fund, investing the same amount of money over the same period, you would have $22,750 (25.5 × 5 = 127.5 percent growth) or $5600 more in your RRSP than with the *S&D* fund. This does not necessarily mean you have the better fund for the next five years. Research indicates that only about 38 percent of funds delivering better-than-average performance in any given year will manage to deliver the same level of performance, relative to other funds in their class, in the following year.

At first glance, it may look as though choosing the best mutual fund is a mug's game. It is, *as long as you base your choice on past performance figures exclusively, supported by the unchallenged recommendations of your commission-based advisor or broker.*

Fortunately, there is a brighter side. More than a handful of mutual funds beat the odds by delivering above-average performance on a relatively consistent basis. The trick is to identify them, which requires research and the honest assistance of a good financial advisor. Looking beyond average annual performance returns, you should favour funds with low volatility (the way in which the fund's returns and losses vary over an extended period compared with similar funds), especially when you are age 50 or older; low fees (reasonable MERs and no loads of any kind); the fund's mandate (what does the fund invest in—steady blue-chip companies? Volatile smaller companies? Special sectors such as mining or communications? Geographical areas such as Asia, emerging economies, Europe?); and qualified managers (Is he or she new? Highly regarded?).

Chapter 12 includes a checklist for identifying mutual funds that suit your needs and are most likely to enrich your portfolio. Meanwhile, here's yet another way that investment industry marketing skews things in favour of commission-based advisors.

Wrap Accounts: The Devil Persuades You He Doesn't Exist

One of the best movies of recent years was 1995's *The Usual Suspects*. Gritty and mesmerizing, it featured superb acting, great cinematography, and outstanding writing. The plot hinges on a statement made by the lead character, played by actor Kevin Spacey (who won an Academy Award for his portrayal). "The Devil's biggest achievement," Spacey's character says, "was in persuading the world that he doesn't exist."

The existence of wrap accounts suggests that someone in the investment industry was familiar with Spacey's line when the industry developed and marketed this product. How else to explain a service that enables a "professional" to earn more money by doing less work? If the investment industry can convince you that wrap accounts are a good idea because you pay a higher price for less service, maybe Satan pulled off his scam after all.

Wrap accounts are derived from a basic idea gone bad, like that casserole you tucked at the back of the refrigerator last month and forgot about.

The basic idea is asset allocation, the practice of shifting components in your RRSP/RRIF according to changing economic conditions and strategies. It's somewhat like piloting a ship across the ocean—you correct your course to adjust for tides and winds, and steer clear of shoals or storms, keeping your eye on your destination. Brokers and financial advisors might call it rebalancing, preferring the term to an analogy associated with shipwrecks and icebergs.

Banks and mutual fund companies promote wrap accounts as a means of constantly rebalancing your investment. Consign your money to one of their wrap accounts and they'll adjust the investment mix as needed, according to your investor profile. These profiles are usually assigned one of three descriptions: aggressive, moderate, or conservative, based on your age, investment knowledge, and risk comfort level. Want to make as much money in as short a time as possible? You're aggressive. Want to preserve your capital and sleep well at night? You're conservative. If you don't feel totally comfortable with either extreme, you're moderate, which is where most people end up anyway. Another plus for investors, wrap promoters add: You receive one consolidated statement each month instead of those pesky multi-page documents listing several mutual funds, bonds, cash, and other instruments.

While wrap account adherents make it sound as though the investment mix in your RRSP/RRIF is being tailored like a custom-fitted suit, you usually buy off the rack. Most wraps consist of mixes pre-packaged according to the three profiles. Rather than being fitted for a wardrobe, it's more like choosing an airline meal—do you want the chicken, the beef, or the pasta? Forget about à la carte.

Pooled wraps are basic wrap plans dressed to go out on the town, which means they're aimed at a more affluent market. The packages are more elegantly wrapped and carry a name that suggests exclusivity. Two of the most prominent pooled wraps are AGF Harmony and Russell Sovereign, the latter a U.S.–based package marketed in Canada through RBC Investments, ScotiaMcLeod, TD Waterhouse, and other brokerages. Instead of everyday mutual funds, pooled wraps may hold funds not available to the great unwashed, although both types of funds may be directed by the same fund managers.

The advantages of pooled wraps, claims the promotion material, include research, consulting, monitoring, reporting, and perhaps custodial services. Plus prestige and exclusivity.

Here's where the Devil comes in.

First, wrap accounts do the same thing that your financial advisor or broker is supposed to be doing to earn his fee or commission. The basic premise of every financial advisor's pitch involves making decisions that you, you ignorant and uneducated slob, are not equipped to make. Advisors boast that they are in tune with investment policies and strategies, enabling them to guide you in buying, selling, adjusting, and otherwise rebalancing investments in your account. If your broker or advisor does this effectively, congratulations. But if he is being paid for this chore through sales commissions and trailer fees, why is he advising you to hire someone else to do the job?

Brian Moore, senior VP of marketing for CI Mutual Funds Inc., a purveyor of wrap accounts, provided an unintentional answer to that question. "Wrap accounts free up advisors from having to concern themselves with asset allocation, oversight, and monitoring the mix of client portfolios," Moore suggested. "What advisors do best is manage the client relationship and build their businesses."[42] Really??!!

If asset allocation, oversight, and monitoring client portfolios, supposedly with the goal of building wealth for clients, is not as important to advisors as managing client relationships (cards at Christmas, phone calls at RRSP season) and building their business (asking for referrals, joining community groups), *why do we train and license these people?* The job Moore describes could be filled by used car salespeople, retired taxidermists, and an uncle of mine who has been cadging free beers at a local Legion Hall for 23 years now. He is *really* good at building relationships.

Wrap accounts can cost you an extra level of commissions or service fees, since you are now paying for an extra level of management. They also limit the choice of funds available for your portfolio, which means if the mutual funds in your wrap account begin barking and chasing cats up trees, too bad—you lack the opportunity to ditch those dogs for another choice. Many wrap accounts also fail to provide opportunities for investing in sectors such as gold and precious metals. True, sector investing should represent only a minority portion of most RRSPs/RRIFs, but you have given up flexibility and opportunity in return for putting your portfolio on automatic pilot and paying a premium to do it.

Finally, it comes down to performance. A Porsche costs more than a Toyota because it goes faster and turns more tightly. Does it make sense to pay extra for RRSP/RRIF management that produces similar results with your investments? The simple answer is no. Every Porsche might perform the same, but not every wrap account does. In fact, some of the most popular wrap accounts *underperform* the market, charging extra for the privilege of watching your investments lag.

Consider Sovereign Portfolio, the most heavily promoted wrap account in the country, managing over $100 billion in client assets. "Because each Sovereign Portfolio is customized to reflect individual investor needs and goals," boasts its website, "there is an infinite number of Sovereign portfolios." Perhaps. But the number of ways to assess Sovereign's bottom line is limited, and none is encouraging.

Here are average annual returns for RRSP portfolios in the three investor-style categories. Compare them with the average Canadian balanced mutual fund over the same period. Balanced funds invest both in equities—company shares traded on the Toronto Stock Exchange (TSX), for the most part—and guaranteed income sources such as government bonds and T-bills. Many advisors dislike balanced funds for portfolios $100,000 and up, believing better returns are available from a combination of equity-based mutual funds plus bonds. In this instance, balanced funds replicate the promoted benefit of wrap accounts by offering both growth and security.

RRSP PORTFOLIOS – ANNUALIZED TO JUNE 30, 2004, NET OF FEES, CLASS A UNITS			
PORTFOLIO	3 YEARS	5 YEARS	10 YEARS
Conservative	8.53	3.71	5.64
Moderate	9.43	3.32	5.99
Aggressive	12.02	2.12	5.96
Average Cdn. Balanced Fund	9.4	4.6	6.7
S&P/TSX Total Return Index	21.8	9.5	10.2

SOURCES: SOVEREIGN WEBSITE, MAY 31, 2006; GLOBEFUND.COM, JUNE 30, 2006. REPRODUCED WITH PERMISSION.

By running your fingers down the list of 500-plus Canadian balanced mutual funds and selecting one at random, you would be likely to choose one that outperformed an equivalent wrap account assembled by the vaunted Sovereign investment experts. Selecting a low-MER Canadian Equity Index fund mirroring the S&P/TSX would have placed you substantially ahead of the Sovereign wrap account in every period. If I were a Sovereign client, I would ask what I was getting for my money besides exclusivity and prestige, which, the last I heard, rarely adds to the bottom line of anyone's investment.

Are wrap accounts ever beneficial? They are to the advisor or broker who successfully promotes them. To typical RRSP/RRIF owners, they appear to present one more way of having their heads patted while their pockets are being picked.[43]

An Illegal Racket or an Authorized Investment Opportunity?

In September 2003, the Ontario Securities Commission (OSC) issued a warning to investors.[44] Beware, the news release cautioned, of schemes in which investors receive "interest" cheques that are actually a portion of the investor's own money, and account statements showing profits that are not real. The bulletin identified these scams as *Ponzi schemes*, so-named for their inventor, Charles Ponzi, who launched a Boston-based company in 1920 supposedly dealing in U.S. postal reply coupons. When Ponzi promised 50 percent profit in 45 days, and delivered these earnings to the first wave of investors, others joined in, and soon Ponzi was sitting on more than $10 million. In reality, of course, the fraud artist was paying early investors with money from later arrivals. The scheme inevitably collapsed and Ponzi fled to South America, where he died in poverty. His sole legacy was to have his name associated with any fraud similar to the one he originated.

With more than a little irony, industry critics pointed out that the OSC's warning was somewhat hypocritical because the commission was sanctioning hundreds of investment vehicles that appeared to be structured in a similar manner to Ponzi's 80-year-old blueprint. They were not called Ponzi schemes, of course. They were called income trusts.

Until the federal government's October 2006 announcement that income trusts were to be eliminated in 2011, they represented an attractive means to generate cash flow for people converting their RRSPs to RRIFs, a move required by law in the year the RRSP owner turns 69. To some investor advocates, they illustrated the extent to which the industry will go in creating and distributing investment pornography.

Income trusts were not new. Created as a means of generating capital for mature businesses that did not require massive amounts of cash, they proved beneficial for commercial real estate operators and oil producers. When the primary expenditure of these corporations was devoted to property and equipment maintenance, creating an income trust made a good deal of sense. Since an income trust is not a corporation, it is permitted to distribute revenue to investors while avoiding corporate taxation (corporate dividends are taxed first in the hands of the corporation and second in the hands of shareholders, albeit at a favourable rate).

For many years, income trusts were virtually exclusive to commercial real estate operators and oil producers. With the collapse of technology-based share prices and mutual fund values in 2000, however, investors shied away from equity investments. In response, ever-alert marketers in the investment industry saw an opportunity to bring money from disillusioned investors back into the brokerages instead of having investors secrete away money in bonds, GICs, and money market mutual funds, all of which pay brokers/advisors a pittance.

Within months, herds of new income trusts came galloping into the market, driven by shouts of "High yields!" "No corporate tax!" and, of course, "Buy now!" By the end of 2005, income trusts represented 10 percent of the quoted market value of all securities listed on the Toronto Stock Exchange (TSX), 39 percent of all equity capital raised on the TSX, and 22 percent of all new listings.[45]

Literally hundreds of income trusts began blossoming on the TSX like dandelions in May. Many were from the traditional sources of real estate income trusts (REITs) and energy suppliers. Others represented industries and corporations that defied the original premise for income trusts. Here's a small sampling of the latter:

Aeroplan Income Fund
Art in Motion Income Trust
Benvest New Look Income Trust
Boston Pizza Royalties Income Trust
Canadian Helicopters Income Trust
Cineplex Galaxy Income Trust
Clearwater Seafoods Income Trust
Gulf Town Income Trust
Hot House Growers Income Trust
Lakeport Brewery Income Trust
Pizza Pizza Income Trust
Rogers Sugar Income Fund
Second Cup Royalty Income Trust
Sleep Country Canada Income Trust
Sterling Shoes Income Trust
Student Transportation of America Income Trust
Sun Gro Horticulture Income Trust
Swiss Water Decaffeinated Coffee Income Trust
Yellow Pages Income Trust[46]

The morphing of an investment vehicle suitable for real estate operators and oil patch companies into a scheme based on pizza shops, beer companies, decaffeinated coffee producers, and "art in motion" could only occur in a climate of greed and opportunity. Advisors, eager to promote promises of exceptional growth, pushed income trusts on investors who were seeking safer alternatives to stocks. Or perhaps it is more accurate to say advisors nudged investors towards these trusts because the claimed returns of many income trusts did most of the selling. When income trusts began paying annual yields of 20 percent, a stampede was born. Like all stampedes, it easily drowned out voices of caution such as those of Paul Cherry, Chairman of the Canadian Accounting Standards Board. "The income trust sector has somehow convinced people that the cheque they get is a measure of economic performance," Cherry warned. "That's just drivel. The notion of yield has been distorted from a marketing point of view. It has never been part of financial statements."[47]

Cherry claimed that many income funds were paying portions of the investors' capital back to the investors, along with the designated stream of earnings—a clear echo of various Ponzi schemes foisted on trusting investors down through the years. Consider: If 5 percent of capital coming in is added to 10 percent of earned revenue going out each year, the trust can claim a 15 percent annual yield. Promoting that figure would boost the value of trust units skyward, adding to the wealth of the fund managers.

Noting that one research firm estimated that business income trusts were inflating their claimed income—the source of the distribution streams flowing money to investors—by 58 percent, Cherry cautioned: "… the unit holder's equity is shrinking each year. In 99 times out of 100, the distributions are going to be substantially higher than the earnings." Eventually investors would be left holding nothing while the issuers who inflated the earnings numbers would long have sold their units at a premium and gone yachting in the Caymans.

Accountant and investor advocate Al Rosen trumpeted a similar warning: "… the distributable cash figure itself is an invention of each trust," Rosen pointed out. "Company management teams decide the process they will use to calculate their distributable cash. Thus, by definition, the figures are not very comparable between companies because there aren't any standard financial reporting rules, or even quasi-regulatory guidelines for companies to use."[48]

Rosen made a distinction between those who operated income trusts purely as a get-rich-quick scheme and those who legitimately considered them a means of expanding their business through the valuation spread, i.e., the value of units based on an inflated cash flow. Whatever the motive, Rosen suggested, the same disastrous end is a certainty for investors. When companies employ the funds to expand their firm or acquire new businesses, investors would assume the increased revenue was "cash," even though it had not been earned, an assumption that could have driven income trust unit evaluations to stratospheric heights. "I cannot overstate how faulty a presumption this is when it comes to valuing a business from a fundamental viewpoint," Rosen added.

No one appeared to be listening. Not investors, many of whom kept scrambling after new income funds. Not scads of advisors, who pocketed commissions from the sales. And, according to Rosen, not senior officials at the Ontario Securities Commission (OSC). When Rosen suggested that the commission reflect the actions of the Securities and Exchange Commission in the United States, which overrules accounting standards boards in the interests of protecting investors, the response from the OSC was: "You don't expect us to start setting accounting rules, do you?"

When the federal government dropped the hammer on income trusts, its declared motive was to limit the potential loss of corporate tax revenue. Despite cries of anger and rage from investors who might have placed more faith in the operations of some income trusts than they deserved, Ottawa might well have limited the potential loss to investors as well.

Or Perhaps You Prefer a Plate of PPNs?

Anyone who doubts the dominant role that marketing plays in the investment community need only examine principal-protected notes, or PPNs, and the substantial promotional effort devoted to them since 2005.

Income trusts exploit investors' greed, and PPNs exploit their fear—in this case, the fear of losing money. Purchase a PPN, the purveyors of these devices promise, and you can't lose because you are guaranteed to receive at least the full value of the money invested, thus "principal protected." (Other names may be hung on them as well, such as *linked notes* or *return notes*. Same dog, same breed.) If, however, the investment portion happens to make money between now and the PPN's maturity date, often 10 years down the road, you'll earn a profit. You can't lose!

Did investment industry wizards wave their wands to conjure up carriages out of pumpkins and gowns out of sackcloth? Not a bit. Dig into the details and you discover that a PPN consist of two parts: about 70 percent of your money goes into a guaranteed investment, such as a GIC or bond, and the balance goes into an equity investment, usually a market index or mutual fund.

Here's where the magic comes in, but all the stardust from the magician's wand settles in the seller's pocket, not yours.

Assume you invest $10,000 in a 10-year PPN. What's the worst that can happen? After 10 years you get at least the $10,000 back, suggesting you haven't lost a thing—*but you have.* Even at current low interest rates, the same $10,000 in a government-guaranteed bond would return about a $5000 profit over 10 years, and the guarantee on its return is as solid as you can find in the real world.

"Ah," you may think, "but I could earn even more than $5000 because part of my money is going into equity investments." Dream on, McDuff.

Here are the hard facts:

- Your money is tied up for several years. Try to withdraw it prior to the maturity date and you may forfeit the guarantee on the principal and pay a penalty. If that happens, your "can't lose" opportunity becomes a "can't win."

- The guarantee is only as good as the company selling you the PPN. PPNs are not considered deposits and thus are not covered by the Canada Deposit Insurance Corporation or the Régie de l'assurance-dépôts du Québec. If the issuer of your PPN goes out of business before the maturity date or the underlying security proves worthless, be sure you have enough cash on hand for a glass of beer and prepare to cry in it.
- Many PPNs have more fees than a dog has fleas. Among the means of sliding money from your PPN investment into someone else's pocket are *sales commissions* to whomever sells you the PPN; *management fees*, to whomever chooses the investments; *performance fees*, which skim the cream from exceptional investment returns; *structuring fees*, to whomever designs the program; *operating fees*, to whomever runs the show; *trailer fees* (you didn't expect to avoid them, did you?); *early redemption fees*, in case you try to bail out; and *swap arrangement fees*, if you look for a better investment from the folks who sold you this turkey.

It may be possible to make more money from a PPN than you would earn from splitting the $10,000 yourself, putting $7000 in a long-term bond and investing the balance in a blue-chip stock or quality mutual fund. It may also be possible to remove your own appendix.

The greatest value of PPNs is this: They demonstrate the means the investment industry employs to persuade you that its primary objective is to make you wealthy and help you sleep at night. In this case, you pay a very high price for 10 years of good sleep. Meanwhile, most of the folks who devise and promote these goodies sleep very well in a much better bed than yours.

A Guide to Investment Divorce

Carol MacKinnon smiles in the sunlight that floods the deck of her cottage. Set above an inlet of Bowen Island, in British Columbia, the home represents a fulfilment of sorts for the 52-year-old leadership trainer and musician. Inside are her piano, her cello, and the various accoutrements of a varied and interesting life. Her dog naps at her feet and birds flutter around her feeder. Life is good—certainly better than three years earlier.

"I worked all of my life," she reflects. "I never wanted to work past 65 if I could help it, so I put everything I could afford into my RRSP." A single woman with ailing parents, Carol was determined to achieve financial independence and recognized the importance of obtaining independent advice. "I was a financial illiterate," she laughs. "I didn't understand mutual funds. I just knew I didn't want to be in the stock market because I figured that was a place for gamblers, and I didn't want to gamble with my money—I'd worked too darn hard for it! Of course, I didn't know that I was already in the stock market with the mutual funds I owned."

In the 1990s, Carol was employed in Toronto, where she struck a close friendship with a co-worker whose husband was a sales agent for a large insurance company. "She was a chartered accountant, he had a lot of experience; they lived in a large home in an exclusive Toronto neighbourhood, and both drove expensive sports cars," Carol recalls. "They were the picture of success. After a while, the husband suggested I transfer my account to him. I knew people in the investment community were paid by commission, but these were my friends. I trusted them. So I moved my account to him and kept maximizing my RRSP contributions every year. I was working long hard hours, and I knew this was the time, in my 40s, when I should be putting away every penny I could afford. So I did."

In 2000, Carol moved to Vancouver to be closer to her ailing parents on Bowen Island, keeping her account with her Toronto insurance agent friend and his wife. When the media began reporting news of falling stock prices in tech and internet shares, and the losses began to be reflected in her account statements, Carol grew concerned.

"I called my friends two or three times," she says, "asking if I was still okay, if my account was in the right mix, and I visited them as a friend and to discuss my account. Each time, I was told everything was fine, that my account was still around $400,000 in value, and I could retire any time I wanted."

Not likely. Within a year Carol's RRSP had dropped by more than $100,000, with no end of the slide in sight. "I watched my savings slipping away, all the money I had worked so hard to make," she says. "I didn't need to see it grow as much as stay where it was, or close to it. But everything I owned just kept going down, down ..."

Carol began to question the suitability of the investments chosen for her. Many of them appeared based on the same kinds of investments that seemed to be the hardest-hit. "You're panicking," she was informed by the insurance agent during one telephone conversation. "Do you really think that Nortel will not recover?" By this time, Carol's RRSP had lost $200,000, about half its value, and her retirement dreams were sinking with it.

When Carol found herself being intimidated by empty, often angry, responses to her queries, she began sending email requests for explanation. These produced accusations that she understood neither the market nor the investing strategy being used, and was not appreciative of the work being done on her behalf. One of these messages arrived in the winter of 2001 from the financial advisor and his wife at their winter home in Florida. "You're being foolish, you're losing your nerve," she was told. "We're the experts, so trust us!"

"That's when the penny dropped," Carol remembers with a rueful smile. "That's when I asked myself, 'Is this friendship really worth it?' I was at the point of real despair. I had never asked for handouts, never looked for special treatment. I had done everything to provide for my security. I understood there could be risks with investments, but losing this much money in such a short period of time just didn't make sense. Half my life savings had vanished in two years. I had hoped to be at least semi-retired, but instead I was back to working 80 hours a week, trying to make up the losses in my RRSP, which was supposed to be growing but was shrinking faster than I could replace the money."

One of Carol's pleasures is music, both vocal and instrumental. In pursuit of this, she joined a church choir on Bowen Island, travelling there by ferry two or three times a week to rehearse and perform. Singing was a way to avoid thinking about her RRSP losses. After choir practice one night in March 2001, her anxieties surfaced and without thinking she blurted out to one of the choir members standing near her, "I'm just so worried about my RRSP. I've lost over half my money in less than two years and nobody seems to care about it!"

"I had no idea who I was saying this to," Carol laughs now. "I had never spoken to this man before, although I had seen him at choir practice many times. He was just a nice older man, and I was surprised when he told me he happened to be a financial advisor living on Bowen Island and working from his home, although he kept an office in Vancouver. When he offered to review my account and give his opinion, I went along with the idea. I just wanted someone to give me an honest answer."

The answer that the financial advisor, a tall, soft-spoken Dutchman named Hans Merkelbach, gave her was, "Appalling!" Carol's account had been invested in life insurance–owned back-end-loaded segregated mutual funds investing in Canadian, U.S., Japanese, and European equities, each fund carrying MERs as high as 4 percent or more, and each with an abysmal performance. Then things got worse. To transfer her investments from these DSC funds would cost Carol about $13,000 since the DSC would be applied not to the current value of her investments but to the original investment, which was twice as high as the funds were worth.

"When Hans explained this to me, I was shocked," Carol says. "But he wasn't. He told me he had seen many accounts like mine, designed to make money for the advisor first. I was flabbergasted that I was going to have to pay $13,000 of my money to correct a mistake somebody else had made." Now Carol understood what her friends had meant when they kept telling her she couldn't afford to get out of the money-losing funds; the high deferred service charges would take another major bite out of her RRSP assets. "That produced a new level of disgust in me. I wasn't sure what to do with my RRSP, but I knew I couldn't leave it in the hands of my 'friends' anymore. I sent them a letter informing them that I was moving my account to Hans Merkelbach, and I frankly never wanted to talk to them again."

And her friends' response?

A cool smile. "They asked if I really believed someone on Bowen Island could know more about investing than they could, located as they were in Toronto."

Her move proved fortuitous. By early 2004 her account, newly structured by Merkelbach, had recovered much of its value, reaching a balance of about $320,000 and climbing. Had she kept her portfolio unchanged from the way it had been assembled by her Toronto advisors, the balance would have drifted to about $130,000 (from about $400,000) on that same date, even after the market recovery of 2003.

"The effective word here is capitulation," Carol says, sipping her tea and scratching her dog's ears. The ferry from Vancouver sounds its horn as it rounds the corner of the inlet, approaching the island dock. The sun's early spring warmth is like a blessing. "There comes a point where you just have to surrender, where you have to let go because the evidence tells you to accept what has happened. It is a real spiritual moment of darkness. I was giving up on a friendship and giving up on dreams of the retirement lifestyle I thought I had worked for. I just had to move on."

Like all salespeople, financial advisors appreciate the value of nurturing personal relationships with clients. Unlike most relationships, however, this one is asymmetric, and the investment industry tries to keep it that way. Over and over, Canadian RRSP/RRIF investors are told they are not sufficiently knowledgeable to make good investment decisions and, to the extent that most Canadians lack awareness of basic investment strategies and instruments, this is correct. Unfortunately, as in Carol MacKinnon's case, the asymmetry of knowledge is used as a club to deflect concerns that clients may express about their own money.

If clients cannot understand and appreciate the investment strategy being proposed by financial advisors, the fault lies not with the clients who are rightly concerned that the strategy meets their goals, but with the financial advisors' ability to communicate. And when clients are honestly confused or distressed about the efficacy of the investment program, they deserve more than a response limited to "Trust us—we're the experts." They do not deserve bullying and

disdain over their concerns. Yet this is precisely the way many financial advisors, brokers, and mutual fund salespeople have been treating
Canadians for years. And no one seems to care about it.

Segregated Funds: They Are a Good Deal for Somebody, But Probably Not You

Some of MacKinnon's RRSP was invested in segregated funds, a
mutual fund hybrid that blends aspects of two industries—the investment industry and the insurance industry—into one product that
assures substantial gains for the salesperson.

Over most of the 1990s, every major mutual fund and insurance
company in Canada trumpeted its version of segregated (or "seg")
funds, claiming they delivered the best of both worlds: the growth
potential of equity-based mutual funds, and the guaranteed principal
of GICs. It was like the travel industry promising the comfort of a sea
cruise and the speed of a transatlantic flight at the same time. Who
could resist?

Seg funds appeared to be the Holy Grail of investment faith. If the
value of the fund rose substantially before the end of the 10-year
term, you could lock in your profits at that point for another 10 years.
And if the fund lost money over a 10-year locked-in period, your
segregated investment didn't lose at all because the original investment would be there to be redeemed.

In reality, seg funds were old vinegar in new bottles, poured in
because Canadians had grown wary of the benefits of whole life insurance peddled to them since Sir John A. was a pup. Whole life
insurance was a package that promised both a life insurance premium
to your beneficiary while you worked, and a pot of gold, or at least
loonies, at the end of the rainbow when you retired. Eventually
people realized they would be further ahead by purchasing cheaper
term insurance and investing the difference in their RRSP, getting

control over their future and a tax break at the same time. Insurance companies retaliated with seg funds, hooking them onto familiar mutual funds from reassuring names such as Trimark and CI Management.

Here is how the seg fund promoters explained things.

REGULAR FUND vs. SEGREGATED FUND PERFORMANCE		
	MUTUAL FUND ($)	SEG MUTUAL FUND ($)
Initial Investment	10,000	10,000
10-year/10% average return	20,000	20,000
10-year/2% average loss	8000	10,000
After Five Years		
10% average gain	15,000	15,000 (locked in)
After Another Five Years		
8% average loss	9000	15,000

Ten thousand dollars in both a regular mutual fund and a seg version of the same fund would grow in value at the same rate (for the purpose of this illustration), so an average 10-percent annual return would double the value of both in 10 years. If both funds lost money over that 10-year period, the regular mutual fund would have a lower value than the original investment—you would be out of pocket. If both funds gained, you could lock in the seg fund's gain and extend the term for another 10 years, ensuring you would not lose the gain you already earned, while committing yourself to maintaining the investment for the next 10 years.

Seg funds grew popular enough for insurance firms to tighten the rules in their favour. Most seg funds now guarantee only 75 percent of your original investment and require a 15-year lock-in period (as Carol MacKinnon's did), sucking much of the bloom from this particular rose.

It might be said that MacKinnon's life insurance friend placed a substantial portion of her RRSP assets in seg funds as a form of guarantee for several years. It might even be argued that this constituted a conservative strategy intent on preserving her capital. But it would be a weak argument at best. Here's why:

- It is difficult to lose a portion of your principal over 10 years of investing in quality funds. In only one 10-year period between 1925 and 2000 did any North American index lose money (1929 to 1938, when Canadian stocks declined a total of 0.02 percent over the entire span). So why bother paying extra to protect yourself against a loss that will likely not occur?
- That seg funds originate with insurance companies and not investment specialists should tell you something about their true value. They are essentially insurance products, not investment vehicles.
- Like all insurance products, seg funds come with a premium, paid by the investor (who else?). In this case, the premium is buried in much higher MERs for the same kind of fund sold without the seg/insurance factor.
- The elevated MERs make it difficult to achieve the same returns as non-seg versions of the same fund.
- Seg funds are totally inappropriate for RRIFs, which require you to withdraw fixed amounts each year. Withdrawing cash from seg funds before their mature date means forfeiting the guarantee, and the guarantee remains the only justification for paying the higher fees on seg funds.
- The biggest benefit of a seg fund is creditor protection (they may not be available for seizure in the event of a lawsuit and might

be shielded from bankruptcy) and estate creation (you can name a beneficiary to receive a seg fund when you die).

"There was no hope that Carol would make money from those funds," Hans Merkelbach says.[49] "The kinds of losses suffered by Carol can shatter people's lives. If you are 50 or 60 years old or older, you will not be able to recover these losses, and it is foolish, maybe even criminal, for advisors to say in effect, "Stop your whining!"

Among a small group of investors, Merkelbach has become something of a legend for his contrarian views on the role of a financial advisor. He issues annual report cards to each of his clients, revealing the performance, positive or negative, resulting from his counsel over the previous year. Serving about 150 clients, Hans and his wife live an idyllic life in a spectacular custom-built home on the shore of Howe Sound, B.C., where eagles nest in the tall pines, cruise ships pass by on the water, and snow-capped Mount Garibaldi shimmers in the distance. Although he maintains an office in Vancouver, Merkelbach prefers to work from an office on the second floor of his home, overlooking the water and the mountains.

"All Money Is Serious Money"

Merkelbach lacks a university degree, placing greater value on the experience he gathered as a bond trader and investment manager for insurance companies and mutual funds before obtaining his securities trading licence. "Degrees don't help an advisor do a better job for clients," Merkelbach suggests. "For some advisors it limits their ability because they become accustomed to doing things by the book. They're textbook-taught, so they make decisions according to whatever the textbook says, instead of what the market situation and the clients' needs tell them to do. Figuring things out for yourself takes hard work, and that's not something that many advisors take the time to do."

Merkelbach is especially dismissive of advisors who belittle investor concerns about losses. "All money is serious money," he states, "and should be treated seriously."

In Merkelbach's view, the majority of financial advisors sell products instead of investment advice. "As long as we have people in this business who cannot make a decent income from fees paid to them by their clients, we will have the commission system," he observes. "And as long as we have the commission system, we will never have full transparency. Embedded compensation ensures that real power in the industry is in the hands of the mutual fund sponsors and financial advisors, not the investor. Clients, especially those with RRSPs and RRIFs, must grasp this idea."

No critic of the DSC is more bitter than Merkelbach. "The DSC has hurt clients more than anything else in this business. It has been a bonanza for the mutual fund industry and a disaster for investors." He does not, however, retain as much distaste for high MER levels. "Sometimes a relatively high MER is not only acceptable, it is necessary, based on the amount of work needed by the manager to run the fund," he explains. "It's one factor in choosing a fund. You have to look at others as well."

Merkelbach's approach to making investment decisions on behalf of clients, in addition to accounting for each client's individual needs and expectations, rejects broad applications of the buy-and-hold system. "It works relatively well when equities and bonds rise in tandem, but works poorly during bear markets," he points out. Nor is he a great fan of asset allocation: "It's a 'popular mechanics' kind of diversification, a simplistic approach that can be compared to throwing darts at a board." Hope, Merkelbach suggests, plays a role in successful asset allocation. "Any time you find yourself hoping in this business," he says, "the odds are that you are on the wrong path, or that you did something stupid that needs correcting. During a bear market, the idea of moving investments such as mutual funds back and forth according to their performance levels will likely prove futile."

In mid-2004, with the prospect of rising interest rates, the return of inflation, and global uncertainty, Merkelbach favoured Canadian federal and provincial bond funds, noting that these had outperformed every market sector over the 20 years between 1984 and 2004. He was also advising clients to move into resource sectors such as gold and precious metals, commodities, energy, and inflation-indexed government bond mutual funds.

Most of Merkelbach's clients were prepared to take his advice, and why not? In 2003, the accounts of all of Merkelbach's clients grew in value by an average of 34 percent. Those who had retained him as their advisor on or before November 1, 1999, when Merkelbach began plotting and issuing his annual report card, watched in glee as their portfolios produced a total return over the next 50 months—to December 31, 2003—of 110 percent, achieved through the worst period of a serious bear market.

Start by Asking Questions and Seeking Answers

Merkelbach's performance on behalf of clients proves that Warren Buffet's maxim—First, never lose money—is attainable. There are other Merkelbachs in the Canadian investment industry, to be sure. Identifying them is a serious matter. Here are some dos and don'ts, based on observations from many people on both sides of the investor-advisor fence, that are worth following when dealing with advisors:

- Don't feel you owe loyalty to a financial advisor or broker who a) does not appear as concerned as you about losses suffered in your RRSP/RRIF, b) chooses not to explain rationales for decisions or recommendations, c) contacts you only within 60 days of the deadline for RRSP contributions, d) appears uncomfortable or dismissive when answering questions about MERs, DSCs, and similar matters, e) proposes only funds with DSCs, or f) responds to questions or concerns in a dismissive manner.

- Don't choose a new advisor or planner based on a pitch made at financial seminars or forums. You are a fish, the seminars are barrels, and the advisors, brokers, and planners are armed. Get the picture?

- Don't respond beyond a polite "No, thank you" to an unsolicited telephone call from an advisor or broker offering assistance. As a lad I visited racetracks, where colourful characters offered to pick winners for me. Advisors making cold calls are their progeny.

- Don't be impressed with a financial advisor's education level or status within his or her company. Formal education is less important in an investment advisor than intelligence, long experience, empathy for client concerns, personal integrity, and a willingness to work hard. Membership in a brokerage's President's Club, Chairman's Club, Gold Key Club, or similar group means the member sold more products than most others in the organization. You're not looking for an outstanding salesperson; you're looking for an outstanding advisor, and the two do not always coincide.

- Don't accept a financial advisor's boasts about gains in a bull market. From 1995 to 2000, a dart-throwing chimpanzee could have produced a winning portfolio.

- Don't permit yourself to be bullied or intimidated. If a financial advisor suggests that the proposed strategy, or any element of it, is too difficult for you to understand, ask for a simpler strategy—or a better advisor.

- Don't forget whose money it is, and who should profit most from it.

- Do start by asking friends, relatives, business associates, and others how they feel about their advisor. How much attention do they get? How comfortable are they recommending him or her?

- Do note if the advisor begins by asking a number of key questions before proposing a plan or revamping your existing portfolio. These should be questions about your income, assets, financial goals, health, marital status, pension program, and investment knowledge and experience. Answer directly and honestly. If your investment knowledge is low, don't try to impress the advisor by suggesting you're practically Warren Buffet's guru.

- Do ask about the advisor's success on behalf of clients during the bear market of 2000 to 2003. Did the advisor break even or gain? If not, how much did she lose on average? What was the advisor's strategy? How would she change it? Once you pass 50 years of age, a main criterion in choosing an advisor you can rely on is that she has a risk-averse investment strategy, also known as capital preservation.

- Do ask to see a sample statement from the advisor's firm. Don't worry about the figures—just decide if you can make sense of it. Are the assets clearly indicated? Can you understand key elements such as gain/loss, book value, and foreign content?

- Do note the advisor's familiarity with, and ability to discuss and recommend, a wide range of products. Which mutual fund companies, and funds within them, does he favour and why? Would he recommend no-load funds that pay no commission or trailer fees, if the funds fit your needs? If so, how would he charge for his services? How does he feel about bonds? Some mutual fund salespeople are very good at selling mutual funds (surprise!) but not so good at understanding and responding to individual investor goals and concerns.

- Do favour someone who listens more than he talks, rather than vice versa.

- Do note the advisor's or broker's general appearance and carriage. You don't need a Ben Affleck or Belinda Stronach handling your portfolio, but you should favour someone who is well groomed, confident, respectful of your concerns, and open in his or her responses.
- Do ask how the advisor is compensated for her services. If by commissions, are those commissions negotiable under some circumstances? Would she consider switching to a fee system at some point?

Some of these questions may seem intrusive and so may be difficult to ask. If you feel this way, or if you sense any antagonism or resistance on the part of the advisor, keep reminding yourself whose money it is, and who deserves to profit from it.

ARROGANCE, DISASTER, AND DEATH OF A WHISTLE BLOWER

A speech therapist working in public schools, Jocelyne Robidoux took steps to ensure a degree of future financial security, investing in both an RRSP and a non-registered account. While living in Winnipeg in the mid-1990s, she opened accounts with Aurum Financial Group, which was later folded into Assante Financial Group Inc. When she moved to Thunder Bay, Ontario, in 1999, Jocelyne chose to continue dealing with the newly named firm. After Assante's acquisition of Aurum, statements received from her advisor listed the current value of the portfolios periodically accompanied by transaction slips that made little sense to her.

As Jocelyne relates it, she noticed an alarming drop in the value of her portfolios, excessive even in light of the general market decline that was occurring. "I called the advisor and asked for an explanation," she says. "I knew markets went down as well as up but none of this made any sense." The advisor promised to send a summary of all the trades made in her accounts. When they failed to arrive, she called again and again, even offering to meet with the advisor during a scheduled visit to Winnipeg that summer. "It seemed odd to me that he couldn't find the time, since we hadn't met for over three years."

A detailed statement arrived in September, nine months after Jocelyne Robidoux's first enquiry. "The statement confirmed what I suspected. Mutual funds in my portfolio had been sold and replaced by other funds without my knowledge or approval." The funds sold by Assante were valued at $64,000, and much of the proceeds were used to purchase Assante Artisan Portfolios, which included newly issued proprietary funds with no earnings record; these funds were based on high-risk investments and carried above-average MERs.

On the assumption that reversing such an obvious error would be easy ("I thought it would be like taking a defective toaster back to the store—you just talk to the manager and you get your money back"), Jocelyne met with the Assante manager while on a Christmas vacation in Winnipeg. "I asked the manager to reverse the trades and replace the new funds with the funds I had agreed to invest in years earlier, but later I was informed by the compliance officer at the Assante branch that my advisor was claiming we had discussed the trades by telephone, and that was an outright lie!"

On the branch manager's suggestion, she filed a complaint with Assante's compliance office in Toronto, launching a process that dragged on for more than two years and would have exhausted a less determined individual. During this period, she discovered that her advisor was not licensed by the Ontario Securities Commission to trade securities in Ontario. Jocelyne also learned that the advisor was claiming she had placed telephone calls to him instructing him to sell the disputed mutual fund units and purchase funds from Assante, CI, and AIM. Copies of telephone records revealed that no calls took place on the days the advisor claimed to have received instructions, and on one of the dates he submitted, Jocelyne proved she was out of town on business.

Despite possessing documents supporting her claims, when Jocelyne sought legal advice in late 2002, a lawyer advised her to forget about legal action because the legal fees would exceed the amount of her claim, and there was no certainty of success. Determined not to give up, she decided to represent herself and filed a claim against Assante and the advisor for $13,000. "That was the amount of money I lost when they switched funds on me," she explains. "It should have been about $25,000 if I had added lost dividends and my costs."

In October 2003, Assante submitted an offer, through its Winnipeg law firm, of $5000 to settle the matter. As is usual with settlements of this kind, Jocelyne would have had to sign an agreement never to discuss any aspects of the settlement and its terms. She rejected the $5000 offer, determined to pursue the matter in court.

Two months before the scheduled trial, a second offer arrived by fax from Assante's lawyer. Along with an increased offer of $7000, the lawyer's letter noted, "... you are going to have great difficulty establishing liability and damages, such that you will not be entitled to anything at the conclusion of the three-day trial. Moreover, you risk an order of costs against you, which may be significant."

The attempt to intimidate her failed, and one day before court proceedings were to begin, yet a third offer arrived by fax from Assante's lawyer, this one finally agreeing to her claim of $13,000. Jocelyne accepted it, anxious to put the entire experience behind her. "Besides," she recalls, "I had run out of options. The trial was to be held in Thunder Bay, and I would have had to pay my travel and accommodation costs."

Unfortunately for Assante's lawyer, the requirement for Jocelyne Robidoux to sign a release preventing her from discussing any aspect of the settlement was missing from the $13,000 offer. If it wasn't included, did Jocelyne have to agree anyway? No, advised a lawyer she consulted on the matter. The offer was basically a contract, and if the contract excluded a requirement to maintain silence on the matter it could not be added later without her agreement.

"I called the lawyer, who happened to be a woman, the next day and told her I would not sign a release," Jocelyne says. "She told me that she would have to consult with her client. Meanwhile, I assumed the money was mine."

But it wasn't, the Assante lawyer claimed. A letter soon arrived bearing hints of panic among the lawyer's threats. "If you refuse to provide the release," the lawyer scolded, "you will have failed to comply with your obligations pursuant to the settlement agreement, and the settlement funds will not be paid to you." Then, in case the message wasn't clear enough: "I can confirm ... that I now have in my trust account the settlement proceeds in this matter, in the sum of $13,000." Get me off the hook, the lawyer was saying in effect, and I'll give you your money.

Jocelyne Robidoux refused to be intimidated. In a telephone call to the Assante lawyer, she repeated her lawyer's observation that an offer is like a contract and both parties were bound by its terms, which did not include a release. She had signed an agreement that made no mention of a confidentiality clause, and she expected the lawyer to comply with its terms, which included giving the $13,000 to her, the person to whom it had been designated.

This prompted a third threatening letter: "If you do not fulfil your obligations pursuant to the settlement," the lawyer wrote, "you are not entitled to receipt of the settlement proceeds."[50]

It was another attempt at bullying with no legal basis, and the Assante lawyer knew it. Again, Jocelyne Robidoux refused to budge. Her position was clear: The money was hers, the error was the lawyer's, and she demanded the cash. A week later, it finally arrived.

Jocelyne Robidoux thus became among the rarest of wronged investors, someone who had received a settlement from her broker/advisor and remains free to discuss all aspects of the event. The experience converted her into an active investor advocate, someone who speaks out against various industry practices, and demonstrates the risks that investors face when confronting an investment firm with deep pockets and tough-minded solicitors. More than that, it revealed the inner workings and values of an investment firm that, from its birth to recent years, has generated an inordinate amount of criticism from clients and regulators alike.

Assante sprang from the imaginative ambition of Winnipeg businessman Martin Weinberg, who blended an agency to manage the multi-million-dollar earnings of professional sports stars with financial services for small investors. The small investor management resources were built, in part, by absorbing several other investment houses and brokerages over time until, by 2000, Weinberg could boast at age 40 that he headed one of the largest professional sports representation firms in North America and the largest non-bank-owned financial services firm in Canada. The company had expanded into the U.S. under the corporate name Loring Ward.

The firm's primary appeal to investors was based on the freedom of its advisors to construct portfolios from literally thousands of available mutual funds. In contrast, bank-owned brokerages were expected to favour funds managed by the parent bank, leaving clients to wonder if these really were the best funds available. In a similar fashion, Investors Group (IG), Canada's largest independent financial services company and a Winnipeg neighbour of Assante, trumpeted the "appeal" of its in-house managed funds, available to IG clients exclusively. But investors noticed that IG funds charged higher MERs and produced lower returns than average third-party funds, and they expressed their dissatisfaction by moving their accounts. Only then did IG agree to add third-party funds such as those managed by Trimark, Templeton, Fidelity, and others to its menu.

While IG was broadening its selection of funds, Assante moved in the opposite direction. The firm that had bragged about the independence of its advisors when it came to selecting mutual funds introduced its own line of in-house funds, with incentives for Assante staff to favour them.

"Assante began by promoting the idea that their advisors could be totally objective because they could select the perfect fund for each client's needs," *National Post* columnist Jonathan Chevreau comments. "The credibility of this 'off the shelf' approach helped build Assante's client base in the beginning. When Assante began promoting its own in-house funds, it kept claiming to be independent even when evidence surfaced that the advisors were told to push the in-house funds as a means of boosting the value of Assante shares."[51]

Credibility was not the only thing that suffered as a result of Assante's shift toward in-house self-managed funds. As Chevreau pointed out in his *National Post* column of July 15, 2003—a column that proved pivotal in this tale—Assante's funds boasted the second highest average MER of all funds sold in Canada.

What were investors receiving in return? Not much. In mid 2003, 28 percent of assets in the firm's Artisan RSP Maximum Growth Portfolio were invested in index funds, for which an appropriate MER might be 0.25 percent. Of its international assets, fully 40 percent had been passed along to AGF, CI, and Fidelity to manage, with 13 percent in two Altamira-managed index funds. Unit holders of these funds paid Assante an MER of 3.0 percent. Just what was Assante doing to earn its excessively high MER?

Things were even worse for U.S. investors, where Assante's Loring Ward targeted investors with more than $100,000 in assets. Of three

Assante portfolio management services aimed at wealthy Americans, two were *100 percent invested in indexed products*. Again, it is unclear just what these clients were receiving in return for the fat MERs being applied to their portfolios. It is very clear, however, that Assante and its advisors were earning enormous revenues in return for little effort.[52]

Mutual fund managers are free to set any MER level the market will agree to pay, of course. But Assante, which had built its credibility and its extensive client base on the premise that its advisors chose investments according to their suitability for client needs, was changing the rules. Moreover, these changes were being made to benefit Assante and its staff in a far more lucrative manner than they were benefiting the firm's clients.

Getting Rich on Other People's Money

From January 2000 to October 2002, Stephen Gadsden managed the Assante office in the Toronto suburb of Aurora. Gadsden, who is now an outspoken investor advocate severely critical of many industry policies, alleges that he attended an Assante presentation in April 2002 where he and other branch managers were enticed to favour Assante in-house mutual funds. The inducement, according to Gadsden, was made by the firm's executive vice-president, with Assante's own vice-president of compliance in attendance.

Gadsden claims that he and other Assante branch managers and representatives were advised that selling Assante proprietary mutual funds would boost Assante Corporation's cash flow and enhance its balance sheet. In turn, this would generate favourable publicity in the financial media, boosting the value of publicly listed shares held by Assante employees and ultimately generating substantial profits for Assante employee stakeholders.[53]

Gadsden also alleges:

- Assante branch managers were encouraged to convert up to 80 percent of their client accounts, consisting of mutual funds managed by companies other than Assante, to Assante in-house funds
- The Assante executive pointed out that the firm's in-house mutual funds earned greater revenues for the company than third-party funds, thanks to their substantially higher MERs
- Assante branch managers attending the presentation who questioned the plan received a veiled threat to conform with the strategy or risk losing their business
- The Assante vice-president of compliance remained throughout the presentation and discussion, his attendance perceived as a silent endorsement of the program
- After voicing his concerns at the meeting and during the months following, Gadsden was fired by Assante for "… transgressing corporate compliance policy"

A number of incidents, including Jocelyne Robidoux's experience, appear to support Gadsden's allegations. Among them is a February 2004 ruling by the Ontario Securities Commission ordering Assante to cease subjecting its representatives to quotas when promoting in-house funds to their clients. Assante was also ordered by the OSC to eliminate any incentives, monetary and non-monetary, that encouraged Assante brokers and salespeople to push the proprietary funds on clients. Beyond this cease-and-desist slap on the wrist, the firm appears to have suffered no penalty.[54]

Boosting the sale of higher-profit items is neither new nor surprising to consumers; General Motors, after all, clearly prefers its customers to purchase Cadillacs rather than Chevrolets. But comparing motor cars to mutual funds does not address a parallel transaction. Purchasers of new cars are actively involved in the buying decision. They are equipped to assess and determine the relative merits and values of competing products, and they enjoy the protection of a warranty should the vehicle fail to live up to its promised performance. None of these opportunities was available to Assante clients. Gadsden's allegations indicate that Assante clients would have little or no role in the switch to the in-house products, were not equipped to judge the wisdom of the decision, and had no recourse to a warranty when the performance of the Assante funds proved less than satisfactory.

Controversy and an Apology

Assante's promotion of in-house funds and other events attracted the attention of various commentators in the financial press, most of it unflattering and much of it originating in the *National Post* during the last months of 2002. None of the *Post*'s negative stories about Assante was challenged in court, but it was clear that *Post* reporters and columnists, especially Jonathan Chevreau, were reporting smoke wafting from Assante's camping grounds. Was a fire or two raging there?

One Chevreau column covered Assante's attempts to prevent a departing senior advisor from moving his business to a competitor—business the advisor had built up through personal contacts and service over the years. Another column related its version of Stephen Gadsden's allegations that top Assante executives had pressured branch managers to switch up to 80 percent of client accounts to Assante in-house funds.

The stories made an impact. Assante clients began asking embarrassing questions, and Assante sales staff began complaining to management about the *Post*'s coverage. Whatever happened next is speculative, but facts confirm that a senior editor at the *National Post* sent the following letter to Marty Weinberg, Assante President and CEO:

June 13, 2002

Dear Mr. Weinberg:

   *We sincerely apologize to Assante for any inaccuracies in a
number of articles that referred to Assante, published in the
National Post from November 16, 2002 to December 5, 2002.*

   *We have appreciated the opportunity to learn more about
Assante through recent meetings with some of your senior staff. It
is through this type of helpful backgrounding that the Financial
Post can be sure that it has the fullest perspective on the operations
of your company.*

   *We sincerely appreciate the open and standing offer on your
part to comment on reports on the activities of your company and
on the financial advice business.*

                              Yours truly,[55]

This is remarkable correspondence from a top-level news
medium to a supposedly aggrieved company. Newspapers and other
media sources commit errors from time to time, and the subjects of
their errors have every right to demand a retraction or correction.
Yet apologizing for "any" inaccuracies appears to be a forelock-
tugging exercise of fealty-based obedience, along the lines of "I'm
sorry if anything I said offended you." It is the nature of a free press
to offend from time to time. In the legal lexicon, "offend" does not
equal "libel." And how did "learning more about Assante through
regular meetings with some of your senior staff" provide the *Post*
with an opportunity to improve service to its readers, supposedly a
newspaper's primary obligation?

If the *National Post* had indeed published inaccuracies about
Assante, it had every obligation to correct these in a public forum,
openly explaining its errors and setting the record straight according to confirmable facts. Instead, there was nothing open about
the process. On June 13, 2002, the same date that appears on the

Post's letter, Marty Weinberg circulated a copy of the letter as an e-mail attachment to every Assante employee with this opening comment:

> For a long period of time we have been working hard to get our story out and to continue to enhance Assante's investor relations and media profiles.
>
> From an investor relations perspective I am sure you are aware that we have made great strides in research coverage, trading volumes and price.
>
> From a media relations perspective, you can see from the accompanying letter, we are making some headway here too.

Weinberg signed off his inspirational message to the troops with:

> Please note that we have provided the National Post assurance that the attached letter will not be reproduced or distributed in any form.

If letters such as the *Post*'s act of contrition have a value, this one might have been tagged for a billion dollars two months after it arrived on Weinberg's desk, for on August 22, 2003, the world learned that CI Fund Management Inc. had purchased Assante for that amount. The letter likely improved the prospects of Assante's passing a "sniff test" by CI, since it practically guaranteed that any future Assante stories would be filled with sunshine and flowers, or at least devoid of criticism and questions.

Why would CI Funds be interested in Assante and pay such an enormous amount to acquire the firm? Because CI wanted a sales force, and Assante provided 1500 salespeople with their own list of clients and portfolios. As a second tier of motive, Sun Life Financial

Services owned 34 percent of CI Funds. An in-house sales force with ready-made books of clients and portfolios just might entice Sun Life Financial Services, awash with cash, to purchase the remaining 66 percent at a premium price, a move that would slip tens of millions of dollars into the pockets of CI shareholders—a group that included, of course, many executives of CI Funds.

This potential river of profit, however, would flow towards CI shareholders only if Assante's character were free of any hint of impropriety and remained that way, a process that appeared threatened by a Jonathan Chevreau column that appeared in the *Post* on August 26, 2004. Either unaware or undaunted by the senior editor's letter, Chevreau wrote a column about a disgruntled former employee and his charges of unethical conduct by an Assante branch manager.

Serious Allegations from a Disgruntled Former Employee

Chevreau's column of August 26, 2004, related the tale of two opponents whose backgrounds and personalities could hardly have been more contrasting.

Brian Mallard headed Saskatoon-based Brian Mallard Insurance Services Ltd., an Assante branch. Mallard might have been 3000 kilometres from Bay Street, but for several years his influence on the investment industry could not have been stronger if his offices had been in the CN Tower. In addition to an impressive alphabet following his name—CLU, Ch.F.C., RFP, CFP—Mallard has held high positions with various investment industry bodies. These include a Past Trustee of the Institute of Chartered Life Underwriters and Chartered Financial Consultants; Member of the Canadian Tax Foundation, Canadian Pension and Benefits; Member of the Board of Directors of the Canadian Associations of Insurance and Financial Advisors (CAIFA); Chair of the CAIFA Task Force on the Regulation of Distribution of Financial Products and Services; and Founding Chair of Advocis, an organization representing Canada's financial advisors and insurance salespeople.

Clearly not a man to be trifled with, Mallard nevertheless was challenged by a former employee of his Assante office named Kent Shirley. Gifted with obvious athletic ability, Shirley served on a championship fencing team, leading to an admitted association with steroids and performance-enhancing drugs that may or may not have affected his emotional state.[56]

Shirley was employed at Mallard's office, selling mutual funds and insurance, from 1996 to 2004. During this time he took an eight-month leave of absence to deal, he claimed, with stress-related problems. In January 2004, Shirley was fired and within a few weeks had launched a wrongful dismissal suit against Mallard and his company. In his suit, Shirley charged that Mallard had failed to abide by an agreement he had with Shirley, and harassed Shirley during Shirley's tenure with the firm. But it was Shirley's allegations that Mallard "condoned, engaged in and required Shirley to engage in unethical and/or illegal conduct" that proved most explosive. The charges alleged that Mallard

- provided insider information to clients that enabled them to make investment decisions with information not generally available to the public
- overbilled clients by charging work performed by Shirley, whose hourly rate was $80, at Mallard's hourly rate of $200
- granted personal loans to clients
- offered advice on stock investing and assisted in making stock trades while not properly licensed to do so
- issued personal guarantees on client accounts
- condoned the practice of having other staff members sign his name on forms requiring his signature[57]

Mallard filed a defence denying the allegations and launched a countersuit against Shirley's claim of wrongful dismissal in which he painted Shirley as an inept and sloppy employee. According to court documents filed by Mallard's attorneys, Shirley arrived for work in an unkempt state, demonstrated erratic behaviour, failed to complete paperwork, and engaged in "… appropriate [*sic*] personal conversations with female staff."[58] Other allegations included charges that Shirley admitted some drug abuse, that he failed to complete a Certified Financial Planners course as promised, and that he had not returned Assante shares owned by Mallard but in Shirley's possession.

Mallard had every right, and even an obligation, to respond to Shirley's claims with appropriate legal action. No one, however—especially Kent Shirley—anticipated the power that Mallard unleashed in a second legal action when reports circulated that Shirley had repeated the charges in his lawsuit to the Saskatchewan Financial Services Commission and distributed documents allegedly acquired while Shirley was employed by Mallard's firm.[59]

In this second lawsuit, Mallard charged Shirley with defamation of his character, alleging that his former employee not only had "misappropriated confidential and proprietary documentation" relating to Mallard and his company, but had distributed the material to representatives of the business press and various internet sites. "The disclosure by internet," Mallard's suit charged, "has resulted in a world wide distribution of confidential and proprietary information, in breach of the fiduciary duties of Shirley to the plaintiffs. In addition, the Disclosure has included false and defamatory statements about (Brian Mallard Insurance Services) in general and the Plaintiff Brian Mallard in particular."[60]

Indeed, various websites across Canada had been buzzing with tales of the legal duel, repeating Shirley's charges against Mallard and posting documents that appeared to support them. These were

devastating to Mallard's reputation as one of Canada's most prominent mutual-fund investment dealers. His lawsuit included a
request for a court injunction preventing Shirley from discussing
any aspect of the case, and $1 million in exemplary and punitive
damages. It also asked the court to have all related documents seized
from Shirley, preventing him from either destroying or disseminating them.

The court agreed to the seizure request with an Anton Piller order,
a legal device unknown to the vast majority of Canadians, most of
whom would be amazed to learn of its power.

Derived from a 1976 British legal decision,[61] an Anton Piller
order provides authority for a court to search premises and seize
documents without prior warning in order to prevent the destruction
of incriminating evidence. No search warrant is issued, the subject of
the order has no grounds for appeal, and the initial action is
conducted under a veil of secrecy. The power of this order is best
expressed in the execution of this order as described by the one filed
by Mr. Justice D. B. Mason, Court of Queen's Bench of Alberta, on
October 28, 2004.[62] Among its directives:

- A forensic accountant team was authorized to search or seize "the
  Defendant's computer(s), computer equipment … material
  relating to telephone charges, software, computer files and disks
  (including hard drives of any computers) and any material
  which may be used as evidence …"
- Each occupant of the residence was ordered to disclose "… the
  whereabouts of all Relevant Documents of which he or she has
  knowledge, whether on the premises or elsewhere …" and his
  or her name and address.
- Every locked cabinet, safe, container or any other storage facility
  must be unlocked.
- The premises were to be photographed or videotaped.

- The individual whose premises were to be legally invaded and pillaged could not communicate in any form through any medium with anyone about the order and its execution for two days.

Not complying with any of these or several other directives in the six-page court document would lead to a charge of contempt of court. Remember, this involved not a criminal matter but an otherwise routine civil case between two private parties. Kent Shirley had been neither charged nor convicted of doing anything illegal, yet his treatment under the terms of the Anton Piller order are reminiscent of those prescribed against people suspected of committing a capital crime.

In a swoop worthy of a raid on a major drug dealer, KPMG forensic auditors (KPMG provided accounting services to Mallard's firm) carried off all the evidence Shirley referred to in his reported testimony to the SFSC.

Shirley, already unstable as a result of several influences including his claimed wrongful dismissal, sought help from various sources. Among the people he contacted in December 2004 was me. In a telephone call to my home, Shirley asked my assistance in preparing and publishing a book on his experiences in the investment industry, prompted by my book *Free Rider*. He was coherent but his voice was strained, like a man holding himself together emotionally. I suggested that he find himself a ghost writer, explaining that I had recently completed *The Naked Investor* and faced several other writing assignments.

Our conversation was followed by an e-mail from Shirley on December 10, 2004. In it, he repeated his claim about having "... first hand info on what may turn out to be the largst [sic] scandal in our industry, and many from the SRO's etc involved. I have al [sic] the evidence but am not very good at writing ..."

Kent Shirley contacted several others as well, most notably Joe Killoran who has devoted the last ten years or so to the role of full-time investor advocate. In his missives to Killoran, Shirley indicated that he remained under restrictions of the Anton Piller order. Killoran, for his part, encouraged Shirley to continue speaking out and disseminating material to support his charges, contrary to the Anton Piller order, while maintaining a positive outlook.

On Christmas Eve 2004, Kent Shirley was found dead in his parent's home, an apparent suicide.

The Progress of a Damage-Control Juggernaut

Various investor advocates who had been following the Mallard–Shirley duel with mild interest became understandably disturbed at the news of his death. Meanwhile, the rumour mill among investor advocates suggested that columnist Chevreau, who had first written of the case several months earlier and been provided with documents supporting Shirley's claims, decided to break an apparent self-imposed silence. It is believed that he drafted a column headed "Death of a Whistleblower," but if so it never appeared, suggesting to me that the column was "spiked" by *Post* editors. Chevreau neither confirms nor denies this.

For his part, Mallard and his lawyers began executing the same game plan applied to Shirley, this time directing it at messengers. Robert Kyle, another investor advocate, had been posting news of the Mallard–Shirley suits on his website investorvoice.ca. In a letter to Kyle, Mallard noted that "… the web site's information is incomplete as it relates to my statement of defence and counterclaim." Adding that he had referred the matter to his lawyers, Mallard closed with, "Your posting maligns my reputation and is a basis for defamation. I hope you can supply another motivation."

In an extended reply, Kyle offered to "... cooperate fully with you by adding these affidavits ... Our purpose is congruent in this regard. I want to be factual and present complete information. In an honest effort to address your concerns and to be fair to both parties, I would be pleased to place on site all documents of public record."

Instead of accepting Kyle's offer, Mallard's lawyers pressured United Online, Kyle's U.S.–based internet service provider, to close Kyle's website or face legal action, and United Online capitulated.

Sometime during the legal choreography, the file on Shirley's testimony to the Saskatchewan Financial Services Commission was closed. Queries on the matter were directed to the Ontario Securities Commission and the Mutual Fund Dealers Association. The OSC deflected questions back to the SFSC; the MFDA simply described the matter as closed, with no further comment. The SFSC declined to make any comment. No one at the SFSC can provide a reason for not pursuing Shirley's allegations against Mallard, and no further action is contemplated. The file is essentially dead and buried.[63]

Neither was any action taken by regulatory groups to whom the transcript of Shirley's testimony was reportedly provided, including the Ontario Securities Commission, the Mutual Fund Dealers Association, the Financial Planners Standards Council, or the Honourable Ralph Goodale, then Federal Minister of Finance. Their determination appears supported by the Court of Queen's Bench of Alberta and the Honourable Justice Mason, who restricted wide distribution of court documents within the legal parameters of "implied undertaking." The term, as defined by Mallard's lawyer Richard Billington, dictates that parties involved in litigation are not to use any information gathered as a result of the proceedings for any purpose except the litigation, and no one else is permitted to assist them by using material gathered as a result of the process.

"Both the plaintiffs, Brian Mallard and his companies, and the court in this case have been very diligent in ensuring that the private litigation is kept private between the parties," Billington comments, "and that the court's process is respected and not interfered with from outside."[64]

Mallard's legal efforts to stifle the release of details of his operation might have been effective but they have also proved expensive. Mallard has either boasted or complained, depending upon the point of view, of spending "… more than $500,000 in legal fees …" to defend himself against charges submitted to "… the MFDA and other quasi regulators …"[65]

The lawyer representing the estate of Kent Shirley declined comment. Through the summer of 2006, the action continued with no prediction of its length or outcome.

Here's Your Hat …

To many industry observers, Assante's history appears besmirched with an inordinate number of legal and regulatory concerns. In 2003, for example, the Ontario Securities Commission found that 50 Assante salespeople had been dealing in securities with Ontario residents while not possessing a license to do so in that province. This finding was followed by an investigation and the resultant ruling that banned the firm from setting quotas and offering incentives for Assante representatives to promote in-house funds, as alleged by Stephen Gadsden. And a number of class action suits have been filed alleging that Assante, among other firms, received secret commissions from handling the sale of various limited partnerships.

Meanwhile Joe Canavan, newly appointed Assante Chairman and CEO, began openly discussing changes he was implementing to improve the firm's image and operations. Canavan, a personable industry veteran who previously held top-level positions with major investment firms, was frank about his efforts to reshape Assante into a firm that provides "full-blown wealth management versus people who are just selling mutual funds."

To achieve this, Canavan focused on the quality of Assante people. "Advisors who were marginal have been encouraged to merge their practices with more serious professional advisors," he explained, "a guy who brings with him maybe a decade of experience and a more successful practice." How does an advisor "merge" a practice with a more highly regarded colleague? Here's Canavan's delicate explanation: "We've made it financially feasible for the advisors to do that because we think the clients are better served that way." The term "financially feasible" suggests "buy-out," but Canavan moved forward to describe the critical qualities for future Assante people. "We're really looking for a history of positive compliance," he continues. "Good practice management, good governance. We don't have time or tolerance for people who play outside the line."[66]

In an earlier interview with Jonathan Chevreau, Canavan had been more direct. Noting that a full audit of the firm's 260 branches was underway at the time, the Assante CEO said, "We want people to know that people we would deem as black hats, we want out. We want nothing to do with them."[67]

The Assante audit was scheduled for completion at the end of 2005. In early 2006, Brian Mallard declared he would no longer be associated with Assante. Announcing Mallard's departure, an Assante news release declared, "We [Assante and Mallard] have fundamentally different views on carrying on business within the financial services sector."

Richard Billington made it obvious that I would be afforded no opportunity to interview Brian Mallard for this book. I am thus unable to confirm the colour of Mr. Mallard's hat.

SRO or SOL? The Failure of Self-Regulated Organizations to Protect Investors

She is not someone you'd expect to play the role of stubborn crusader, laying siege to monuments of stone and gold-tinted glass. But as Patricia Cosgrove relates her experience on behalf of her mother, Norah, and their treatment at the hands of various organizations claiming to protect investors, her voice grows steely with resolve and barely restrained outrage.

"Things in my mother's account were wrong from the beginning," she says. "The Know Your Client form, which she never saw, claimed she had previous experience investing in stocks, and that her investment objectives were to be 50 percent income and 50 percent growth equity. That is simply not true. Many of the investments chosen for my mother were high-risk, including Nortel, Celestica, Laidlaw, Mitel, and a CI Pacific sector mutual fund. Most of the mutual funds carried seven-year deferred service charges, sold to my mother when she was in her mid-80s. Does that make sense?"

Patricia's mother, Norah, 92 and more alert than some people 50 years younger, sits to one side, absorbing her daughter's words. We are in her west-end Toronto condominium. Norah's voice retains her British accent, and she carries herself with the dignity and gentle nature of a proper Englishwoman born in Edwardian times.

Patricia Cosgrove's litany of complaints against the Ottawa office of a bank-owned brokerage includes familiar criticisms—incorrect information posted on KYC forms; churning the account to generate commissions; resistance by the broker to discuss concerns about losses; and investments that defy age-appropriate guidelines for someone of Norah Cosgrove's age. "How can you justify changing a Know Your Client form to say that an 85-year-old woman has increased the risk exposure of her portfolio to 75 percent, and claim that her fixed assets had increased by $200,000 when no such change occurred?" Patricia asks. "You can't." Yet this is what Norah Cosgrove's file at the brokerage states, motivating Patricia's charge that the information was altered.

According to Patricia Cosgrove, the broker pressured her mother to move a substantial portion of her portfolio into the Sovereign wrap account, selling a number of Norah's Government of Canada bonds paying 9 percent interest to pay for the Sovereign units. "I understand the broker made 2 percent commission on the sale of the securities to go into Sovereign," Patricia says, keeping her voice soft and steady. "For her part, my mother suffered a total capital loss of over $60,000."

Concerned about her losses, Norah insisted on moving her account and shortly afterward purchased a condo in Toronto to be near her daughter. Demanding that the broker be punished and the losses suffered by her mother restored, Patricia began a process of complaint extending more than three years, achieving little beyond elevating her outrage and revealing unsettling attitudes on the part of the Ontario Securities Commission (OSC), the Investment Dealers Association (IDA), the Ombudsman for Banking Services and Investments (OBSI), and the regulatory process in general.

"The response of the IDA was incredible," she recalls. "The most disturbing comment was their claim that they found insufficient evidence to move the file to a formal investigation. 'Your mother is 90,' one senior IDA official said. 'What kind of a witness would she make? And after all, she could be dead within a year. You have to realize that our resources are limited and we have to get the best bang for our buck.' Is this IDA policy, to ignore broker misbehaviour if the client is old?" The IDA's response, Patricia says, was to send "a letter of caution" to the advisor, but it refused to do anything regarding the advisor's right to hold a licence.[68]

(The IDA disputes Patricia Cosgrove's story. In a written statement Paul Bourque, Senior Vice-President, Member Regulation, says, "The IDA does not now, and never has, based the decision to proceed with an investigation and/or prosecution on the age of an individual. It is ludicrous to suggest that this was the case here."[69] A decision on this dispute was handed down by the Ontario Human Rights Commission; all parties have agreed to keep its ruling confidential.)

When the IDA continued to refute her charges, Patricia Cosgrove turned to the OSC. On reviewing the documentation she provided, the OSC noted that there was nothing on the incorrect KYC form or any of the records to indicate that Norah disagreed with the form's directive increasing her portfolio to 75 percent equities. "She never saw the form," Patricia almost screams in frustration, "so how could she disagree with it? [The broker] told me there is no regulatory requirement that new account application forms must be signed or reviewed by the client—yet these are the same forms used by the brokers to justify their investment strategies. It's insane!"

A meeting with the OBSI in October 2003 proved equally fruitless, except in its ability to raise Patricia's blood pressure still further. "[The ombudsman] told me that my mother didn't really need the money she lost. Seniors like my mother didn't need much money after they pay their rent or condo fees and buy groceries, there really aren't that many expenses for them to cover. When I asked about the wisdom of putting such a large portion of a 90-year-old woman's portfolio into equities, he shrugged and said his own late father had maintained a significant amount of his investments in equities. Well, his father had been a stockbroker, which is an entirely different matter. When I sent a letter challenging him on his attitude toward seniors, he refused to respond."

With none of the regulatory agencies prepared to acknowledge her assertion that her mother's portfolio had been mishandled—"by this time I had honestly given up on the chance of recovering the lost money and just wanted someone to agree that things had been done wrong"—Patricia turned to small claims court as a means of making her point. A pre-trial hearing was set for March 23, 2004, in Ottawa.

"I went there from Toronto with all my files and a power of attorney permitting me to represent my mother," she says. "I know something about small claims court. It's supposed to be a court of equity, an opportunity for individuals like my mother and me to be heard. But I couldn't believe what I encountered when I arrived."

The first thing she encountered was the co-chairperson of litigation from one of the largest and most prestigious law firms in the country, who had travelled from Toronto to spend the day defending the brokerage against the claims of 92-year-old Norah Cosgrove. "I was stunned to see so much money being spent on such a small matter," Patricia says. "I mean, how much does it cost to have a lawyer of this stature travel to Ottawa for the day? Maybe $1000 an hour? Maybe more?"

Patricia Cosgrove was not intimidated by the presence of the heavy-duty lawyer, who remained pleasant and cordial. The attitude of the pre-trial judge, however, was in sharp contrast to that of the lawyer. "He was rude to the point of insulting, telling me that the power of attorney for my mother was deficient, and waving off my description of the case by saying he had no idea what a KYC form was, didn't know a thing about investments, and didn't understand what 75 percent in equities meant. All of his comments indicated that he thought I had nothing to complain about. Needless to say, it got nowhere."

Few investors are as fervent in their search for answers and accountability as Patricia Cosgrove. At the core of her case is the claim that details on her mother's KYC form were altered. These changes would have permitted the broker to increase the proportion of high-risk equity investments and DSC mutual funds to an inappropriate level. Changing information as entered on a legal document without the knowledge or approval of the signatory smacks of forgery, especially if the altered information benefits the person who changed it. How often has a financial advisor or broker been charged with forgery under these circumstances? Rarely, if at all.

This fact alone is evidence that investors face a less-than-equitable environment when launching challenges against the investment industry. The problem grows more ominous when investors seek legal counsel to pursue their cases. Do not expect your family lawyer, the one who crafted your will and handled the purchase of your home, to fill this role.

Some law firms specialize in representing plaintiffs against brokerages and financial advisors. If you choose to follow the legal route, be prepared to pay a hefty retainer, followed by monthly charges extending over perhaps a year or more, with no prospect of having your day in court and limited chances of recovering anything beyond a portion of your claim. As Patricia Cosgrove discovered, the battlefield of legal challenge to the investment industry is strewn with client casualties, and all the heavy artillery is on the other side. Small claims court? If Patricia Cosgrove's experience fails to dissuade you, remember that the maximum you can recover there is $10,000. Which leaves little choice but to venture into the dark and confusing Valley of the SROs. Good luck, pilgrim.

SRO stands for self-regulated organization. To the investment industry, the term indicates that its members are conscientious enough to look after themselves without government interference, thank you very much. To cynics, self-regulation means no regulation at all. The truth meanders somewhere in between.

The Investment Dealers Association: Things Are Getting Better

The Investment Dealers Association (IDA) remains the most prominent of the SROs and for years it was a regulatory target for Canadian investor advocates because it played both sides of the street. The IDA's original mandate depicted the organization as "the national self-regulatory organization for the Canadian securities industry. We regulate the solvency, educational proficiency, and sales and business practices of Canadian investment dealers and their registered employees ... The IDA provides front-line regulation of day-to-day activities involving clients and their investment dealer firms. Recommending unsuitable investments, performing transactions without client approval, or encouraging an excessive number of transactions are all examples of improper practices that can warrant a complaint to the IDA."[70]

Well and good, but until April 1, 2006, the IDA also served as the investment industry's lobbying group, promoting its members' activities to various levels of government and the public at large and, in the process, enhancing efficient capital markets in Canada. This latter function clearly suggested a responsibility for the IDA to keep those pesky unwashed investors down on the street and out of certain corporate executive suites where they might start demanding answers to abusive questions. Imagine an organization that simultaneously encouraged the expansion of the country's highway system and fostered more protection for the environment and you have an idea of the IDA's dual and sometimes contradictory role.

All of this changed on April 1, 2006, when the IDA relinquished its function as a trade association, a chore since assumed by the new

Investment Industry Association of Canada, leaving the IDA to concentrate on regulation. To boost its effect in this area, the IDA and Market Regulation Services Inc., responsible for ensuring that stock market trades are conducted according to the rules, plan to consolidate their functions under the IDA umbrella.

(Readers of the first edition of *The Naked Investor* may recall the response of IDA president Joe Oliver* to a 2001 suggestion from the Ontario Securities Commission (OSC) regarding the splitting of dual responsibilities. The OSC, echoing a government-appointed committee charged with investigating the IDA, acknowledged that the IDA was not impartial in its policing of the industry, and that penalties imposed on member firms and their employees were too lenient. The OSC's solution was to propose that the IDA either protect investors through an exclusively regulatory role or lobby on behalf of its members, but not play both sides. Oliver dismissed the OSC's charges of a lack of impartiality and practically bragged that he had persuaded the government committee to back off, "because such a move [to separate the duties] was not justified."[71] Sometime over the next five years Oliver was apparently persuaded to change his mind.)

Focusing on regulatory matters should produce an IDA that is more responsive to investor concerns. If that's the case, the organization may expect to hear more often from disgruntled clients of its member companies, although the complainants will have to limit their expectations. That's because the IDA's powers are restricted to investigating complaints and imposing penalties on member firms and their employees found guilty of violations. No matter how strong your argument about losing assets because of broker or advisor malfeasance, the IDA cannot refund money to you, except under extraordinary conditions. It's not a bank; it's a police force. Well, sort of.

---

*Oliver has since announced his retirement, planned for mid-2007.

"The primary mission of the organization is to protect investors," Paul Bourque states.[72] As IDA's Senior Vice-President, Member Regulation, Bourque applies his experience as a former Crown attorney, first in Ontario and later in Alberta. Following stints with the B.C. and Ontario securities commissions, he returned to Alberta to serve as Deputy Minister of Justice, moving into his current post in 2001. This is the kind of person you want standing up for your rights as a small investor. But, is the IDA the kind of organization to do the job, even with its focus on ensuring that regulations are respected?

The IDA trumpets its role as protector of investor interests and assures the public that investors do not pay for the IDA's regulatory services. As columnist Doug Steiner observes dryly, that's like saying you don't pay for the warranty protection on your new car.[73] And consider the IDA's publication of an investor's guide for bond trading. A nice idea, but nowhere does the investor discover that the IDA helped set up the rules on which it is advising investors.

According to Bourque, about 20 percent of calls received by the bureaus are investigated. But why do 80 percent never make it past the initial inquiry? "Most are service complaints," Bourque responds. He is a tall, elegantly dressed man who carries himself with the quiet assurance of someone familiar with the environment of both boardrooms and courtrooms, grappling with the complexities of civil law and the personalities of aggrieved plaintiffs. "Perhaps the broker hasn't called them in a year, which we categorize as a simple service issue. Other complaints are out of our jurisdiction, or deal with criminal matters." Where evidence of criminal activity is evident, such as fraud or embezzlement, the matter is referred to local law enforcement officials. Whatever the basis of their complaint, investors cannot count on compensation.

"Let's face it," Bourque points out, "a client who feels that his or her account has been mishandled wants compensation above all, and that's fair. But we're not the place to provide it. If clients cannot get a settlement from their broker or advisor, or the company they're dealing with, they should talk to the Ombudsman for Banking Services and Investments." If OBSI cannot help the investor gain satisfaction, the IDA will assist in setting up an arbitration process for claims up to $100,000. But don't expect IDA to write you a cheque—with one possible exception.

Bourque made his assessment that the majority of investor complaints related to service issues in mid-2004. The IDA's statistics on investor complaints for the following year belied that statement, suggesting that other, more serious issues were being raised:

MOST FREQUENT REASON FOR INVESTOR COMPLAINTS, JAN DEC 2005[74]		
RANK	**REASON**	**NUMBER OF COMPLAINTS**
1.	Unauthorized/discretionary trading*	322
2.	Unsuitable investments*	222
3.	Other	188
4.	Service issues	111
5.	Misrepresentation*	99
6.	Undetermined	44
7.	Supervision*	38
8.	Manipulation & wash trading*	28
9.	Internal control violations*	27
10.	Falsification/forgery of documentation*	23
*Regulatory issues		

Of these 1102 complaints (the total number received in 2005 was 1271), 749, or almost 70 percent, are not service issues but regulatory issues, and serious ones at that.

In response to criticism about the IDA's inability to protect investors in the most practical manner—returning assets lost as a result of inappropriate actions by its members—IDA President Joe Oliver suggested a turnaround in the IDA's position regarding investor restitution. "Clearly a wrongdoer should not profit from his misconduct," Oliver stated in May 2006, "and a victim should not suffer from it."

If investors' hearts undoubtedly skipped a beat at this acknowledgement, investors almost swooned at Oliver's announcement that the IDA would indeed begin supporting the concept of restitution of assets to investors who clearly suffered losses at the hands of IDA members. Hats were tossed in the sky. High-fives were exchanged. Plans to canonize Oliver were formulated.

Then Oliver outlined the five restitution provisions: The funds must be available, i.e., in the wrongdoer's possession; the loss must be clearly attributable to the misconduct; the individuals entitled to the restitution must be clearly identified; the amount must be readily ascertainable; and the funds must be easily and efficiently distributable. Oh, and the wrongdoer must still be registered with the IDA.[75] The same issue of *The Globe and Mail* in which this report appeared also noted that the earth risks being struck by an asteroid of substantial size sometime within the next 10,000 years. Suggestion: Scan the sky for asteroids. Do not scan the media for IDA investor restitution.

When the Going Gets Tough, the Tough Get Out

What about discipline for the wayward broker or advisor, assuming that he or she is employed by a member firm of the IDA? The association will launch an investigation and impose a penalty, if warranted, which might include fines, a directive for the offender to undergo retraining, and a temporary or permanent ban from employment in an IDA-member company.

Fines remain the most prevalent discipline, with penalties beginning at $10,000, and here is another area where investor advocates
can feel that progress is being made. Past criticisms of the IDA
frequently noted that, as a member-based organization, it cannot
penalize someone who is no longer employed by a member firm,
any more than a golf club can penalize a player for cheating on her
scorecard if that player resigns from the club. Thus, a broker or
advisor hit with a $500,000 fine by the IDA might decide that his
future in the business isn't worth a half-million-dollar re-entry fee
and look for another career. When the going gets tough, a member
can simply resign rather than pay the imposed fine. More likely, a
tainted broker may find himself persona non grata with the firm as
the firm defends itself against charges by his clients.[76]

Bourque acknowledges this weakness in the strategy, but notes
that any broker/advisor who chooses to jump ship rather than pay
the imposed penalty cannot return to the fold. "Failure to pay a
fine," he emphasizes, "will result in the IDA refusing an individual
the required registration to allow them to work at an IDA member
firm."[77] Since securities dealers in Canada must be members of the
IDA, this represents a barrier against penalized members re-entering
the industry in this country.

According to its own records, the IDA collects less than 20 percent
of all fines it levies, a situation that is easily explained by one industry critic. "The advisors have outlived their usefulness at that point
and are usually unceremoniously cut adrift by their employers," he
says. "Their licence is dependent upon their being employed in the
industry, and the regulator does not (perhaps cannot) pursue them
for monies due because they are no longer members. That has not
prevented many of them from moving to the US and starting the
same game all over again."[78]

Other critics of the IDA point out that enforcement of its rules is
influenced in favour of the companies making up the organization

(who pay the membership dues to keep it operating), and against individual employees. The implication of lower fines to brokerages than to their employees suggests that employees can walk away from the association and even the industry, but the association needs those member firms and the fees they provide.

The IDA defied this assessment at the close of the market timing investigation in 2004 (see Chapter 5) when it imposed fines and disgorgement of fees totalling more than $42 million on four major investment firms—TD Waterhouse, BMO Nesbitt Burns, RBC Dominion, and HSBC Securities—for their participation in the practice. The following year, with no market timing issue to generate fines, the association still managed to swell its coffers by almost $1.8 million in penalties imposed on its members.

The IDA's control over member firms may be tighter than the public assumes, because IDA membership is no longer an option; securities law requires investment dealers to belong to an SRO, which, if the dealer seeks to provide comprehensive services, means the IDA. The choice is as simple and direct for securities firms as for individual brokers/advisors: Either pay your fine or get out of the business. Still, the organization remains a favourite whipping boy for investor advocates.

"Any regulatory agency is going to be subject to criticism that it provides too little, too late in some cases," Bourque sighs. "Whatever you do, some people will say you didn't do enough, and others will say you went too far. In our cases, we're dealing with people who expect to be compensated, and if they're not compensated in full, they're not very happy. Having said that, I think we have a good process for taking complaints, investigating them, and moving forward the ones that we believe offer some success in applying discipline. So basically, I think it's a pretty good system."

The Investment Industry Association of Canada (IIAC): The View from the Other Side of the Street

First things first: the IIAC is not an SRO. In its own descriptive words, it is "A professional industry association, re-assuming the original role of the IDA when it [the IDA] was founded in 1916."

The newly hatched IIAC, created in April 2006, identifies three goals in its mandate:[79]

1. To promote cost-effective securities regulation and public policy initiatives that support well-functioning and efficient markets with high standards of integrity
2. To assist the Canadian securities industry to succeed in an ever-changing business environment while meeting its business objectives and regulatory responsibilities
3. To act as the authoritative voice for investment dealers in Canada's capital markets

Individual investors will likely have little reason to contact the IIAC regarding their concerns in the future. There may be much to gain, however, in monitoring the IIAC's moves to influence the shape and power of regulations in a manner that makes life easier for the organization's members.

The Mutual Fund Dealers Association: Is You Is or Is You Ain't My Dealer?

If you purchase mutual fund units from your broker to insert in your RRSP, does this make your broker a mutual fund dealer? Yes, but this does not mean the brokerage is a member of the Mutual Fund Dealers Association of Canada (MFDA). The distinction between CIBC Wood Gundy and CIBC Securities Inc. may be relatively minor to you, but it is important enough for each to be a member of a different self-regulating organization. CIBC Wood Gundy is an IDA member,

CIBC Securities Inc. is a member of MFDA. Just to make things more complex, both the IDA and MFDA share the same mailing address in Toronto. If your broker or advisor firm is not a member of one, it's probably a member of the other. Or not. The MFDA began as the kid brother of the IDA in the 1990s, sharing the same president. Since 2003, however, the MFDA has been a stand-alone operation, although they're on the same floor in the same office building. Like the IDA, the MFDA is an SRO. It fulfils a dual, perhaps contradictory, role of protecting investors from abuses by its members and protecting its members from abuses by whomever.

Leaving regulation of funds and fund sponsors to the 13 securities commissions in Canada, the MFDA restricts itself to regulating only the sale of mutual funds by its members and, in its mission statement, stresses that it "has been created, in part, to protect [the] public confidence." The public confidence, retail investors might suggest, would be protected and perhaps enhanced if the SROs appeared more dedicated to addressing concerns such as inappropriate fund recommendations, questionable sales techniques, excessive fees, and poor fund management.

The Ombudsman for Banking Services (OBSI) and Investments: If He Can't Help You …

If the problem with your bank includes banking fees, commissions, interest rates, or credit-granting procedures, or is before the courts, forget about the ombudsman. You might also want to know, going in, that OBSI makes recommendations in favour of substantial compensation for the consumer only about 15 percent of the time, with small adjustments recommended in an additional 5 percent of situations. Why so low?

"By the time a complaint has moved into the formal investigation process, it has already been reviewed at various levels of our members," former ombudsman Michael Lauber explains. He suggests that the low percentage of substantial adjustments proves the system is working because most legitimate claims have been settled before clients encounter the OBSI: "Our existence puts pressure on members to be more responsive to customer concerns and resolve them promptly."[80]

Critics of the OBSI point out that investors should not fool themselves into believing the office maintains strict impartiality, although it's admittedly a difficult chore. If the OBSI agrees to investigate your complaint, its regulations require you to accept that no OBSI ruling or observation can be used as evidence in any other legal action, and that none of the organization's staff can be subpoenaed as a witness on your behalf. Nor will OBSI conduct a forensic audit in pursuit of your complaint. It's OBSI's game, after all, so it makes the rules.

Promptness is one aspect where OBSI appears to outpace others in this field, although speed, if that's the word, is relative in these situations. OBSI aims for a 90-day turnaround between accepting a complaint for investigation and issuing a report and recommendations. If OBSI finds in the consumer's favour and a loss of client funds is involved, it is not permitted to recommend payment exceeding $350,000—another OBSI rule, this one designed to limit losses to the banks funding its operation. Complainants are required to sign an agreement releasing the financial institution from being obligated to pay more than $350,000 regardless of the size of the claim. If your loss totals $500,000, be prepared to forget about recovering $150,000 of the amount, assuming OBSI agrees to investigate the situation and you beat the seven-to-one odds against OBSI finding in your favour.

OBSI does not make payments where it rules they are justified; it only recommends that the financial institution make the determined payment, and its proposal is not binding. If a member (financial services provider) does not accept OBSI's recommendation, the ombudsman will make this refusal public.

At least one OBSI statistic is relevant to the point of this book: Of 82 complaints filed with OBSI during 2005 concerning investment issues, about half related to suitability of investments proposed by advisors, assessed against data on the Know Your Client form.

Canadian Investor Protection Fund:
Even If Your Broker Goes Bankrupt, You May Not

You may believe that your chance of going bankrupt is greater than your broker's, and you're probably right. But the possibility still exists. If it helps you sleep at night, about 200 Canadian investment dealers belong to the Canadian Investor Protection Fund (CIPF), which covers members' accounts for up to $1 million each. If you maintain two accounts with a CIPF member—an RRSP/RRIF and an unregistered account—each account qualifies for $1 million coverage. From its inception in 1969 to the end of 2005, CIPF paid $36 million to clients of eligible insolvent brokerages.

The most recent broker bankruptcy involved Thomson Kernaghan & Co., which folded in the summer of 2002, leaving a $3.3 million shortfall. Bankruptcy will always be a risk for any business in any industry. While it's a nice feeling to know the CIPF is there to protect you, assuming your investment firm is a member (it will proclaim its membership on its brochures, contracts, and financial statements), most Canadian RRSP/RRIF owners are more concerned about their personal assets than those of their brokerage or investment firm.

The Ontario Securities Commission:
Is Big Brother Really on Your Side?

Many people living west of Thunder Bay and east of Cornwall grumble about Ontario's concentration of power, especially where finance and investment are concerned. Some point with justification and reasonable outrage at the Ontario Securities Commission (OSC).

On the surface, anything with a province's name in its title should be restricted to that provincial jurisdiction, and that's the official case with the OSC. The practical experience is somewhat different. Like it or not, and most people outside of Ontario do not like it, the OSC sets most of the rules in the investment game.

You may never win a bar bet with this fact, but it's worth knowing anyway: Of all the industrialized countries in the world with a securities industry, only two lack a truly national securities commission. One is Bosnia-Herzegovina. The other is Canada. (By the time you read this, the fact may no longer be true. In April 2004 rumours swept the world, or at least corners where people who care about these things lurk, that Bosnia-Herzegovina was about to finally establish a national securities commission. So was Canada, via a proposal dubbed *Blueprint for Uniform Securities Laws in Canada*, launched in January 2003 but with no firm action apparent as many as four years later. The smart money is on the Bosnians winning this race.) This drives a lot of people crazy, from Canadian nationalists who are ashamed that one of the world's great capitalist democracies has never been able to agree on a single securities watchdog, to foreign investors who believe they'll be operating a publicly traded company in 1 jurisdiction and discover they're actually operating in 10. Or more. (For a list of provincial and territorial securities commissions or administrators, see the Appendix.)

When it comes to securities commissions, Canada is like a squabbling family of siblings dominated by a bigger older brother whom everybody respects but nobody likes very much. Each province retains the right to establish and manage its own securities trading operation, but the OSC, by virtue of Ontario's economic clout and the presence of the TSX in Toronto, dominates the scene. It's not purely resentment that prevents smaller provinces from facilitating a national commission, which would continue to be dominated by Ontario anyway. Other provinces, especially Alberta and British Columbia, fear that an Ontario-led national securities commission would have a bias toward large corporations, leading to a failure to recognize the unique needs and concerns of smaller companies in the east and west, and the way they represent regional concerns.

Most dominant of all, perhaps, is the notion that the OSC is poorly administered, to the point of derision by many industry observers. One highly respected academic who has studied securities regulators on an international scale refers to the OSC as "probably the most poorly governed securities regulator among those of the OECD [Organization for Economic Co-operation and Development—the world's 26 most developed nations] countries."[81] The OSC also makes demands on others that it refuses to adhere to itself. For example, it advocates that the majority of a corporation's board members be independent of the company's senior management, yet its own board is composed exclusively of OSC commissioners, who also make up the compensation committee.

This would just be business as usual in Canada were it not that the OSC has generated its own coterie of critics and sceptics over the years, many charging that the commission is overpopulated, overprotected, overpaid, and underworked.

Susan Wolburgh Jenah, OSC Vice-Chairwoman, admits that critics of the OSC have a point regarding its role in investor protection.[82] The solution, she suggests, lies first with investors themselves. "We're not there when they are having the conversation with a broker who is trying to get their business," she explains, suggesting that investors must assume the front line of their own defence against bad investment advice. "We're not expecting people to read long prospectuses. We're just trying to identify areas where people can be the most vulnerable and say, 'Here are things to look out for.' We want [investors] to become our allies in preventing abuses through investor protection." As an example, Ms. Wolburgh Jenah cites elaborate packages of educational material made available without charge to retail investors through the OSC.

All well and good—arming investors with knowledge and aware-ness is also the goal of this book. This is the equivalent, however, of telling people to keep their wallets in a safe place and be careful when walking down dark streets. It's good advice, but when you're mugged or attacked, you want the long arm of the law to sweep in and deliver swift justice. When it comes to investor protection, many Canadians feel that the enforcement responsibility has been assumed by members of the same gang who left you broke and beat up in the alley—in this case, the IDA and MFDA. What can these SROs do to convince us that the public concern is being addressed where investor protection is concerned? Well, how about if some outside individuals, people like you and me, sit on the boards of these SROs with a mandate to question policies that do not appear to be in our interests? Wouldn't that be good idea?

Ms. Wolburgh Jenah agrees. In fact, she believes the situation has already been dealt with. "Currently, I think the IDA have a third of their directors representing public interest groups," she suggests. "The IDA's position historically has been, 'We are an industry group, we need to have a lot of representation on our board from industry people.' But you would want to have ... a majority or 50 percent of people on the board, perhaps an academic, who has never worked with the industry, who has no ties to the industry ..."

So in mid-2004, when I interviewed the Vice-Chair of the OSC, she believed one-third of the IDA board consisted of "public interest directors," and that the proportion should be perhaps half. Providing a list of IDA directors taken from the association's website, I asked her to identify which of the members of the 2004–2005 board repre-sented investor interests. She found it difficult to identify one. Two years later, the size of the board had been drastically slimmed from 23 to 13 members (see page 198), but little else had changed. Can you spot the "public interest people" who have "no ties to the industry"?

INVESTMENT DEALERS ASSOCIATION
BOARD OF DIRECTORS 2006–2007

Donald W. Black, C.M., S.O.M.
Deputy-Chairman, Greystone Managed Investments Inc.

Roger Casgrain, CFA
Executive Vice-President, Casgrain & Company Limited

Kenneth G. Copland
President, KGC Ltd.

Anne-Marie d'Amours
Managing Partner & President, Capimont Technologies Inc.

Michael A. Grandin
Chairman & Chief Executive Officer, Fording Canadian Coal Trust

Daniel Leclair
Former Executive Vice President, Finance and Chief Financial
Officer of Hydro-Québec

Ronald Lloyd, Chair
Chairman, Chief Executive Officer, Credit Suisse Securities
(Canada), Inc.

Phipps Lounsbery
Managing Director, Debt Capital Markets, CIBC World Markets Inc.

Daniel Muzyka
Dean and Professor, University of British Columbia

Joseph J. Oliver
President & Chief Executive Officer, Investment Dealers Association
of Canada

Brian J. Porter, Past-Chair
Chief Risk Officer, Scotia Bank

H. Sanford Riley
CEO & Chairman, Richardson Partners Financial Limited

Ruby Wallis
Vice President, Director & Chief Compliance Officer, FirstEnergy
Capital Corp.

SOURCE: IDA WEBSITE, WWW.IDA.CA/ABOUT/ORGANIZATION/DIRECTORS_EN.ASP,
ACCESSED JULY 2006.

Professor Muzyka is the only 2006–2007 board member not
employed by or associated with an investment or securities firm, but
as RBC Financial Group Professor of Entrepreneurship at UBC's
Sauder School of Business, he can hardly be considered a representative of investor interests.

Sloths, Turtles, and Snails

Perhaps the most common criticisms of the OSC are directed toward
the amount of time it takes to get anything done. In an industry that
measures its transfer of thousands of securities representing millions
of dollars in nanoseconds, the OSC trundles across the microproces-
sor landscape like an ox cart.

Columnist Eric Reguly of *The Globe and Mail*'s Report on
Business once compared the OSC's activity level "with the reflexes of
a superannuated sloth."[86] Reguly was noting that the OSC had been

alerted in 1998 to the practice of equity monetization, a trick used by top executives of high-flying companies selling shares to the public. The mechanics are unimportant, but monetization enabled executives who sensed an imminent drop in the value of their company's shares to unload their own shares without publicly declaring the sales, thereby avoiding hefty tax hits. It took two years for the OSC to acknowledge the problem. Creeping into action, it introduced new regulations riddled with more loopholes than macramé underwear. As a result, almost no incidence of equity monetization was reported until the spring of 2003, about five years after the alarm was raised. Just for fun, some regulations were not made retroactive, meaning that anyone who had managed to cheat shareholders, investors, and the taxman in the past could relax. By the time even this vapid ruling was handed down, the bull market that spawned monetization concerns had long faded away.

And while investment industry heavyweights such as the Ontario Teachers' Pension Plan Board were decrying the soft dollars flowing into mutual funds and warning of the conflict of interest they represented in mid-2003, the OSC addressed the problem by promising to "assess the impact of 'soft dollars' on market efficiency, analyst bias and competitiveness."[84] Not a word on investor protection.

Where broker and advisor misconduct is involved, the OSC's reaction is so dawdling as to be almost humorous, except to investors claiming advisor and broker misbehaviour. Seven months after the smooth and devious Patrick Kinlin was convicted and sentenced to prison for defrauding dozens of clients out of millions of dollars, the OSC announced it would hold a hearing into Kinlin's activities. (For details of Kinlin's nefarious activities and ignominious end, see Chapter 11.)

In defence of the OSC, it is not alone in responding to the need for modifying investment rules with all the reflexes of a rusty drawbridge.

Canadian securities commissions have grown notorious for being sluggish to the point of near paralysis. Among the critics is Barbara Stymiest, former CEO of the TSX. Stymiest recalled, as an example of this country's lethargy in this area, an incident concerning the U.S. Securities and Exchange Commission (SEC) when it introduced regulatory changes in mid-2002. The changes were a response in part to investigations into the activities of Enron and Tyco executives. Dubbed the Sarbanes-Oxley Act, the new rules dictated tighter standards and heavier penalties for senior executives who abused their positions at the cost of shareholders.

Acknowledging the cross-border structure of North American corporations, the SEC wrote the Canadian Securities Administrators (CSA) in October 2002, listing the proposed changes to take effect January 30, 2003, and asking for comments and suggestions from the OSC and other CSA members. The CSA, recognizing the meaningful gesture of the SEC and its implications not only for corporations with Canadian links but for the universe of corporate governance generally, leapt into action and managed to reply on February 19, four months after receiving the letter and about three weeks following the introduction of the legislation. In the Canadian securities industry, this was considered prompt. "One of the [CSA] administrators," Stymiest explained, "calculated a couple of years ago that the average rule change used to take seventeen months."[85]

Eventually OSC chairman David Brown announced new rules, reflecting the U.S. Sarbanes-Oxley Act, with great fanfare at the end of March 2004. He also boasted that the average time it took the OSC to start investigations against a company under investigation had been reduced from 20 months to just 11 months, suggesting that the OSC had geared up from the speed of a tranquilized turtle to that of a snail in heat.[86]

Message from a Caring Government to Aggrieved Investors: *Get a Move on, Damn It!*

By now, it should be clear to readers of this book that the process of identifying and collecting losses in their RRSP/RRIF due to inappropriate activities on the part of their financial advisor is complex and drawn out, often taking several years. Organizations such as the OSC and IDA acknowledge the virtue of patience in these matters. Yet the government of Ontario has proposed reducing the period during which aggrieved investors can obtain restitution from six years to two years from the date on which the claim is discovered or *ought to have been discovered* by the person making the claim. Should Ontario succeed in this venture, other provinces are almost certain to impose a similar limit on their citizens.

In effect, if six months after you ought to have discovered that units in the *Standback & Duck Emerging Markets Technology Fund* were not suitable for the low-risk, income-generating portfolio you had requested of your financial advisor .... and he had assured you they were ... and you learn their total value will now buy you a double-double and a cruller at Tim Hortons ... you have 18 months to recover your losses, or somewhat more time than it takes the OSC to open a file on the matter.

The proposed legislation lit a firestorm among investor advocates and citizens' groups, who in the past have spoken with the polite voices of shy panhandlers to passers-by. The Small Investor Protection Association (SIPA) and United Senior Citizens of Ontario rallied their members to protest the move; the Canadian Association of Retired People (CARP) described it as a form of seniors' abuse; and to their credit even the OSC and MFDA denounced the proposal.

Ken Kivenko, among the country's most knowledgeable and persuasive investor advocates, provides six convincing reasons for trashing this seriously flawed law:

1. The multiple levels that investors must negotiate is excessively time consuming, and control of the speed of this process rests in the hands of the dealer/broker. Under the new legislation, it will be in the dealer/broker's interests to delay the process as long as possible in the expectation 24 months will pass and the door to a settlement will effectively slam shut.

2. It can take an extended amount of time for investors, especially senior citizens, to learn the extent of their losses. Book values that obscure poor performance, investment terminology heavily laced with jargon, and the fact that some mutual funds report semi-annually all delay an investor's awareness of serious losses due to inappropriate investments.

3. Advisors may encourage aggrieved clients to "hang in there" as their assets decline like a car on a well-greased roller coaster.

4. Investors dealt serious blows to their financial plans often demonstrate cognitive dissonance in being unable to accept reality and its impact.

5. The stress of serious losses to a hard-earned retirement nest egg generates an emotional response in many people that effectively blocks their ability to take action for some time.

6. The last resort for those investors who qualify by virtue of dealing with a bank-owned investment firm is OBSI. Among OBSI's rules is the provision that investors must have exhausted all other avenues without receiving a settlement, and OBSI's own process may take several months.

"The Act actually encourages corporate foot-dragging to consume as much time as possible," Kivenko notes. "This hardly seems an Act … in support of the public interest."

So consider the plight of RRSP/RRIF investors who believe they have a legitimate claim worth pursuing and expect regulatory agencies to assist them when the investment firm rejects their allegations:

The IDA points out its inability (except under the most unlikely circumstances) to reimburse investors with funds lost as a result of actions by its members and chooses to retain any disgorged funds instead of returning them to the investor.

The OSC maintains a tradition of somnolence reminiscent of Dorothy Parker's response to the news that Calvin Coolidge had died: "How could they tell?"

The odds against OBSI finding in favour of aggrieved investors are about seven to one, making it a long shot at any racetrack.

And the government of the largest province in the country proposes legislation that ensures investors have even less chance than they already do of effectively pursuing their case against bad advice and self-interested management of their retirement portfolios.

If investors are indeed sheep, perhaps it's time that some of us morph into wolves.

THE BANKS: GATHERING US BENEATH THEIR UMBRELLA

Sunil and Bharati Kumar* were relatively pleased with life. Their two children had just completed university, their small video production business was doing well, and their RRSPs were growing in value.

Their overall financial situation, while not at a critical state, remained somewhat perilous, as it had for several years. They carried a mortgage on their home of almost $200,000, representing about 50 percent of its market value, and maintained a line of credit that frequently nudged their secured limit of $50,000. "Given the cyclical nature of our video production business," Sunil explains, "we were always operating close to the limit. We might get a big production contract, but full payment wouldn't be due for months down the road. Meanwhile, we had expenses to cover, equipment to lease, and so on. Fortunately, our bank manager was understanding, and we had been with the same bank, same branch, for over 20 years. We kept everything there—our household account, our company's current account, our leasing plans, our home mortgage—everything except our RRSP accounts."

*Pseudonyms

The RRSPs, which exceeded $500,000 in 2003, were maintained at the full-service brokerage of a rival bank. "We opened our accounts there years ago," Sunil says, "on the advice of a business associate who had nothing but good things to say about the advisor, a man named Harris. Harris proved as good as our associate said he was. Harris would call every couple of months to discuss things, suggest certain investments, tell us if he was investing in the same thing that he was proposing for us, and let us know when he was getting out of it. We've always made contributions to our RRSPs every year because this is really an unpredictable business. We knew we could sleep better knowing we had money salted away and were investing it wisely."

"He was wonderful, that broker," Bharati adds sadly. She is a dark-haired, petite woman, her steadiness balancing her husband's more emotional nature. "He helped make us a lot of money in our RRSP accounts."

In the fall of 1999, a new branch manager arrived at the Kumars' bank. Much younger than the somewhat folksy manager the couple had dealt with for several years, he was friendly and helpful but not nearly as laidback. "He reminded me of somebody who had just stepped out of a motivational meeting," Sunil recalls, "filled with ideas and ambition, and totally dedicated to making you as much of a success as he saw himself to be."

Within a few weeks of arriving on the job, the new branch manager invited Sunil and Bharati in for a chat and a review of their accounts. "Nothing to worry about," he assured them. "You've been a good customer of the bank and I just want to make sure you stay that way."

The bank manager was as positive during the meeting as he had been during the telephone call, looking over the personal financial statements that the Kumars had provided at his request.

"He seemed to fasten on our RRSP balances," Sunil says. "I remember he whistled at the amount on our last statement. Then he asked why we weren't with the bank's brokerage arm."

"We explained that we were happy with our advisor," Bharati adds. "So why change?"

The bank manager noted that his bank-owned brokerage was rated higher for customer satisfaction and performance than the one the Kumars were using. "You should be with us," he said, meaning his bank's brokerage arm. "You won't give up a thing in service, and you'll save money." The manager reminded them that the Kumars' mortgage was scheduled for renewal the following year. Consolidating their financial activities with his bank would put them in a much better bargaining position when it came to negotiating interest rates for their mortgage and operating loan. "I can probably knock at least a quarter-point off the interest rate on your current account overdraft," he said, "and it would make things easier to raise your operating loan credit in the future, if you need it. You've got a lot of clout in your RRSPs—over a half million dollars' worth. You should be using it. Bring everything under one umbrella with us, and we'll bend over backward to save you money and keep you happy."

"It kind of made sense," Bharati says.

"Of course, we owed Harris, our guy at the other company," Sunil says. "We told the branch manager that, but he shrugged and said, 'Business is business. It's your money, and if you can get the same kind of service from our outfit, which is just around the corner from here, and save a few hundred dollars a year on interest charges, why wouldn't you do it?'"

The Kumars promised to give the idea serious thought. Over the next week, the bank branch manager called twice, urging them to make the switch. During his second call, he asked if he could have the registered representative from his bank's brokerage call and make an appointment—"Just to review your account, give you a second opinion." The Kumars agreed.

"To make a long story short, we switched," Sunil says. "The new broker seemed like a pleasant fellow. He made several suggestions about selling some of our mutual funds and buying others. He even brought the papers needed to transfer the account to his brokerage. So we did. I sent our former broker a letter thanking him for his help in the past. He didn't respond. I didn't expect him to."

None of the new mutual funds appeared to perform better over the next year than those that had previously been held in the Kumars' RRSPs. In fact, returns were mediocre at best. Nor did the new broker contact the Kumars before mid-February, when he called to ask how much the couple would be putting into their RRSP from the previous year's earnings, reminding them that a decision was needed before the end of the month. "I get really busy around then, as you might expect," he said, "so I'd appreciate it if you would get back to me in the next few days."

"Nothing about a review, nothing about strategy or anything like that," Bharati says. "He just wanted to know how much we would be contributing. It was so different from Harris, our other broker."

The Kumars instructed the broker to purchase units in the bank's money market mutual fund while they decided on a longer-term investment.

"We sat down one night in March to talk about it," Sunil says, "and that's when it hit us. Our RRSPs weren't performing as well as they had been and the service—well, there was no service to speak of. We'd given up big potential earnings on over half a million dollars in our RRSPs to shave maybe a quarter percent off our bank loan and mortgage. It was a bad deal."

"Friends told us that all the banks were open to negotiating mortgage rates," Bharati adds, "and there's no way they would have let somebody else take over our mortgage if it came down to a competitive battle to keep our business. So why even think of transferring our RRSPs to them? After 20 years with the same bank, we had all the clout we needed."

They decided that night to return their RRSPs to Harris, their previous broker.

"He was a little cool," Sunil says. "And he pointed out that our bank's money market funds couldn't be held in our RRSPs if his bank-owned brokerage was handling our accounts. It sounds like a really stupid law, but it didn't matter much, because we could cash them out and buy something else."

The real blow came when Harris announced that he was no longer accepting new clients. In fact, he was reducing his client load in preparation for moving into semi-retirement. "He said he expected to keep working for another 10 years, but with a reduced client list," Bharati says. "If we had stayed with him, he would have kept us as clients. That's the feeling I got. But ..." She shrugs.

The Kumars were passed on to a junior financial advisor, who failed to impress them. By the end of the year they were searching for another place to take their RRSPs that would have an advisor as good as their old friend Harris, and not having much luck.

The Bank Act prohibits tied selling, defining it as "the practice of linking the purchase of a product or service to a bank loan." Is that what happened here?

"The issue is whether or not there is coercion," former banking ombudsman Mike Lauber explains. The Kumars' experience, he suggests, was something else. "Their situation was not coercive tied selling. It was incentive selling."

Just to confuse things, banks also engage in cross-selling. This involves a bank representative finding a way to sell you two goods or services when you intended to purchase only one. Visit your branch to buy a Canada Savings Bond, for example, and you might receive a sales pitch for a safety deposit box in which to keep it.

Back to tied selling. Is it a major factor for the ombudsman in his role of protecting bank customers?

"We have not had a complaint on this for several years," Lauber replies. "One of the issues that we have considered is, if the customer is approached on a coercive basis and declines the transaction, what are the damages?" No damages, beyond the opportunity for a possible lower interest rate, were linked in this case.

The Kumars fell victim to a powerful sales pitch that cost them potential growth in their RRSP and marked the end of a beneficial relationship. That the idea originated with their bank, which controlled much of the couple's fiscal obligations, added impact to the new manager's proposal. Canada's chartered banks no longer carry the weight of the near imperial authority they held a few decades ago, nor are they the source of last resort for financial assistance. But they continue to represent a repository of trust, leavened with a friendly corporate persona delivered via TV commercials and other media. If the bank claims it can save us money, we tend to believe it. Should we?

Bank-Owned Brokerages: Too Much Concentration?

The deregulation of banking fostered the entry of chartered banks into the investment industry. When it happened, conservative middle-class Canadians who regarded stockbrokers as equally alien and unknowable as Afghanistan camel drivers found it more comfortable to deal with their neighbourhood bank branch than with brokerage firms such as Wood Gundy; Richardson Greenshields; Burns Fry; McLeod, Weir, Young; and Dominion Securities. By the early 1990s, when Wood Gundy was absorbed by CIBC; Richardson Greenshields by TD Bank; Burns Fry by Bank of Montreal; McLeod, Weir, Young by ScotiaBank; and Dominion Securities by Royal Bank, they were dealing with them anyway.

Simultaneously, Canada's chartered banks grew more approachable. Everyone, it seemed, wore a friendly smile and had a bundle of cash ready to foist on you. Canadian humorist Stephen Leacock's essay about being rattled every time he entered a bank was no longer simply dated—it was incomprehensible. Why be nervous about entering a bank? Banks were the fiscal equivalent of a neighbourhood pub, the one where everybody knows your name and they all want to buy you a drink, or maybe sell you a savings bond.

Except, in some instances, the bank-owned brokerages.

In recent years, these firms have appeared to generate an alarming number of complaints from small investors about the manner in which advisors handle investor accounts. On the surface, this is hardly surprising. Not only do the bank-owned brokerages handle the majority of RRSP and RRIF accounts; their client list is often less sophisticated than those of the few remaining independent brokerages.

This second factor cuts both ways, of course. On one side, it may be argued that unsophisticated investors do not fully appreciate investing philosophies and the inherent risks involved in pursuing a strategy—thus the greater number of unwarranted complaints. It is also true, however, that this very lack of sophistication makes it easier and more tempting for some advisors to place their interests ahead of those of their clients. Not only are the clients less likely to understand or complain about inappropriate investments or misunderstood risks, but they also are less likely to pursue complaints based on unnecessary losses, and are even less prone to launch a legal joust.

Investors who challenge a bank brokerage risk finding themselves financial cannon fodder. Patricia Cosgrove's experience (see Chapter 9) of facing down a senior litigator hired by the bank's investment arm at an hourly fee likely exceeding $1000 in response to a potential $10,000 loss in small claims court is a dramatic illustration of the counterattack small investors risk facing. The only inference to draw from her experience is that the bank could not risk losing even a diminutive challenge to the practices of its brokerage for fear that, like the small Dutch boy removing his finger from the dike, a deluge would follow.

Why Can't Bankers Just Be Bankers?

Canada's chartered banks enjoy privileges of size and freedom as attractive as any in the industrialized world. They are also, as a result, among the most profitable banking operations found in any country. Bankers are still business people, however, and nothing inspires business people more than the prospect of expanded operations and profits. Surely, however, a limit exists and the banks might have reached it with their recent proposal to sell insurance.

At first glance, this appears an innocuous and even inevitable move. After all, banks provide mortgages and personal loans along with investment services and products. In some ways, they already serve as a source of insurance coverage, selling short-term health coverage for tourists and business travellers. Segregated mutual funds sold by banks may also be construed as an insurance product. So what's the big deal about the chartered behemoths moving into automotive, home, and life insurance?

Most Canadians feel well served by their insurance providers, and little evidence exists that they need yet another source for this service. Competition, as every free-enterpriser attests, is good, but capitalist hegemony is dangerous. The banks' ambitions are firmly rooted not in filling a needed service but in lining their own pockets, while gaining a degree of power that many consider dangerous. According to one source, about one out of every five Canadians who applied and was approved for a personal loan, line of credit, or mortgage from a bank claims to have been pressured to give more business to that bank in return for favourable rates otherwise not available.[87] How do we benefit by providing banks with power derived from being the primary source of insurance coverage for individuals?

The risk of excessive power in the hands of banks relates to their access to personal information on bank customers, and its potential for misuse. Banks, most people believe, possess enough personal information on their customers. Your bank already knows where you live, what you do for a living, how much income you earn, how many dependants you have, your S.I.N., your age, your marital status, your credit record, your current debt, your available assets, and much more. The banking industry claims, with some justification, that this data is either necessary to provide various banking services on your behalf or is mandated by law. Fair enough.

But consider the additional information gathered by companies providing life insurance, especially related to your health records. Insurance providers have legitimate reasons for intrusive questions such as the following: Have you ever been treated for a sexually trans-mitted disease? Do you have a heart condition or cancer? Have you ever suffered from depression or another mental condition requiring treatment? These are identical to the kinds of questions that would be posed to customers seeking life insurance coverage from bank-operated companies.

Banks declare that they would erect an impermeable wall between information gathered by their life insurance providers and data made available to staff approving personal loans and mort-gages. No one familiar with large, multi-layered corporations bent on maximizing earnings and limiting risk—and what industry qualifies for that description more than Canada's chartered banks?—believes this to be true. The prospect of a loan officer having the opportunity to scan a customer's personal health history before setting the interest rate, or approving the loan at all, would inevitably prove a reality.

Canada's banks do a good job at banking and a not-bad one at investment services (with caveats—see below). We do not need them as insurance providers.

First Rumblings of a Revolution?

The investment industry tends to laugh off claims that sales pressure is applied at the expense of the well-being of clients. Bank-owned brokerages, which are frequently accused of exerting pressure on their client service staff, declare that they function within the guidelines of the IDA and provincial and territorial securities authorities. But from time to time, someone shines a light on the inner workings of the giant brokerages, with revelations that are neither attractive nor reassuring.

This occurred in April 2003 when journalist Jonathan Chevreau printed a resignation letter from a financial advisor in his *Financial Post* column. The advisor, a man in his mid-40s, had built an impressive income-generating portfolio over the years, a tribute to his investing skills. The income this produced, along with the advisor's admittedly frugal lifestyle, enabled him to emphasize benefits to his clients over income for his employers. He had guided most clients into portfolios as low-cost, diversified, and tax efficient as his own. In fact, the annual cost to the broker's clients hovered around 0.65 percent of assets, exceptionally low considering the quality of the service provided.

In fact, it was considered too low by the bank-owned brokerage, which Chevreau dubbed *BBB* (for Big Bank Brokerage). For some time, Stan, the pseudonym hung on the advisor by Chevreau, had resisted pressure by his superiors to "peddle" wrap accounts and other high-fee investment products. The BBB pressure on Stan and other advisors, he claimed in his letter, was not unique. "As with every other firm on the street," he wrote, "all manner of perverse incentives are in place. All manner of investment pornography is on hand to distract not just clients but advisors too. The most striking thing is not the pilferage of clients' wealth, but how otherwise honest and well-meaning people can be seduced into doing the wrong thing by careful systems design."[88]

The advisor referred to the bank's inactivity fee, which applied a $15 charge each quarter ($60 annually) to non-registered investment accounts in which no trading activity—buying, selling, or exchanging mutual funds, bonds, or stocks—had taken place.

Bank executives defend such a fee by pointing out that they are required to print and mail statements each quarter, along with a tax summary each year. Besides, there were compliance officers to be paid (for sheltering the brokerage from harm), research departments to be maintained (identifying stocks to be bought and sold), executive salaries to be covered ("Churn the old ladies to buy the Mercedes"— sardonic Bay Street poetics), and so on. Were these not accounted for in the bank's existing fee structure? Apparently not—or not well enough. In effect, the bank reversed the concept of user pay into "pay if you don't use it."

Canada's chartered banks are open to another level of criticism, related to multi-levels of power and influence they exert. Consider the following scenario.

A couple in their seventies, persuaded by a well-known investment guru, seek to increase the size of their retirement nest egg through leverage. The man has suffered a heart attack and stroke. His bank-owned brokerage promotes the investment of $100,000 in a tech-based bank-managed mutual fund, purchased at a 9-to-1 leveraged ratio—the elderly couple put up $10,000, and the bank loans them $90,000 secured by the couple's equity in their home. When the fund tanks with the collapse of the high-tech industries, the fund's value is a fraction of its original cost, and the bank demands full payment of the $90,000 loan plus interest.

In effect, the bank has—

1. Made money from the sale of its own fund
2. Made money from interest on the money loaned to purchase the fund
3. Transferred risk (of the fund losing money) from itself to an elderly couple with serious health concerns
4. Obtained virtually 100 percent security via a claim of equity in the couple's home
5. Achieved all of this with a totally inappropriate investment vehicle considering the couple's age and status

Based on the above, a case could be made to impose restrictions on chartered banks involved in such multiple-level actions of advising and financing investments of this kind. By the way, this is not an imaginary event. It is based on an actual case that, unfortunately, cannot be presented in more detail here (to the chagrin of the elderly couple who experienced it) because of a gag order demanded by the bank before any settlement deal could be reached, and a confidentiality agreement certain to be imposed afterward.

For the record, I have dealt with bank-owned brokerages for almost 20 years, with results ranging from spectacular (thank you, Harley) to frustrating. My current broker (Hi, Rob) is a bright, hard-working, and trustworthy guy whose opinion I seek and respect.

The point is not that bank-owned brokerages are to be avoided, but that they are indistinguishable from most of the other players in the game when it comes to 100-percent trustworthy service. Every broker and advisor possesses more means of extracting money from your retirement savings than you are aware of, and any advice offered to you may result from pressure on him or her to maximize the bank's revenue rather than an honest desire to maximize the performance of your RRSP or RRIF.

Vultures, Jackals, Ghouls, and Everyday Thieves

Helen Rentis is not a woman to be trifled with, nor someone you would expect to be easily deceived. As a 16-year-old high school graduate, she began her working career in a secretarial position with Mills, Spence & Co., which metamorphosed first into Burns Fry and eventually to Nesbitt Burns, the brokerage arm of the Bank of Montreal. She was also employed in the legal industry, filling a sales position with Butterworths, the leading distributor of law books in Canada. She raised two children as a single mother following the break-up of her marriage, kept a close and supportive relationship with her aging parents, maintained her youthful figure into her 50s, and assembled impressive balances in an RRSP and a non-registered portfolio from years of dutiful contributions and astute management.

These kinds of achievements give a woman confidence in dealing with people, not to mention a sense of independence and self-sufficiency. In short, if you were to choose someone to defraud and swindle, Helen Rentis would not be a good candidate.

She proved this on the day in 1991 when she received a cold call from a young man at Midland Walwyn. "He obtained my name from a list of investors in a popular tax shelter," Helen Rentis recalls. "I had no intention of handing my account over to some stranger via a telephone call, although I recognized that Midland Walwyn was one of the leaders in the brokerage field."

She was, however, considering a new brokerage firm to deal with. Her firm, Richardson Greenshields, had transferred her broker from the downtown Toronto office, convenient to Rentis, north to its suburban Richmond Hill office. The downtown location of the Midland Walwyn office where the cold-calling broker was located was appealing for its convenience, perhaps. But nobody was going to persuade her to move her account on the basis of a single telephone call.

The young broker assured her that he understood her position. "He asked if it would be all right to perform an analysis, at no cost or obligation, of my investments and those of my parents that I was watching over for them," she says. "I went along with the idea, and for several months he gave me his assessment along with examples of the kinds of investments he was doing for other clients."

The young broker explained that, in addition to the usual trading in stocks, bonds, and treasury bills, he employed a unique strategy in commodities trading that was producing excellent results from derivatives—options, puts, and calls. The maximum risk of loss, according to the broker, was 7 percent.

"I was not familiar with that kind of trading," Helen Rentis explains, "but it seemed an acceptable risk to me. He gained my confidence over time, to the point where I thought it might be a good idea to move everything back downtown. Besides, I would be dealing with Midland Walwyn, right?" Better returns were especially appealing to Rentis because she was not a member of her employer's pension plan; this was not a matter of greed but of taking prudent steps to generate a secure financial future, exactly as the investment industry preaches. As a client of Midland Walwyn she also believed that her investments would be secure and that trading in her accounts would be overseen by the brokerage.

Ever cautious, Helen permitted the broker to use only a portion of the portfolios for his trading system and, with that decision, Michael Holoday, the Bay Street whiz kid, had himself another client.

From the beginning, Holoday reported phenomenal profits with every commodity trade—that is, when Helen could decipher the statements. "I was on the road quite a bit at the time," she says, "and I would come home to piles of statements from Midland Walwyn. I just couldn't understand the ones on options and neither could my accountant. When I complained about them, Michael told me that most of his clients had the same problem so I should just ignore them. He would provide easier to understand summary statements on the multiple trades being made. My accountant could use them to calculate the profits on investments outside my RRSP, report them to Revenue Canada, and pay income tax on them. And that's what we did."

In the early 1990s, Michael Holoday was being portrayed as a kind of boy genius, enjoying special status as the youngest member of Midland Walwyn's Chairman's Club, reserved for the top 5 percent of all Midland Walwyn brokers—an achievement he managed to reach within three years of obtaining his trading licence. How did he rise so far so fast? "Michael's ploy from the beginning was to gain the trust of his clients," Helen emphasizes. "I had no cause for alarm, nor did I receive any calls from Midland Walwyn informing me that, as I discovered only years later, he had virtually wiped out my account within the first few months of opening it."

Holoday's use of personalized account statements was not limited to Helen Rentis. He used this ruse on all his clients, persuading them to ignore confusing (or distressing) commodity statements and accept his personal assessment of their account status which, of course, was always positive. And all the clients did, through his tenure at Midland Walwyn and his move (under a cloud of suspicion) to aggressive First Marathon Securities, where he was awarded the impressive title of Managing Director, Futures Division.

Holoday's lifestyle matched his new title. Instead of the small apartment he occupied when Helen Rentis entrusted her account to him, he now resided in Forest Hill, one of the most exclusive neighbourhoods in Toronto; owned a fleet of cars, including a Jaguar, a Porsche, and a Ferrari; hosted parties at a large cottage on Lake Simcoe; and began construction of a beachfront villa in Barbados. He even married a leggy blonde woman who played the role of Successful Executive's Wife perfectly.

Mistakes happen, but over the next few months, mistakes in Helen's accounts kept happening over and over. "Finally I told Michael I wanted my money out of my commodity accounts," she recalls. "He promised to do it, but days and weeks went by and nothing happened. Every time I asked about it he had one excuse or another. Finally, I called him just before I was to leave on a business trip. 'I want my money, Michael,' I said. 'No more excuses. Just close out the accounts and send me my money.'"

Holoday protested that he had just doubled the value of her account.

"I shouted through the telephone, 'So sell the damn thing!'" recalls Helen. "And he promised to. But there was nothing to sell. It took me months to discover that my commodity accounts had been basically empty for years."

It was little consolation, but as events unfolded, Rentis discovered she was not alone in being deluded by Michael Holoday.[89] When he was finally ejected from First Marathon in late 1994, dozens of clients appeared with ransacked accounts and similar stories of Holoday's extensive deception.

As the facts emerged through a long police investigation and criminal trial, it became apparent that Holoday was no ingenious con man. He cheated his victims with any technique at hand, from promising safekeeping for a client's stash of Canada Savings Bonds (promptly cashing them himself) and selling units in a fictitious about-to-be-launched mutual fund, to dispensing promissory notes backed by First Marathon through his position as Managing Director, Futures Division.

Nor can his clients be classified as greedy. Almost all were realistic in their expectations, although these expectations were exploited by Holoday's sales pitch and his position at the two brokerages. Without exception, all of the clients relied on Holoday's exalted position within each brokerage to confirm that their investments were appropriate and their statements accurate.

Perhaps most telling was the manner in which the two brokerages that employed Holoday responded to revelations of his frauds. Both steadfastly denied any responsibility for their star broker's antics. Clients who called First Marathon to inquire about the status of their accounts, after news broke of Holoday's dismissal, were told by the firm's compliance officer, "You've been cheated. I suggest you hire a lawyer." No offer was made to replace the money swept from their accounts. When one client protested that he had trusted Holoday because he was First Marathon's Managing Partner of the Futures Division, the compliance officer sneered, "That was only a title."

Some clients worked through their emotional distress before throwing up their hands and trying to forget about the experience. Others took legal action, seeking redress through civil suits launched against Holoday's former employers. First Marathon's blanket defence to the lawsuits was to claim the clients were "authors of their own misfortune" for trusting Holoday and his schemes. Two former clients were the subjects of countersuits launched against *them* by First Marathon, the brokerage claiming $10 million from each to cover damages that the brokerage refused to acknowledge in the first place.

The brokerage fought every claim launched against it tooth and nail. Most civil cases were eventually settled through arbitration, although a handful remained in dispute a decade later. Thanks to confidentiality agreements, no information on the final settlements, including the proportion of losses reimbursed to the former clients, has been revealed. "I never thought a brokerage could turn on you that way," mused one of the ex-clients.

Why Blame the System When You Can Blame the Victim?

As we have seen, inappropriate investments in your RRSP account (or elsewhere) can lead to losses that you may never recover, with the advisor and brokerage defending themselves in a number of ways, most related to the inevitability of risk and uncertainty.

Fraud and embezzlement differ from bad advice because the proof is often easier to establish and the action can involve criminal courts, where exposure is more widespread and punishment more severe. The common factors, however, are that you lose money and you retain similar low expectations of recovering more than a token amount.[90] Here's one more: Your expectation of protection by the professed guardians of the investment industry should be similarly low, based on past experience.

Remember the OSC? Its stated goals are to "provide protection for investors from unfair, improper or fraudulent practices; foster fair, efficient capital markets; maintain public confidence in the integrity of those markets."[91] Unlike the SROs, the OSC (and related provincial commissions that emulate its structure and objectives) possesses teeth to force settlements, ban participants from the industry (not just member dealers), apply and enforce fines, and generally wield a regulatory club.

No one expects any regulatory or enforcement body to engage in every corner of its jurisdiction, snooping where it is neither needed nor welcome, but the OSC and its counterparts across the nation do not inspire confidence in their ability to deter licensed fraud artists from dipping their greasy hands into your hard-won RRSP assets. To many observers, the OSC's attitude toward controlling licensed securities dealers is like that of a police officer who ignores reports of armed and suspicious-looking characters until the bad guys get around to shooting somebody.

Consider Patrick Kinlin, as notorious as Michael Holoday and cut from the same bolt of cashmere. Like Holoday, Kinlin loved the good life, especially if it was being charged to someone else's tab. He lived in lavish homes, enjoyed expensive clothes, ate at exclusive restaurants, and favoured pricey cars, owning both a Mercedes and a Porsche. He proved especially adept, with his silver mane of hair, elegant bearing, and honeyed voice, at romancing middle-aged women who were in possession of liquid assets. Basically an insurance agent, Kinlin had been licensed by the OSC to sell mutual funds and insurance products exclusively. In the late 1990s, however, he started pushing phoney bonds onto his clients. When word of Kinlin's illegal activities got back to the OSC, it began investigating his actions. In the middle of this investigation, one of Kinlin's clients called the OSC to check on the insurance man, whose profligate living had raised a red flag. Kinlin, the client was told, had "a clean record" at the OSC. Based on that notification, the man handed Kinlin $60,000. Soon afterward, Kinlin fled Toronto and was arrested in a Pennsylvania hospital where he was being treated for an understandable nervous disorder. Needless to say, the client never saw his $60,000 again. Nothing in OSC policies regarding suspicious activity by licensed dealers seems to have changed. Once again, small investors must take it upon themselves to don their own armour for protection instead of relying on regulators.

They Love Themselves, Not You

Detective Jeff Thomson of the Toronto Police Services Fraud Squad is as familiar with people like Kinlin and Holoday (he was instrumental in investigating and convicting the latter) as anyone, although he probably loathes them more than most. With a powerful physical presence and an expression that can transform itself from warm laughter to a threatening scowl in an instant, Thomson has a good deal of sympathy for victims of fraud and embezzlement.

"They don't expect to be taken by these guys," Thomson says over lunch in a sports bar across the street from Toronto Police Services Headquarters.[92] "They expect these fraud artists to help them, because that's how the bad guys present themselves." When someone offers to help you, Thomson points out, your guard is automatically lowered. That's why the victims of fraud and embezzlement can be among the last to recognize and acknowledge that they have been scammed.

Going through life in a highly suspicious state of mind is neither wise nor healthy, Thomson admits. Fortunately, it is also unnecessary. "All you need to remember are a few warning signals," he advises. "Hearing or sensing any of them should turn on a red light somewhere in your mind, and that's when your guard should come up." He is sympathetic with most of the victims and despises the fraud artists. "They all have two characteristics," he says of the fraudsters. "They don't give a damn about other people. And they love themselves."

Here are Thomson's suggestions for avoiding fraud and embezzlement. They're neither infallible nor complete—the scum who prey on trusting elderly people are adept at developing new tricks—but they provide some armour worth wearing whenever you encounter an unfamiliar and promising investment opportunity.

If It Sounds Too Good to Be True, It Probably Is This is the oldest rule in the book. Unfortunately, thousands of people ignore it every day. If anyone tells you they can double your money within a dramatically short period—less than a year, for example—without incurring a major degree of risk, reply with three words: "No, you can't." Or simply walk away.

Do Not Be Overly Impressed with First Impressions You don't know what a swindler looks or sounds like, so do not trust your instincts to warn you about one. These people may be smooth and fast-talking, or so shy and soft-spoken that you feel compelled to give them your money. They may boast about their educational achievements, or brag that they were school dropouts who clawed their way to success. They may be men or women, as young as your grandchild or as old as your parents.

One quality shared by many is their lifestyle. Fraud artists almost invariably pursue extravagance in their dress, their possessions, and their social life. Extravagance is the reason they commit fraud in the first place, and the image of success it conveys adds extra appeal to their schemes. Clients begin to believe that an investment advisor making so much money for himself must be able to generate similar wealth for his clients. In reality, the criminals are not just living beyond their means—they are living beyond the means of their clients.

George Nelson Allen, a stockbroker convicted of defrauding several clients out of $7.5 million, lived in a sprawling suburban home (which he transferred to his wife for $2 before investigators could freeze his assets), and drove a Jaguar valued at $110,000.

Allen's embezzlement technique, familiar to Thomson, was to sell "corporate investment certificates" in two fictitious companies. The certificates paid interest far higher than current market rates and could be cashed on 30-days' notice. "It was a classic Ponzi scheme," Thomson recalls. "He was always robbing Peter to pay Paul." Allen had no compunction about grasping money from any source, and no apparent conscience regarding the damage he was inflicting. One of his victims was a young man awarded $600,000 after losing the use of his legs in an auto accident. Allen took every penny. When a married couple saw their entire life savings of $850,000 vanish through Allen's fingers, it almost destroyed the family and nearly drove the husband to suicide.

"He always looked wealthy and successful," Allen's victims would recall. "He was well groomed, well dressed, and drove that flashy Jaguar."

Upon conviction, Allen was sentenced to four years in prison. The courtroom audience, mostly comprising Allen's victims, broke into applause as he was handcuffed, and one ex-client shouted, "You're a scumbag!" at the ex-broker's back.

"In 27 years as a police officer, I've never seen cheering in the courtroom before," says Jeff Thomson. His wry smile suggested that it was well deserved.

If "You Have to Act Now!"—Don't Con artists do not want you thinking too much before you hand over your money. If someone insists that you "act now!" and sneers at your insistence on thinking things over, take a hike.

Michael Holoday was brilliant at persuading people to jump at his schemes, many of them short-term investments—as short as one week—providing promissory notes indicating that he would be paying 5 percent interest for a seven-day loan, which works out to an annual interest rate of 250 percent. When his scheme collapsed around him, one element of Holoday's defence was to point out, correctly, that this interest rate was illegal under the Criminal Code of Canada and, as a result, he was not obligated to pay it. Besides, he argued, non-payment of a loan is a civil, not a criminal, matter, and he should not be subject to criminal charges as a result.

This illustrates one more quality to expect from these people: chutzpah.

Never, Ever Fall for a Scheme to Extract Money from Your RRSP, RRIF, or LIRA Tax-Free The money in your RRSP or RRIF is free of income tax until you withdraw it as cash. This is fair, since you did not pay income tax on the contributions you made nor on any growth that took place over the years. Still, it hurts to find the Canada Revenue Agency (CRA) standing there with its hand out when you're ready to enjoy the benefits of all that saving and investing.

Enter the fraud artists.

While you cannot withdraw funds from your registered plan without triggering income tax, you can move the investments within it, perhaps selling bonds to purchase shares in a company, assuming they are eligible as an RRSP investment. This rule inspired a number of scams in which investors were offered the opportunity to invest in a growing company with RRSP assets, and the company would return as much as 75 percent of the share price in cash to the investor. Newspaper advertisements still appear from time to time, offering an RRSP loan free of tax. Buy $100,000 worth of shares in Ungava Enterprises Inc. and receive $75,000 in cash that the CRA needn't know about. Boy, is this a good deal or what?

You probably know the answer. Unfortunately, hundreds of people each year discover too late that their money has covered only a transaction fee or a down payment, in the case of legitimate corporations. Even if shares are transferred into the RRSP, their actual value will be more apparent than real, and clients eventually discover that $100,000 has effectively vanished from their retirement savings. Then things get worse.

The CRA takes a dim view of any attempt to avoid paying taxes. They'll demand immediate payment plus interest and perhaps a penalty as well when such activity is suspected. While the bilked investor is dealing with this blow, there is always the risk that the shaky company whose shares the investor purchased goes bankrupt. If this occurs, the corporation's creditors may appear on the investor's doorsteps demanding payment, even though the purchased shares are now worthless. Yes, it has happened.

Do Not Trust the Internet To those engaged in fraud and embezzlement, the internet is like a commuter train delivering them to work each day. "Work," in this case, means persuading trusting citizens to part with their money, which vanishes into cyberspace before being deposited in offshore bank accounts.

That's what happened to about 13,000 people in 60 countries around the world who invested in a "bank debenture trading program" promising 120 percent annualized returns. The "program," operated by an organization calling itself the Tri-West Investment Club, claimed to be associated with Haarlem Bank via something called the Haarlem Universal Corporation, and included among its directors a Vice-President of Lloyd's of London. All of this could be accessed on the Tri-West website, where investors could obtain every bit of information needed to participate, including instructions on transferring their deposits.

It was, of course, yet another variation of the old Ponzi scheme. The alleged kingpins behind Tri-West, including Canadian Alyn Richard Waage, were eventually collared. Waage admitted his guilt and promised to make restitution to his victims, who should not be hanging by their thumbs waiting for it.

You wouldn't fall for a deal pledging such high returns, would you?

Not unless you were among the people who responded to a fictitious website supposedly launched by the OSC in March 2001 as a means of alerting people to the dangers of investing blindly through the internet. The website promised monthly returns of 30 percent or more from "international debentures" eligible for RRSPs. Within six weeks the site scored over 16,000 hits. Many visitors expressed keen interest in the prospect, and some offered to send $50,000 or more in cash without obtaining more information. P.T. Barnum would be pleased.

Never Invest in Something You Do Not Understand Stay clear of anyone who promises substantial earnings while being unable to explain the deal in terms you can understand.

This goes for friends, relatives, and colleagues who rave about the returns they are receiving, or more likely are expecting to receive, from an investment. "I don't know how it works," they may say, "but it's making me money and that's all I care about."

Your grasp of the investment's mechanics will be about the same as your eventual grasp of any profits.

Beware of Investments Sold through Affinity Groups Fraud artists feed on your trust. Unless you believe and trust their promises, they won't collect a penny from you.

Religious groups, service clubs, and community organizations are typically composed of people who enjoy each other's company and confer their trust easily. The members of a Toronto mosque did just that in the summer of 2000 when a charming young man named Salim Mohammed Damji began discussing a new investment opportunity. Damji, who told some people he was a dentist and others he was a physician—in reality he was neither—claimed his company, Strategic Trading Systems, had developed a teeth-whitening product called Instant White. Colgate Palmolive was prepared to buy the rights to Instant White for $400 million, and Damji was offering friends, relatives, and almost everyone in the close-knit Islamic community an opportunity to purchase shares in Strategic Trading Systems. "When Colgate buys us," he promised, "you get back $20 for every dollar you invested."

He had little except his word to back up his promises, but that was enough to persuade over 5000 people to hand Damji a total of $70 to $80 million before the scheme collapsed 18 months later. Less than $5 million was recovered; Damji lost much of the balance through bad investments, real estate purchases, and internet gambling.

"It's the nature of an affinity group," Detective Jeff Thomson explains, "plus the special character of the Islamic community. In their culture, a handshake is a binding contract. Damji took advantage of that, plus the trust placed in him by members of his mosque and even members of his own family. That's the power that fraud artists have inside their own ethnic and religious group."

In November 2002, Damji was sentenced to prison for six years and three months, with no directive for him to make restitution. Many of his victims were forced to sell their houses to settle loans made for their investment in Damji's scheme, and some required treatment for mental and physical hardships directly related to their experience.

And while the world at large welcomes a future of true ecumenical equality, investment swindlers practise it every day, on thousands of trusting individuals. Consider these two cases:

Financial planner Earl Crackower was Mr. Popularity in his corner of Toronto's Jewish community. A past president of Toronto Freedom Lodge, a Jewish charity, Crackower celebrated weddings, anniversaries, and birthdays with his clients. When they were ill, he visited them in hospital, and when they or their loved ones died, Crackower was at the graveside, comforting those around him. Who could fail to trust such a man? None. And when his frauds caught up with him, none of the 43 clients and their families who trusted him with over $3 million of their life savings recovered a penny.[93]

One former client whose parents lost over $560,000, splitting the family and leaving everyone in it struggling, called Crackower "an embarrassment to humanity." Others at his trial said they felt foolish for trusting him, commenting that the comfortable retirement they had anticipated through all their working years had vanished in an instant.

For his part, Crackower's lawyer noted that his client occasionally purchased lottery tickets in the hopes of paying everyone back with his winnings. Oh, and one thing more: He was remorseful. In July 2006, the remorseful Earl Crackower was sentenced to five years in prison. As a first-time offender in a white-collar crime, he would be eligible for day parole after serving less than one year.

A few miles down the highway in Hamilton, Ontario, financial planner Bob Adams promoted an investment opportunity that none of his clients had heard of before, but almost all of them agreed to purchase. After all, good old Bob was an elder in the Hamilton Christian Fellowship, a "deeply religious" man whose sermons in the fundamentalist Christian organization often left worshippers writhing on the floor in a state of euphoria.

Adams's investment opportunities involved limited partnerships issuing Standby Letters of Credit that could yield as much as 31 percent annually virtually risk-free. None of Adams's clients could fathom what Standby Letters of Credit were, or how they managed to earn such high interest with no risk. But could such a pious man be anything but scrupulously honest?

Well, yes, he could. When everything came crashing down and the dust began to settle, Adams and other members of his limited partnerships were short of U.S. $4 million entrusted to them by about 100 clients. Three of Adams's partners were eventually convicted and sentenced to jail terms ranging from 22 months to three years. No charges were laid against Adams despite the judge's observation that Adams should be the subject of "appropriate investigation."

For a short time, Adams operated a café in the Ontario hamlet of St. George before declaring personal bankruptcy. In May 2006, however, former clients of Adams were amazed to discover that he was once again dispensing investment advice in Cambridge, Ontario, as Bob Adams, Chartered Financial Planner, and had been a featured speaker at a nearby Pentecostal Assembly. The title of his talk: "Biblical Principles of Financial Success."

A newspaper story on the Bob Adams saga revealed that the Ontario Securities Commission had not applied any restrictions on Adams's endeavours.[94]

When the Punishment Fails to Fit the Crime

Our justice system makes a clear distinction between crimes committed with a stroke of the pen (or computer key) and those committed with the use of a threat, a fist, a knife, or a gun. Rob a bank of $20,000 and you may receive a nine-year prison sentence; with acceptable behaviour you will be eligible for parole in three years. Steal $20 million from trusting citizens through scams and embezzlement and you may also receive a nine-year sentence; behave in the same manner, however, and you'll be back on the street in just one and a half years because your crime was "non-violent."

That's assuming, of course, that you are caught and convicted in the first place. To give it a hip-hop beat: Crimes in the street get you more time than crimes in the suite, and the punishment is lighter when your collar is whiter. There are practical reasons for this. No offence to neighbourhood muggers, but white-collar criminals are a little higher on the intellectual level and work with more sophisticated tools than a lead pipe. Tracking a street thug employs snitches and descriptions. Tracking an investment mugger may take months or even years of following paper trails and computer records.

A study conducted by Osgoode Hall Law School noted that "people from poor and working-class backgrounds charged with committing street crimes are less able to resist the use of criminal law, whereas the business and professional classes who engage in corporate [or financial] wrongdoing are better able to avoid the criminal label as a result of their influence and financial resources."[95]

The entire legal process tends to favour a softer, more complacent treatment of white-collar criminals, beyond the distinction between supposedly passive and violent methods of stealing other people's money. Under the federal Criminal Code, a conviction of breaking-and-entering carries a potential life sentence for the offender even if nothing more valuable than a beer is taken from the fridge. The same man committing fraud faces a maximum sentence of 10 years, no matter how many tens of millions of dollars he stole and how many lives he devastated. And while Statistics Canada spews detailed figures on street crime every year, it produces only a smattering of statistics on white-collar crime.

The underlying philosophy suggests that white-collar crime is either victimless or merely a crime against property exclusively, with no link to personal suffering. Anyone who has endured a severe loss in their life savings, especially in their middle years or beyond, will reject this as nonsense. Virtually every conviction of fraud and embezzlement conducted against trusting individuals leaves the victims feeling twice-abused—first by the fraud artist and then by the legal system.

The victims of Michael Holoday received some satisfaction when he was sentenced to a total of seven and a half years for his misdeeds at brokerages Midland Walwyn and First Marathon, plus another 15 months for writing bad cheques while awaiting trial on the earlier charges. They were less than thrilled, however, to learn that Holoday served most of his time at the minimum-security Beaver Creek facility set among the lakes and woodlands of Muskoka, where inmates reside in winterized log cabins and cook their own meals in a communal kitchen. "That's not prison, it's summer camp," sneered one of Holoday's victims. And many were further appalled to learn that Holoday was released to a downtown Toronto halfway house in August 2002, having served just 16 months.

Patrick Kinlin, who carried out scams similar to Holoday's, was released on day parole after serving less than a year of his five-year sentence. Salim Damji's immense fraud, which cost friends, relatives, and members of his Islamic community an estimated $80 million, served barely a year of his six-year three-month sentence before receiving day parole, leaving him free to walk among the people whose lives he had damaged to such an enormous extent. Nelson Allen's four-year sentence for pocketing $7.5 million of investor funds meant he would be back on the street in just eight months. Those are Canada's parole rules; non-violent crimes qualify first offenders for release after just one-sixth of the sentence has been served.

David Blow, who masqueraded for years as an insurance agent in a Toronto suburb, avoided trial by admitting he had defrauded 65 victims of $7.3 million. When he was sentenced to 43 months in prison in February 2001, the court considered that he had been held in a detention centre for five and a half months, all of which qualified him for day parole after serving about seven months behind bars. If you care to look at it from a salary or wage angle, that's about $1 million a month.

The rationale for this lenient treatment is based on the apparently lesser impact of white-collar crimes versus that of appalling offences such as sexual assault, robbery with a weapon, and murder. That's reasonable, but it fails to address the true impact of crimes in which victims lose virtually all their worldly possessions. Fraud artists lacking financial resources receive a court-appointed attorney to defend them against criminal charges, while their victims are frequently left too destitute to retain a lawyer and recover their losses (or attempt to) in civil court.

Victims are often left defenceless in other ways. "Over 80 percent of all frauds involve people more than 60 years of age," states fraud investigator Jeff Thomson. "They had assets saved for their retirement, and they came from a generation when people were more trusting of others. That's what makes them the favoured target. Of course, they are also the least able to recover their losses, so they are also the most tragic."

Whatever the age and status of the victims, the shock of losing a substantial portion of their life savings often results in depression, family strife, divorce, and even suicide. White-collar offences are "victimless crimes"? Says who?

Admittedly, prison sentences are ineffective as a deterrent to these scam artists. Investigators claim the rate of recidivism with fraud artists and embezzlers is among the highest of any criminal activity, including murder and armed robbery. Within months of being released onto the streets of Toronto, Michael Holoday was found collaborating with an internationally sought fraudster who had set up internet sites promising high returns for investors and employing good old Ponzi-scheme principles. Patrick Kinlin was even brasher. He spent his day parole hours chatting on pay telephones, promoting a phoney retirement home and picking up donation cheques at mail drops. When the scam was discovered, Kinlin's parole rights were revoked and he languished in a prison cell for a few weeks before succumbing to a heart attack. Few mourned his passing.

"These guys never learn," said one investigator familiar with both the Kinlin and Holoday cases. "They consider their time behind bars as an educational opportunity, where they can pick up new ideas and maybe meet new partners in crime."

If incarceration provides neither a deterrent to the fraudsters nor a gratification for their victims, perhaps our best course of action as citizens is to assume responsibility for preventing scams. It will cost us something in trust, normally an admirable and beneficial human characteristic, and require us to temper our greed to a substantial degree, which is not a bad goal in itself. In this manner, we can avoid being victims and prevent the fraudsters and embezzlers from succeeding. It is, like it or not, our best defence.

LOOKING OUT FOR YOURSELF
AND YOUR MONEY

"I'm not an angry guy," Stan Buell insists. "I may be outraged, but I'm not angry."

We are relaxing over coffee on a promising spring day in the affluent Toronto suburb of Unionville. Buell's real estate office is a short walk up the street from Starbucks. He has arrived at my request to discuss the Small Investor Protection Association (SIPA), an organization Buell launched in 1998. Trim and stylishly dressed, Buell appears substantially younger than his 66 years, and the spring in his step is that of a more youthful man.

Like most of SIPA's 500 members, Buell was the victim first of broker malfeasance and later of the failure of regulatory bodies and the legal system to support him. "I prefer not to discuss my own experience because people will assume I launched SIPA as some sort of revenge," Buell says, "but I didn't. I started SIPA to help others, after I went through my own nightmare."

Buell's nightmare consisted of returning from a five-week trip abroad to discover that his six-figure investment portfolio entrusted to his broker in his absence had vanished, leaving him a $70,000 debt. He spent years attempting to recover his losses, encountering unhelpful industry regulators and the brokerage's attempts to prevent the case from being heard in civil court. Meanwhile, Buell remained distracted from earning a living, drawing on the remainder of his personal savings to cover his living expenses. Thanks to unflagging energy and unfailing optimism, he managed to put the incident behind him, but the experience left him sensitized to problems of small investors who are at the mercy of the investment industry. When he heard a story of advisor wrongdoing in 1998 that was even more devastating in its impact than his own situation, he decided to do something about it.

"It concerned an elderly man and woman who had worked together all their lives to build a thriving business," Buell relates. "When the husband was stricken with terminal cancer they sold the business. Soon after, the husband died, believing that at least his widow would live her life in financial comfort and security. But that wasn't the case. The widow put her money, which included the proceeds from the sale of the business, the sale of their house, and their last $160,000 of savings—a total of over $900,000— in the hands of a financial advisor she trusted. The entire amount was gone within three years, placed in high-risk investments that benefited only the advisor through commissions. It was terrible, and it got worse when nobody seemed able or willing to assist her. Nobody really cared."

Buell cared enough to start SIPA, holding the organization's first meeting in the basement of his church. "About a dozen people showed up," he recalls, "and we've been building slowly but steadily ever since. Now we have about 500 members in nine provinces."

Instead of bragging about the organization he spawned, Buell regrets the necessity for his group. "Investors need an organization with the power to offer them protection," he suggests, "and that power will not come from the SROs. An industry-sponsored association cannot properly look after the concerns of individual investors, because its focus is on the people who pay the association dues—and that's the brokerages and mutual fund companies."

No one representing small investors sits on the board of directors of the SROs or the provincial securities commissions, Buell points out. He notes that the industry giants are very effective, however, at defending their own interests: "The larger companies protect themselves from anything that might affect their image. The financial press may cover frauds and scam in detail, but when a bank-owned brokerage is taken to court over its involvement in the Bre-X fiasco, which cost small investors untold millions of dollars after it collapsed, very little is heard about it."

Buell's denunciation of large financial firms represents the root of his criticisms about the industry. He is not an advocate, for example, of do-it-yourself investing by most RRSP/RRIF owners. "Investors need good brokers and financial advisors," he insists, "and I really believe most advisors are bright, hard-working people. Many problems are caused not by individuals but by a system that forces advisors and brokers to compromise their principles in the name of pushing profits higher and higher." When the pressure gets strong enough, Buell says, even good people will bend both the rules and their own principles to satisfy upper-management demands to produce more profits. "The first place to fix things is at the top, not the bottom," he suggests.

Buell drains his coffee and prepares to return to his work as a successful realtor. Is he still sensitized to investor horror stories? "Oh yes," he sighs. "And I still hear about them. A few weeks ago I received a call from a doctor who worked hard all of his life with the goal of retiring at 55. He set aside every dollar he could spare through his working career only to discover, in his 50s, that it had vanished through his broker's hands. He had nothing whatever to show for it. When I spoke to him he sounded suicidal, so I made a point of driving to his home to lend him support."

Buell understands the pain the doctor experienced—how much it hurts to face the realization of loss and the refusal of an industry to address the situation.

How many Canadians have been victims of bad investment advice that produced an intolerable and unnecessary drain on assets in their retirement portfolios? It depends on whom you consult. The investment industry claims the number is minimal, and that victims are the product of their own excessive greed, or that the number reflects the same degree of criminal activity found in every profession.

No one knows the extent of abuse suffered by Canadian investors at the hands of brokers and advisors or by the system as a whole, thanks in part to the veil of secrecy created by confidentiality clauses inserted into settlements and supported by the investment industry. It does not take deep undercover detective work, however, to deduce that thousands of Canadians endure preventable losses in their retirement portfolios year after year. Many are told their losses represent normal investment risk levels, and they are cowed into accepting this explanation by their advisor. Others blame themselves or are too embarrassed to acknowledge the evaporation of substantial portions of their assets. Those who take their cases to the SROs, the provincial securities commissions, or the civil courts and obtain little or no redress assume the attitude "You can't fight City Hall" and try to erase the experience from their memory.

Nothing drove this realization home more dramatically than my research and preparations for this book. Several more accounts of fiscal abuse by financial advisors could have been included here, many representing flagrant exploitation of investor trust and unacceptable behaviour by advisors. Stories included the promotion of risky age-inappropriate instruments to elderly investors, the use of bank loans on a highly leveraged basis for investors persuaded to purchase funds managed by the same bank (a nice win-win situation for the bank), performance awards for brokerage advisors who elevated their production through such actions, and so on. In all these cases, the wounded investors were willing and often eager to provide me with details of their experiences. Wherever the investors had retained legal counsel, however, they were directed—sometimes harshly—by their lawyers to say nothing about their claims publicly until a settlement was reached. In the event of a settlement, of course, they would be subject to a similar gag order, usually couched in a euphemism such as confidentiality agreement or non-disclosure agreement, and thus the secrets are maintained ad infinitum. Linked to these disclosure rules will be a disclaimer that the settlement agreement does not constitute wrongdoing by the firm in question.

Lawyers will argue that such confidentiality is critical to launching a successful suit against an advisor or brokerage, ignoring protests from investor groups that operating behind an opaque curtain of secrecy enables the investment industry to claim that abuses are limited in extent and impact. Nor can the actions of some law firms on behalf of their small-investor clients be considered altruistic—not when the same firm plays on both sides of the fence, acting on behalf of brokerages against investors and investors against brokerages, and prefers not to be publicly identified with either side for fear of restricting its earnings opportunities. Whatever motive the legal community may posit, secret settlements inevitably result in other clients of the brokerage firm remaining in the dark on occasions when the malfeasance by the same advisor is being practised on their portfolios.

Gag orders do not keep settlement terms totally secret from observers—only from those who might criticize the industry's policies. A typical directive used to keep investors from discussing their lawsuits before and after settlement might read:

[The plaintiff] will not disclose terms and conditions of the settlement offer to any third party except financial advisors or lawyers, except as required by law and excepting any communication with securities regulatory or other enforcement authorities and self-regulatory organizations.

In case you missed it, this means everyone in the industry with an interest in the facts, including lawyers, brokers, advisors, the IDA, and other SROs, can be privy to the details, but not the press and the public.

Given the concern of law firms not to be associated with one position over another lest it limit their potential client lists, how can we avoid suspicions of self-interest when they direct their small-investor clients to avoid public discussion of their cases? One investor who had been eager to describe his experience to me was directed by his lawyer not only to avoid any media contact but also to refrain from identifying the firm representing him. Why? Because this same firm had defended one of Canada's celebrity investment gurus in a legal case, arguing against charges that its client's actions had been detrimental to the interests of investors. The legal team obviously wishes to ride two horses at once, with each trotting in opposite directions. Nothing prohibits lawyers from doing this, and the legal profession can make a strong case against such restrictions. Some firms, however, focus on either one side or the other, choosing to fight battles for small investors exclusively, or be retained by brokerages and advisors to repel investor charges of inappropriate actions. They, at least, deserve some respect for choosing an ethical position (ethics are, of course, a moral quality and not a legal one).

How Many Anecdotes Does It Take to Make a Statistic?

During presentations I make to community and service groups on the subject of mistreatment of RRSP holders by the investment industry, I ask if anyone with an RRSP or RRIF has felt that her account was mismanaged, or believed he had suffered unacceptable losses in his portfolio. Typically more than half of those present raise their hands. It's easy to locate malcontents in any gathering, but the stories narrated to me during and after the meetings indicate that the majority of these people are neither perpetually disgruntled nor excessively greedy. Too often, their losses are the apparent product of a commission-based sales system that rewards industry practitioners first and investors only incidentally.

When investor horror stories spill onto the financial pages of newspapers, how many private experiences does each publicized tale represent? A dozen? A hundred? A thousand? No one knows, but while each tale differs in character and setting, all are similar in the unfolding of the plot. Consider these, culled at random:

- A Toronto couple in their mid-70s had their retirement portfolio invested in quality bonds and stocks in large established corporations. Encountering an affable stockbroker at a social event, the couple was persuaded to transfer their account to his firm, with substantial cash added from the couple's non-registered account. After selling much of the couple's blue-chip investments, the broker began trading in penny-stock shares of gold mines, audio-cassette producers, and other high-risk ventures. From 1996 to 2001, while stock markets were recording some of the biggest gains in history, the couple's portfolio fell one-third in value. Their complaints led to an investigation by the IDA, which could dispense punishment to the broker but could not recover their losses. After spending three years attempting to obtain some degree of compensation, all the couple, now in their 80s, had to show for it was a thick file of correspondence.[96]

- In July 2000, a new financial advisor was assigned to handle the accounts of a retired Mississauga, Ontario, couple. This advisor severely criticized the emphasis on conservative fixed-income RRIFs pursued by the previous advisor and persuaded the couple to transfer $330,000 into several high-MER funds such as Global Science and Technology, and Global e.Commerce.

The husband, aged 75, was suffering from terminal cancer; his wife was scheduled for major heart surgery. Following the husband's death and her recovery from surgery, the woman noted that the values of their RRIFs, which had never before lost money, had declined by more than $100,000. As the RRIFs spiralled downward with the collapse of the tech industry, the widow called her advisor to express her concern. In response, the advisor suggested she put away her account statements and pick up a good book instead. In November 2002, the widow finally transferred her account to another securities firm and demanded the first company review her case. When no review was submitted after six months, the widow contacted the Ontario Securities Commission, which yielded a telephone call from an independent adjuster who had been assigned to her case. By year's end, nothing had yet been resolved, although a proposed settlement letter arrived in December 2003 in which the brokerage offered a settlement of just $7461. The amount, less than one-tenth of the widow's claimed loss, was based on a KYC form allegedly signed by the husband. Unfortunately, the date on the KYC form was one year after the man's death.[97]

- An 83-year-old retired printing-paper salesman in Pointe Claire, Quebec, was annoyed to discover that his RRIF was docked almost 4 percent of its total value in redemption fees and termination fees when he transferred the account to another brokerage. His complaint letter generated a rejection from the first brokerage's director of business standards, who wrote: *"It appears you are aware that* [the brokerage] *may charge fees and, on review of the client application, I note that you have initialled this provision, as well as that having to do with the simplified prospectus. The applicability of redemption fees are* [sic] *disclosed in the prospectus and outline the formula used to make the calculation."* The former client noted that the agreement he signed said the company "may" charge fees on redemption, that he had never received a prospectus, and that he had never been charged fees for moving his account in the past. He abandoned hope of recovering the fees.[98]

- An Ottawa man fought for years to have his bank-owned brokerage accept responsibility for losses suffered when the registered representative placed substantial portions of the man's portfolio into high-risk investments that included gold and diamond exploration companies, debt-heavy conglomerates, and the notorious Bre-X Minerals Ltd. Whenever the man questioned the wisdom of these investments, especially the Bre-X ones, the broker told him to relax, adding assurances such as, "I have your best interests at heart," and "Our analysts have checked this company thoroughly." When a hefty portion of his portfolio was lost in the collapse of Bre-X and other dubious investments, the client launched a vigorous battle to recover at least a portion of his losses, to no avail. Working his way through a convoluted trail of compliance officers, branch managers, ombudsman's office, MPs, cabinet ministers, and senators failed to penetrate the brokerage's defence that he was an experienced investor, had approved the investment choices, knew the risks involved, and had no right to claim restitution. Seeking $250,000 in damages, he partnered with other former clients who had suffered comparable losses, all alleging breach of contract, negligence, and breach of fiduciary duty, in a class-action suit. A settlement was finally reached years later, with details unavailable because of a confidentiality order.

- In Kitchener, Ontario, Melville and Marion Hunt won a court decision against their advisor for selling a substantial portion of their investment in BCE Inc. without their permission or direction. The judge agreed that the brokerage breached its fiduciary obligation and instructed the brokerage to pay losses and damages. The brokerage appealed and won, the appellate court ruling that the brokerage did *not* owe the Hunts a fiduciary duty because they had opened a non-discretionary account, and thus had "an obligation to mitigate their losses." Undeterred, the Hunts decided to take their case to the Supreme Court of Canada on the basis that "by denying the existence of a fiduciary relationship between the broker and the client in this case the appellate decision results in financial advisory relationships being treated differently in Ontario than in the rest of the country."[99] In March 2004, the Supreme Court declined to deal with the matter, apparently confirming the Ontario Court of Appeal ruling that the advisor did nothing wrong in selling the Hunts' BCE shares without their permission.

- In Montreal, Quebec, several hundred small investors, many of them depending exclusively on their RRSP for retirement income beyond their Quebec Pension Plan/Old Age Security income, lost virtually all of their $17 million entrusted to former TV repairman William Marston. Having switched from nursing television sets to planning financial futures for clients, Marston embarked on a rocky journey with two institutions. The first was Investors Group, which sued him for not turning over client files when he left the firm, and the second was the Quebec Securities Commission, which charged him with forging client signatures on account transfer forms. Marston, it is alleged, promoted promissory notes on behalf of Mount Real Corporation, assuring his clients that these notes were more secure than bonds. In November 2005 Mount Real was declared insolvent and in February 2006 Quebec's financial regulator, the Autorité des marchés financiers (AMF), suspended Marston's licence. Pleading total innocence, Marston blamed the AMF, the IDA, and Mount Real's auditors for the clients' losses. Through the summer of 2006 while accountants attempted to trace investors' money, investors prepared themselves for the total loss of their retirement nest eggs, and Marston travelled between two homes, his own in Montreal and his wife's in Kingston, Ontario, in his Mercedes-Benz.[100]

- Across Canada the debacle related to Portus Alternative Asset Management remained an ongoing story through the summer of 2006. The hedge fund collapsed in 2005, leaving many questions unanswered. The only one that really mattered to the thousands of investors who were sold Portus units by their financial advisors was "What happened to our $238 million?" The answer may be some time coming, but industry commentators such as Dan Hallett easily pinpointed the danger signs that advisors ignored when promoting the hedge fund. Among them:

1. Portus offered brokers a 5 percent sales commission, a healthy upfront return that might have warped their judgment a little.
2. Portus promised weekly liquidity, yet hedge funds usually have a locked-in period of a year or more, suggesting that the fund was hardly as liquid as its founders claimed. Investors would not have been aware of this anomaly, but advisors surely were, if they chose to consider it.
3. The decision by Manulife Securities to offer Portus was seen as an endorsement, encouraging independent brokers to follow suit. Yet banks and major brokers continued to shun Portus based on their due diligence, something the independent brokers should have heeded.
4. Portus was aggressive in recruiting wholesalers, promising earnings two and a half times higher than normal. Why such an expensive enticement?
5. One Portus fund supposedly required a minimum investment of $250,000, yet the average investment was below $30,000. Why were the rules bent so far?

6. Too many advisors directed too many clients to place too much of their asset base in this one investment vehicle. At most, Hallett observes, it should have been limited to 10 percent.[101]

Road Maps, Detours, and Scenic Routes

Canadians need to invest their RRSPs wisely, not salt them away in Canada Savings Bonds or bank savings accounts paying minuscule interest. Investing is all about risk, and risk, as discussed earlier, can be managed.

We need a broader view of risk, especially for RRSP/RRIF holders 60 years of age and older, people whose trust levels and RRSP assets are highest. As a result, they are most prone to suffering unnecessary losses rooted in broker and advisor actions, both passive (DSC-based mutual funds with high MERs, unsuitable allocation of assets, insufficient portfolio updates) and active (account churning, frauds, embezzlement).

Some critics of the investment industry suggest that RRSP/RRIF owners should assume full management of their investments, drawing on articles in the news media and a constantly expanding library of books for guidance. Others disagree. "People with RRSPs still need professional assistance managing their plans," says Stan Buell. "The ordinary Canadian just doesn't have the proper training, expertise, and facilities to make wise investment decisions." Yet trading the risk of making poor investment decisions on one's own for the risk of encountering an incompetent, avaricious, or criminally minded advisor is not an ideal solution either, especially when the prospect of retrieving losses through the convoluted channels of compliance officers, SROs, securities commissions, and civil law is so discouraging.

A third choice can be described with a simple but effective analogy: View the management of your RRSP or RRIF as an extended journey you have never taken before—perhaps a coast-to-coast motor trip.

Your plan is to follow the main highway, where most people travel. There is a risk, of course, of traffic jams during which you hardly move at all, or of being forced to take a detour until the road ahead becomes clear. Over the course of the journey you'll likely pass scenic sites that tempt you off the main path to admire the view. From time to time you'll encounter other travellers who will rave about a short-cut that you shouldn't pass up. Billboards will suggest you turn off at the next junction for an experience you can't afford to miss. You'll consider each, remaining aware of the risk that these diversions and detours might leave you stuck in the mud and spinning your wheels, or direct you into a blind alley from which you may never escape.

The road map is drawn not in lines but with rules familiar to every qualified financial advisor and knowledgeable investor. There is nothing new and revolutionary here, nor should there be—you are not blazing the Northwest Passage after all. This is the Trans-Canada Highway, the main route you follow unless you have a good reason for diverting your path. This road map should not be construed as my effort to provide financial advice. After all these pages of warnings, disasters, and assorted outrages, I could hardly play the role of advisor at this stage. Instead, these are widely accepted guidelines that provide a straight-and-narrow path. Divert from it as you need to or desire. Just understand why and how when you do.

Rules for the Road to Preserve Your RRSP/RRIF Capital While Pursuing Growth

1. Match Your Age to the Guaranteed Fixed-Income Portion of Your Retirement Portfolio
At age 60, the portion of your portfolio comprising government bonds, GICs, or cash (including money market funds) should be about 60 percent, rising as time passes. This tactic is designed to

preserve your hard-earned capital, not to generate spectacular short-term growth. Simply put, the older you get, the less time you have to rebuild your portfolio if it suffers from major market setbacks or inappropriate investments.

Here is how a conservative approach to your portfolio might be charted (short-term assets are cash or money market funds).

AGE-BASED INVESTMENT GUIDELINE

AGE	GROWTH (EQUITY) (%)	GROWTH AND FIXED INCOME (%)	BONDS/FIXED INCOME (%)	SHORT-TERM ASSETS (%)
55–65	10	20	55	15
45–55	20	25	40	15
35–45	30	30	30	10
25–35	50	20	20	10

The growth/equity portion could be one or more low-MER mutual funds, perhaps a combination of managed and indexed plans.

Once you are committed to this strategy, evaluate government-backed strip bonds for your bonds and fixed income source. Strip bonds are the interest coupons clipped from long-term (15-plus years to maturity) bonds. High-quality strip bonds are exchanged like currency among brokers. You can purchase and redeem them in just about any amount. You don't actually take possession of the bond or coupons. Your ownership is registered in your name as a *book entry* and purchases or redemptions are recorded in the *book,* held by a trustee.

The stripped coupon shows its price at maturity, the date when the bond issuer will replace it with cash. You purchase the strip bond at a discount from its face value. The amount of the discount determines the annual interest rate you will earn. A $10,000 coupon maturing five years from today may carry a discount price of $8000. Your total profit of $2000, divided by the five-year period, produces annual earnings of $400 or 5 percent—about average in mid-2003. Remember that these are government guaranteed, meaning that the federal or provincial government will be there to redeem them, reducing your risk to its lowest attainable level and raising your ability to preserve capital.

Some advisors may propose bond funds rather than the bonds themselves, noting that an active manager can trade bonds for short-term profits while providing long-term security. This loses sight of the goal to preserve capital, although several bond funds have managed to exceed bond yields over the long term. Bond funds can and do lose money from time to time, so choose one carefully and, if your RRSP assets are sufficient to justify it, combine both bonds and a track-proven bond fund.

2. Treat Risk Like Saturated Fats, to Be Avoided or at Least Minimized

Remember that high reward demands risk in similar proportion. While it may be tempting to goose your RRSP or RRIF with potential double-digit returns by shifting a substantial portion of its assets to a sector fund or some other vehicle, the risk is almost never worth it. Losses are inevitable with risky ventures, and losses inside your RRSP/RRIF bring an extra measure of pain. Lose investment money outside your RRSP and you will at least receive a tax deduction to soothe the blow. No such balm is available to soften the loss inside a registered plan. In addition, a key benefit of RRSPs and RRIFs is their ability to generate compound earnings free of taxation. Once a loss occurs in your RRSP or RRIF, you lose the immediate asset plus potential future earnings as well. Manage your risk.

3. Be Realistic in Your Expectations for Growth Events of the late 1990s, when mutual funds recorded annual returns of 20 percent or more, convinced investors and RRSP/RRIF owners that such earnings were possible year after year. Well, they're not, unless you are prepared to micromanage your investment and extend your risk tolerance substantially. History suggests that 10 to 12 percent returns are closer to reality, with the higher figure requiring a larger proportion of investments based on equities. The farther you reach for long-term earnings beyond the historical average, the more you wander from the safe and proven path.

4. When Making New RRSP Investments in Equities, Avoid Lump-sum Purchases Take advantage of dollar-cost averaging wherever possible. Instead of dumping a lump-sum contribution into a mutual fund, or purchasing a large block of blue-chip stocks, make your investment in equal amounts over several months. If you have $3000 to contribute for the coming year (and your cash flow can handle it), make one $500 stock or fund purchase each month for six months. Since mutual fund and stock prices vary—sometimes widely—from day to day, this ensures that you purchase fewer units or shares when prices are high, and more when they are lower.

5. Never Purchase a DSC Mutual Fund There should be no exceptions.

6. Pass on Any Mutual Fund That Charges More Than the Median MER for Its Category Generally, MERs and fund performance move in opposite directions—the more of one, the less of the other. Morningstar, one of the leading investment research firms, awards from one to five stars for mutual funds based on performance versus others within their own category. In 2003, Morningstar related its ratings, with three stars indicating average performance, against the MERs for funds in each category (see over).

AVERAGE MER BY STAR RATING					
	4–5 STARS	3 STARS	1–2 STARS	N/A*	ALL
All Categories	2.30	2.50	2.78	2.73	2.62
Cdn. Balanced	2.31	2.45	2.81	2.63	2.55
Cdn. Bond	1.23	2.05	2.35	1.95	1.94
Cdn. Equity	2.65	2.77	2.93	2.80	2.78
Cdn. Money Market	0.62	0.97	1.54	1.17	1.12
Global Equity	2.78	2.72	3.09	3.00	2.93
Science & Tech	3.08	2.95	2.86	2.88	2.92
U.S. Equity	2.29	2.60	3.10	2.76	2.70

* N/A: Unrated funds (due to limited reports, etc.)

SOURCE: MORNINGSTAR CANADA, OCTOBER 2003. REPRODUCED WITH PERMISSION.

In every category, with the exception of Global Equity three-star ratings, fund performance declined with an increase in MER levels. Keep in mind that Morningstar looks beyond immediate past performance levels to other areas, including volatility (less is more).

7. Be Smart Enough to Ask the Dumb Questions The smartest people I know are the ones who never, ever pretend they know something when they do not. It takes courage to admit ignorance or unfamiliarity with facts before making a decision. Do not permit your pride to overcome your need to know when your financial advisor presents you with investment alternatives. The "dumb" questions worth asking are—

- Why are you recommending this mutual fund/bond/stock?
- How does it fit my current investment strategy?
- What is the management expense ratio for this mutual fund? (If the MER is above the median for this group: What justifies its high expense?)

- Is this a DSC mutual fund?
- What is the fee or commission you will charge for me to buy or sell this mutual fund/bond/stock?

8. Favour No-load/Low-MER Mutual Funds Lest some of the foregoing criticisms and observations on mutual funds have totally dissuaded you from using them, fear not. For small investors with more to do than follow the stock market like a hungry hound after a hare, quality mutual funds remain the best choice for growth. Some of the finest mutual funds are rarely, if ever, recommended by financial advisors, *because they do not offer sales commissions and pay very low, if any, trailer fees.* Chalk up another blow against the commission-based system.

Some no-load fund families require higher initial investments to play in their backyard—typically $5000 to get started (compared with $500 or less for the glitzier operations). Larger opening sums help the funds operate more efficiently, as do frugal marketing and communications policies. I don't know about you, but when a company is spending my money, frugal is fine.

A commission-based financial advisor will require a transaction fee of perhaps $100 to obtain units in no-load funds for your portfolio, and that's reasonable. It's wise to establish this fee beforehand.

9. Do Not Hold More Than Six to Eight Mutual Funds in Your Portfolio Investment advisors arm-wrestle over the optimum number, some proposing as few as 4 or 5, others suggesting 10 or 12. Let's be Canadian and compromise.

Why not hold more funds in your plan? Because you don't need more if the ones you own are chosen carefully, and because too many funds can dilute the benefits of diversification.

The top 10 holdings of large Canadian equity mutual funds are remarkably similar in content and structure. All fund managers draw from the same warehouse of statistics, so it is inevitable that their selections are alike. The secret to effective diversification among funds lies in choosing different sectors, and different fund management styles within the same broad sectors.

Sector selection identifies basic industries or companies assessed by the fund manager as the best available, given the fund's mandate. A Canadian large-cap fund will invest at least 70 percent in companies headquartered in Canada, each with a capitalization—the total value of all shares available for investors—of $500 million or more. Small-cap funds will choose among companies with capitalization under $500 million. Global funds invest around the world; international funds restrict their investments to a slightly narrower range. Emerging market funds target areas such as China, Latin America, and Asia-Pacific. Other funds whose descriptions identify their focus include Health Care, Gold and Precious Metals, Resources, and Bonds.

Management styles are associated with broader equity-based funds, and are categorized as growth or value. Growth funds choose companies with limited assets or earnings but with the promise of a bright future. Tech-based companies such as Nortel were sweethearts of growth funds in the 1990s, and we know what happened to them. Value funds favour proven companies whose share price may be temporarily squashed because of market conditions, bad publicity, momentary disasters, or other reasons. Value fund managers like to say they are shopping for bargains, and the best manage to do so with impressive frequency.

Do not trust a fund's name alone to indicate its management style. Example: One of the largest and oldest mutual funds, Templeton Growth Fund Ltd., is actually a conservative value fund. Best solution: Read the prospectus (snore), ask a trusted financial advisor, or do some investigations on your own.

10. Never Forget Whose Money It Is It's not theirs, it's not his, and it's not hers. It's *yours,* and you have more than a right to know where it is going, how much is being siphoned off, and to whom. You have a responsibility to yourself and your family, especially where RRSP/RRIF investments are concerned, to ensure that as much of it as possible remains in your hands.

Managing your money effectively involves maintaining a good relationship with your financial advisor. Like all relationships, this one depends on full and open communication for its success, and an understanding of each partner's rights.

You have the right to pay the lowest fee possible, consistent with the advisor receiving reasonable remuneration for the work done on your behalf.

The advisor has a right to earn a living, and to provide service commensurate with the amount she is earning from your account. In summary: Find an advisor you can trust. Expect openness and honesty on both sides. Locate a space between vigilance and relaxation, and settle into it.

Through discussions with dozens of Canadians who suffered devastating losses in their retirement savings, I have been struck by the manner in which many blamed their misfortune on themselves. True, better diligence might have helped avoid disaster in several instances. Blaming the system, with its commission-based remuneration, unrelenting pressure on advisors to generate ever-higher earnings, and lax regulatory procedures, may be justified, but it brings little consolation. We can only hope that industry disturbers such as Ken Kivenko, Larry Elford, Stephen Gadsden, Joe Killoran, Glorianne Stromberg, and John De Goey, partnered with principled advisors such as Hans Merkelbach and others placing their clients' needs foremost, will stimulate a structure in tune with the concerns of those relying on their registered savings plans for future security.

It is my view that avoidable RRSP/RRIF losses are rooted deeper than investor inattention and advisor malfeasance. They represent an attitude that permeates the industry at the top levels of many brokerages, including those owned by Canada's chartered banks. The evidence seems to indicate that pressure is applied on individual brokers to maximize their commissions to the detriment of other, more critical, concerns, including the growth and security of the client's investment portfolio.

Big producers of commissions, such as Michael Holoday, are stroked with special perks and recognition. Holoday was feted and praised for rising to become among the top 5 percent of commission producers at his brokerage within three years of earning his broker's licence. No one noticed, until red lights began flashing from other directions, that almost without exception all of Holoday's clients had lost substantial portions of their portfolios, and some had been wiped out within months of entrusting Holoday with their investments. Did no one care that virtually all of his clients were losing money? Apparently not.

Holoday and others of his ilk do not lurk in every brokerage cubicle. If it need be said, brokers and advisors are neither more nor less honest than others in similar circumstances. But when the industry drives itself according to the generation of wealth for itself rather than the success of its clients, and rewards are made not as a reflection of the growth in client assets but by quarterly increases in sales commissions, *every decision, every nugget of advice, and every broker-influenced transaction will be subject to suspicion regarding the ultimate recipient of profit and earnings.* How can it be otherwise?

A final observation on two aspects of life that everyone 50 years and older can confirm and that sanction the activities of advisors who place their own interests ahead of those of their clients.

Canadians 50 years and older may be the last generation to harbour a tangible definition of *trust,* having grown up with the concept that a man or woman's promise was as solid as any contract written in dense legalese. They may recall the years of their childhood when every neighbourhood had a corner grocery store where families sent their children to request "a loaf of bread, a quart of milk, and a pound of sugar, and put it on our bill, please." The grocer duly recorded the order, the child returned home with the food, and every Saturday one of the parents—usually the mother—arrived at the grocer's to settle the bill. The grocer trusted the families to pay what they owed. The families trusted the grocer to record the purchases accurately. It was all achieved without credit cards, ATMs, or promissory notes because it was based on mutual trust. Both the neighbourhood grocery stores and that kind of trust are gone.

The other contributing factor is ignorance of financial and investment basics. Today's seven-year-old child likely knows more about sex than her parents and grandparents know about the investments that make up their retirement savings. Our schools appear to consider the subject of finance and investment considerably less respectable than the use and abuse of sexual organs. When we're adults, the ignorance is reinforced by too many commissioned salespeople assuring us that we are incapable of understanding the means of nurturing our retirement savings, and that our only salvation resides in giving them our money and our ... trust.

Do they deserve either?

As my poker-playing mother used to say: "Kid, even when you trust the dealer, always cut the cards."

APPENDIX

PROVINCIAL SECURITIES COMMISSIONS

ALBERTA

Alberta Securities Commission
Ste. 400 - 300, 5th Avenue SW
Calgary, AB T2P 3C4
Tel. (403) 297-6454 Fax (403) 297-6156
Website: www.albertasecurities.com
Inquiries: Inquiries@seccom.ab.ca

BRITISH COLUMBIA

British Columbia Securities Commission
P.O. Box 10142, Pacific Centre
701 West Georgia Street
Vancouver, BC V7Y 1L2
Tel. (604) 899-6500 Toll-Free (B.C. and Alberta) 1-800-373-6393
Fax (604) 899-6506
Website: www.bcsc.bc.ca
Inquiries: inquiries@bcsc.bc.ca

MANITOBA

Manitoba Securities Commission
500 - 400 St. Mary Avenue
Winnipeg, MB R3C 4K5
Tel. (204) 945-2548 Fax (204) 945-0330
Website: www.msc.gov.mb.ca
Inquiries: securities@gov.mb.ca

NEW BRUNSWICK

New Brunswick Securities Commission
85 Charlotte Street, Suite 300
Saint John, NB E2L 2J2
Tel. (506) 658-3060 Fax (506) 658-3059
Website: www.nbsc-cvmnb.ca
Inquiries: information@nbsc-cvmnb.ca

NEWFOUNDLAND AND LABRADOR

Department of Government Services, Consumer and Commercial
Affairs Branch
2nd Floor, West Block Confederation Building
P.O. Box 8700
St. John's, NF A1B 4J6
Tel. (709) 729-4189 Fax (709) 729-6187
Website: www.gov.nl.ca/gs

NORTHWEST TERRITORIES

Registrar of Securities Legal Registries Division, Department of Justice
Government of the Northwest Territories
1st Floor Stuart M. Hodgson Building 5009 - 49th Street
P.O. Box 1320
Yellowknife, NT X1A 2L9
Tel. (867) 920-3318 Fax (867) 873-0243
Website: www.justice.gov.nt.ca/SecuritiesRegistry

NOVA SCOTIA

Nova Scotia Securities Commission
Joseph Howe Building, 2nd Floor
1690 Hollis Street
P.O. Box 458
Halifax, NS B3J 2P8 / Courier: B3J 3J9
Tel. (902) 424-7768 Fax (902) 424-4625
Website: www.gov.ns.ca/nssc

NUNAVUT

Registrar of Securities Legal Registries Division, Department of Justice
Government of Nunavut
1st Floor, Brown Building
P.O. Box 1000 - Station 570
Iqaluit, NU X0A 0H0
Tel. (867) 975-6590 Fax (867) 975-6594

ONTARIO

Ontario Securities Commission
Box 55
Suite 1903 - 20 Queen Street West
Toronto, Ontario M5H 3S8
Tel. (416) 593-8314 Toll-Free (Ontario) 1-877-785-1555
Fax (416) 593-8122
Website: www.osc.gov.on.ca
Inquiries: Inquiries@osc.gov.on.ca

PRINCE EDWARD ISLAND

Securities Office Consumer, Corporate and Insurance Services Division
Office of the Attorney General
95 Rochford Street
P.O. Box 2000
Charlottetown, PEI C1A 7N8
Tel. (902) 368-4569 Fax (902) 368-5283
Website: www.gov.pe.ca/securities

QUEBEC

Autorité des marchés financiers
800, Square Victoria, 22e étage
C.P. 246, Tour de la Bourse
Montréal, QC H4Z 1G3
Tel. Montréal (514) 395-0337 Québec (418) 525-0337
Toll-Free 1-877-525-0337
Fax (514) 873-3090
Website: www.lautorite.qc.ca

SASKATCHEWAN

Saskatchewan Financial Services Commission
6th Floor, 1919 Saskatchewan Drive
Regina, SK S4P 3V7
Tel. (306) 787-5645 Fax (306) 787-5899
Website: www.sfsc.gov.sk.ca

YUKON TERRITORY

Registrar of Securities Corporate Affairs
C-6 Community Services
P.O. Box 2703
Whitehorse, YT Y1A 3C6
Courier: 2130 Second Avenue, 3rd Floor Whitehorse, YT Y1A 5H6
Tel. (867) 667-5225 Fax (867) 393-6251

NOTES

Preface

1. HANSARD 03/04/05-75, Debates and Proceedings, Nova Scotia Legislature, First Session, Thursday, April 28, 2005—Bill No. 168—*Securities Act.*

Chapter 1: You Are David, They Are Goliath, and You Don't Have a Slingshot

2. All the data and quotations for the Laflamme tale herein are derived from the written judgment of Supreme Court Justice J. Gonthier in the ruling of *PA Laflamme Inc.* v. *Roy,* May 3, 2000.

Chapter 2: Of Foxes and Hedgehogs

3. Roles, Rights & Responsibilities—A Guide to Investors from the Ontario Securities Commission (April 2003), p. 1.

4. General Social Survey, Statistics Canada, 2003; Financial Planners Standards Council.

Chapter 3: Brokers and Advisors

5. In the first edition of this book, Ms. Gibson employed the pseudonym "Hillary Cornell."

6. As defined in the Glossary, short selling involves borrowing someone else's securities, usually shares in common stock, and selling them at a current high price with the strategy of buying them back at an anticipated lower price in the future. Dealing in "shorts" is a sophisticated and risky method of investing, unsuitable for anyone without extensive experience, deep pockets, and large reservoirs of nerve.

7. From IDA Bulletin #3537.

8. Paul Bourque, letter to the author, July 13, 2006.

9. The complete saga of Holoday's career is told in my book *Free Rider: How a Bay Street Whiz Kid Stole and Spent $20 Million* (Toronto: McArthur and Co., 2001).

10. IDA Compliance Interpretation Bulletin #C-130.

11. Personal interview with John J. De Goey, Oakville, Ontario, January 13, 2004.

Chapter 4: Mutual Funds

12. Source of data in this chapter: globeinvestor.com, July 2006, except as noted.

13. A dramatic exception to the policy of annual distributions is Warren Buffet's Berkshire Hathaway operation, whose unit/share value began at U.S.$19 in 1965 and was valued at U.S.$50,498 in March 2004, an average annual return of 22.2 percent. Buffet's operation differs from garden-variety mutual funds because of its closed-end structure, meaning that its shares (not units) are traded on the market just as common shares of corporations are.

14. Investment Funds Institute of Canada.

15. The lunch bill gets even bigger if the fund company applies the back-end fee not to your initial investment but to the market value of the fund when you cash it in, assuming the market value is substantially higher than your purchase cost.

16. For those with a mathematical bent: The formula involved taking the median MER for all mutual funds in the Canadian equity asset category (2.7 percent), expressing it as a percentage of the median of pre-MER returns averaged over the previous five years (6.99 percent), and applying it to the 365 days in 2005.

17. Morningstar Canada.

18. In May 2004, AIM Trimark announced that the Select Growth Fund would no longer exactly mirror the original Trimark Fund.

19. AIC picked up more than Buffet's investment guideline. AIC founder and president Michael Lee-Chin also adapted Buffet's company's name, Berkshire Hathaway, for Lee-Chin's Canadian securities operation, The Berkshire Group, which includes Berkshire Investment Group Inc. and Berkshire Securities Inc., and describes itself as "an independent

investment dealer offering a full range of registered and non-registered products and services including mutual funds, stocks, bonds, tax-assisted investments and other specialty investment products." Since Berkshire and AIC share both top management and a head office location in Burlington, Ontario, some observers question the degree of independent advice provided to its clients.

20. Personal interview with the author, Toronto, February 23, 2004.

21. Power Corporation of Canada/Investors Group financial report.

22. Investor Economics Inc. as quoted by Jonathan Chevreau, "DSC may be on its way out," *National Post,* May 1, 2006.

23. The CSA comprises 13 provincial and territorial securities commissions, a loose-jointed method of functioning in the same manner as the Securities and Exchange Commission (SEC) in the United States and similar organizations elsewhere in the world. In reality, it lacks the power and political clout that a truly efficient national securities organization should have. (For more on the OSC and Canada's lack of a national securities commissions, see Chapter 9.)

Chapter 5: It Shouldn't Be Complex

24. The duplication is not as impressive as it appears. The CFP designation is awarded by the Financial Planners Standards Council and the RFP by the Institute of Advanced Financial Planning. In terms of feeling confident about the advice being rendered, for most investors this would be like flying in an airplane whose pilot graduated from two flying schools. In reality, some of the most successful advisors, as measured by the growth of client assets in RRSP/RRIF accounts, have neither designation.

25. Statement on file with the author. Figures rounded off to the nearest $5.

26. Statement issued by Sprott Asset Management Inc., June 2006.

27. Rob Carrick, "Clients deserve to know annual rate of return," *The Globe and Mail,* July 13, 2006.

28. Investment Company Institute (ICI), May 18, 2006.

29. I am indebted to Doug Steiner, Managing Partner of Ventura VGI, who first described this formula in a column appearing in the April 2003 issue of *Report on Business.*

30. Eric Reguly, "Select few reap unfair gain," *The Globe and Mail,* June 21, 2004, p. B4.

31. Letter, from OSC Chairman David Brown to all publicly traded mutual funds under OSC jurisdiction, November 5, 2003.

32. "Hard Line on Soft Dollars," *The Globe and Mail,* April 5, 2004, p. B1.

33. "Hard Line on Soft Dollars."

34. Ibid., quoting Bob Bertram, Executive Vice-President, Ontario Teachers' Pension Plan Board.

35. Derek DeCloet, "Investor complaints to IDA tripled from 1996 to 2000," *Financial Post,* May 12, 2001.

36. Jonathan Chevreau, "Trimark Opposed Southam Shuffle," *Financial Post,* August 8, 1996.

37. "Securities regulators assailed," *The Globe and Mail,* April 19, 2004, p. B1.

38. Ibid.

39. Glorianne Stromberg, "A Wake-Up Call to the Fund Industry," *Investment Executive,* February 19, 2004.

Chapter 6: Investment Pornography and Red Suits

40. Interview with the author, July 4, 2006.

41. John De Goey, *The Professional Financial Advisor II* (Toronto: Insomniac Press, 2006), p. 138.

42. Jim Middlemiss, "Advisors turn to fund wraps, boosting growth," *Investment Executive,* March 2005.

43. Some pooled/wrap accounts appear to deliver good performance. Here are comparable returns for two of the largest operations as contrasted on their respective websites on July 17, 2006:

	1 YEAR	3 YEARS	5 YEARS
Seamark Canadian Equity (to March 31/06)	24.8%	23.9%	13.4%
Jarislowsky & Fraser Cdn, Equity (to June 30/06)	12.76%	21.72%	14.72%

44. *Regulator warns investors about the pitfalls of Ponzi schemes,* OSC, September 12, 2003.

45. *TSX News Release TSX Group Provides Background Information on Income Trusts and Structured Products,* November 2, 2005.

46. TSX News Release.

47. "The sum of the yield question," *National Post,* June 29, 2006.

48. Al Rosen, "Who do you trust?" *Canadian Business,* May 5, 2005.

Chapter 7: A Guide to Investment Divorce

49. Personal interview with Hans Merkelbach, Bowen Island, B.C., March 2, 2004.

Chapter 8: Arrogance, Disaster, and Death of a Whistle-Blower

50. Based on an interview with the author, June 29, 2006, plus copies of correspondence as quoted.

51. Interview with the author, July 7, 2006.

52. Jonathan Chevreau, "'Active' managers are closet indexers," *National Post,* July 15, 2003.

53. The Gadsden allegations were made in conversations with, and documents provided to, the author in preparation of this book. Among the documents is a sworn affidavit submitted at trial in a proceeding related to the Mallad–Shirley dispute. Gadsden, however, did not appear for cross-examination, and as a result, his affidavit was nott entered as evidence.

54. Ontario Securities Commission, IN THE MATTER OF NATIONAL INSTRUMENT 81-105 MUTUAL FUND SALES PRACTICES AND IN THE MATTER OF THE MUTUAL RELIANCE REVIEW SYSTEM FOR EXEMPTIVE RELIEF APPLICATIONS AND IN THE MATTER OFASSANTE CORPORATION, dated February 10, 2004.

55. Copy of this letter in the possession of the author.

56. Kent Shirley's experience with drugs was outlined in an email forwarded to the author on December 10, 2004.

57. From Statement of Claim, *Kent Shirley, Plaintiff,* v. *Brian Mallard Insurance Services Ltd. Et al,* Court of Queen's Bench for Saskatchewan, Judicial Centre of Saskatoon, March 4, 2004.

58. Statement of Defence and Counterclaim, March 4, 2004.

59. Shirley's distribution of documents obtained from Mallard was reported by Jonathan Chevreau ("Shirley provided extensive documentation

to the Saskatchewan Securities Commission [*sic*], the Mutual Fund Dealers Association (MFDA) and the RCMP"), "Assante lawsuit bears a closer look—mutual fund sales practices at centre of employment suit," *National Post*, August 26, 2004.

60. Amended Statement of Claim, *Mallard* v. *Shirley,* October 28, 2004

61. *Anton Piller KG* v. *Manufacturing Processes Limited,* 1976.

62. Action No. 0401-16581.

63. Confirmed by an email from Ms. Shannon England, Enforcement Assistant, Saskatchewan Financial Services Commission (SFSC), to the author, July 11, 2006.

64. Interview with the author, July 10, 2006. Italics added by the author.

65. Posted under the heading "I am not a crook" on advisor.ca, September 20, 2005.

66. Interview with the author, July 12, 2006.

67. Jonathan Chevreau, "'Black hats' not welcome," *Financial Post,* August 15, 2005.

Chapter 9: SRO or SOL?

68. The broker has since retired.

69. Letter to the author from Paul Bourque.

70. "About the IDA," *Roles and Reponsibilities,* www.ida.ca.

71. "Report seeks IDA revamp,". "About the IDA," *Roles and Responsibilities,* www.ida.ca. *Report on Business,* December 13, 2003.

72. Personal interview with Paul Bourque, IDA offices, Toronto, January 14, 2004.

73. Doug Steiner, "Divide and dither," *Report on Business,* September 2005, p. 21.

74. IDA Annual Report, 2005, *Member Regulation, Enforcement.*

75. Janet McFarland, "IDA sets guidelines for investor restitution," *The Globe and Mail ROB,* May 16, 2006.

76. As of mid-2004, the IDA had obtained the authority in Alberta to obtain a court order enforcing fines against individuals no longer associated with an IDA-member firm or who have left the industry completely rather than pay the fine. It remains to be seen whether the IDA can obtain similar authority in other provinces and just how effective it may be, if and when this authority is granted.

77. Letter to the author, July 13, 2006.

78. Personal email correspondence with James Roache, August 12–18, 2004.

79. www.iiac.ca, website of Investment Industry Association of Canada.

80. Personal interview with Michael Lauber, Toronto, March 31, 2004, and follow-up correspondence.

81. Prof. Joel Fried (University of Western Ontario), "The OSC Swamp: Sobering Thoughts for a Legislative Standing Committee Investigating Problems at the Ontario Securities Commission," *Financial Post*, August 28, 2004.

82. Personal interview with Susan Wolburgh Jenah, Toronto, July 29, 2004.

83. Eric Reguly, "OSC slothlike over monetization," *The Globe and Mail*, March 4, 2003.

84. OSC Statement of Priorities for Fiscal 2003/2004, June 2003.

85. James Daw, "Brown launches securities crusade," *Toronto Star*, April 16, 2003.

86. Rick Westhead, "Governance rules go into effect today," *Toronto Star*, March 30, 2004.

Chapter 10: The Banks

87. Gary McLeod, "Banks and the Insurance Business," *Financial Post*, May 19, 2006.

88. Jonathan Chevreau, "Advisor quits big bank in disgust," *Financial Post*, April 22, 2003.

Chapter 11: Vultures, Jackals, Ghouls, and Everyday Thieves

89. The complete sordid story of Michael Holoday is related in my book *Free Rider: How a Bay Street Whiz Kid Stole and Spent $20 Million* (Toronto: McArthur and Co., 2001).

90. There are exceptions. When RBC Dominion Securities broker Christopher Horne duped his clients out of $7 million, the brokerage reimbursed his clients for their losses, plus interest, and paid legal fees for clients to investigate RBC Dominion's actions to confirm that the company acted in a correct manner. It also paid a $250,000 fine to the IDA for failing to adequately supervise their star broker. (The complete story of Horne's deception is related in Deborah Thompson's *Greed: Investment Fraud in*

Canada and Around the Globe [Toronto: Viking, 1997].) RBC Dominion's actions in this case are considered exemplary. They are also, unfortunately, extraordinary.

91. *Financial Disclosure: What You Need to Know,* OSC, September 2000.

92. Personal interview with Detective Jeff Thomson, Toronto, May 6, 2003.

93. Tony Van Alphen, "Swindler jailed for five years," *Toronto Star,* July 7, 2006.

94. Steve Buist, "Financial adviser faces $51m suit," *The Hamilton Spectator,* May 6, 2006.

95. Tara Perkins, "White collar crime lament," *Toronto Star,* March 3, 2003.

Chapter 12: Looking Out for Yourself and Your Money

96. Rob Carrick, "Financial services consumers need a court of last resort," *The Globe and Mail,* November 8, 2001.

97. Rudy Luukko, "74-year-old widow's case just drags on," *Toronto Star,* December 7, 2003.

98. Paul Delean, "Feeling burned and bitter about it," *Montreal Gazette,* July 22, 2002.

99. Supreme Court of Canada, *Bulletin of Proceedings,* March 12, 2004, pp. 415–32.

100. Don MacDonald, "Fall of an investment adviser," *Montreal Gazette,* February 25, 2006; "Seller of Mount Real notes files proposal to his creditors," *Montreal Gazette,* March 21, 2006.

101. Mark Brown, "Portus shame," *AdvisorNews,* April 2006.

GLOSSARY

Asset   Something of value. Your home is your asset (or at least the portion that is free of mortgage), as is your RRSP or RRIF.

Asset allocation   The process of dividing your assets over various options, including cash, fixed income (e.g., bonds, GICs), equity (stock market shares), and real estate according to an investment strategy.

Back-end load   *See* Deferred sales charge.

Balanced fund   A mutual fund investing in a combination of equities and fixed-income investments, seeking growth with limited volatility.

Bear market   A phase in the stock market when prices decline over an extended period.

Beta   A measure of price volatility compared with similar investments such as an index fund. If the benchmark investment is set at 1.0, investments with wide price fluctuations will exceed a beta rating of 1.0; those with less volatility will be rated less than 1.0.

Blue chip   Large, well-known publicly traded companies with long records of earning profits and paying dividends.

Bond   A means of borrowing money over a long term (up to 30 years). Bonds are issued by governments and corporations and pay a declared rate of interest, usually on a semi-annual basis.

Broker   An individual who arranges the purchase and sale of assets.

Bull market   A phase in the stock market when prices rise over an extended period.

Canada Deposit Insurance Corporation (CDIC)　A government agency guaranteeing deposits in member financial institutions to a maximum of $100,000 per account.

Canada Pension Plan (CPP)　A federally sponsored pension plan requiring mandatory contributions from earned income during your working years and providing monthly income for your retirement (Quebec residents contribute to the QPP).

Capital gains/losses　The difference between the price you pay to purchase a security and the price you receive when you sell it. Income from capital gains is taxed on only 50 percent of the profit earned. Capital losses may be deducted from taxable income (outside of an RRSP or RRIF).

Capitalization　In stock market terms, the total value of all publicly traded shares in a corporation. Companies with capitalization of $500 million or over are considered large cap; those under $500 million are assessed as small cap.

Churning　The illegal practice of making multiple unnecessary trades in a client account for the purpose of generating commissions for the broker and the brokerage.

Closed-end fund　A mutual fund that accepts no new investors. Its units may be traded like shares of common stocks.

Commodities　Any product or material traded publicly, usually in the futures market.

Common shares　Ownership shares in a publicly traded corporation. They provide voting rights and dividends, if available.

Coupon　Portions of a bond removed and submitted in exchange for earned interest.

Deferred sales charge (DSC)　A fee levied on mutual fund unit holders who redeem their investment before a fixed period—usually five to seven years. The redemption fee, expressed as a percentage of either the original investment or the value of the investment at the point of redemption, is reduced for each year the fund is held. DSCs are used to generate front-load commissions (or "loads") to brokers and advisors, recovered with higher MERs (which remain in effect after the DSC redemption-penalty period has passed).

Derivatives   Financial arrangements between two parties based on the performance of a security or asset.

Discount broker   A firm that will buy and sell securities for its clients at a lower cost without providing investment advice.

Diversification   The strategy of spreading an investment portfolio over a wide range of alternatives, industries, and countries. The goal is to avoid wide fluctuations in value over the investment period.

Dividend   Payment to shareholders of a public company based on the amount of profit earned and subject to directives from the board of directors.

Equity fund   A mutual fund investing primarily in shares of publicly traded companies.

Exchange traded funds (ETF)   Units of a mutual fund traded as though they were common shares.

Fixed income   An asset paying a determined level of interest for a specific period. Bonds, GICs, savings accounts are examples of fixed-income vehicles.

Front-end load   In mutual funds, when the sales commission is immediately deducted from the investor's assets placed in the fund.

Futures   The expectation of earning a profit by bidding for contracts to deliver items—usually commodities such as wheat, minerals, or energy—at a date in the future.

Global fund   A mutual fund investing in companies throughout the world with no (or limited) geographical restrictions.

Growth fund   A mutual fund investing in companies with little or no current income but prospects for substantial earnings in the future. Generally considered high-risk investments.

Guaranteed investment certificate (GIC)   Certificate issued by financial institutions guaranteeing a predetermined level of interest to the purchaser over a fixed period—usually one to five years. Redemption before that date may result in penalties.

Income Trust Fund   A mutual fund in which units purchased by investors deliver a portion of before-tax cash flow, from an underlying corporation or group of corporations, into the unit holders' hands, thereby avoiding corporate tax. The fund manager determines the portion of the cash flow diverted in this manner, and the payments may also be derived from capital assets.

Index fund   A mutual fund whose investments exactly match those of the index (e.g., S&P/TSX 300, Dow Jones) it is copying. Indexed funds are considered passively managed because the fund manager makes no investment decisions.

Initial public offering (IPO)   The first time a publicly traded stock is made available to investors.

International fund   A mutual fund investing in countries throughout the world with the exception of North America.

Investment Dealers Association (IDA) of Canada   A self-regulated organization funded by member brokerages and securities dealers to promote the industry's goals and positions.

Leverage   Borrowing money to maximize the size of an investment. If $90,000 is borrowed to add to $10,000 in assets, the resulting $100,000 investment is leveraged at a 9-to-1 ratio.

Liquidity   A measure of how quickly and easily an asset can be converted to cash.

Load   The commission cost of purchasing units in a mutual fund.

Management expense ratio (MER)   The portion of a mutual fund's assets deducted annually to cover the fund's expenses.

Margin   An account in which the investor adds leverage to the investment by borrowing funds from the brokerage.

Market timing   Trading shares in anticipation of a major price change, based on statistics, intuition, experience, and so on.

Mutual fund   A vehicle in which contributions by large numbers of small investors are pooled and invested by professional managers, who are paid by a portion of the MER.

Mutual Fund Dealers Association (MFDA) of Canada   A spinoff of the Investment Dealers Association focusing on the goals of mutual fund dealers in Canada.

Net asset value per share (NAVPS)   Total assets of a mutual fund divided by the number of units owned by its investors. A mutual fund with $1 million in assets and 100,000 units owned by investors has a NAVPS of $10.

Ombudsman for Banking Services and Investments (OBSI)   An organization that investigates customer complaints against financial services providers, including banks and other deposit-taking organizations, investment dealers, mutual fund dealers, and mutual fund companies.

Open-end fund   A mutual fund accepting investments by unit holders with no limit on size or number.

Preferred shares   Shares that earn a fixed or variable dividend without voting privileges but with first claim to a portion of profits.

Price/earnings ratio   The ratio of a stock's price to its earnings per share.

Principal   The amount of an investor's capital that is at risk.

Principal protected note (PPN)   An investment vehicle that guarantees the investor will receive at least the original principal, supplemented by potential profits earned from diverting a portion of the principal to equity investments. PPN terms may range from 3.5 to 10 years. Withdrawals prior to the maturity date may trigger a penalty and void the guarantee.

Sector investing   Assigning a portion of your assets to a relatively limited part of the investment universe. Examples are mutual funds or companies operating in emerging markets or specific geographical areas (Japan, Asia-Pacific, China), specific markets (gold and precious metals, health care, internet-based industries), or investment philosophies. Sector investments tend to be highly volatile and should represent only a small proportion of a total investment strategy—typically 10 percent or less.

Self-dealing   The actions of a parent company of a mutual fund to ensure its economic well-being. Corporation A, the parent company of Mutual Fund B, may spearhead an equity offering by a client company, Corporation C, to ensure that C is able to pay debts owed to A, and then pressures its Mutual Fund B to purchase substantial amounts of the share offering and ensure success.

Self-regulated organization (SRO)   An association of industry members whose goal includes policing the members' operations in lieu of direct government oversight.

Short selling   The strategy of borrowing publicly traded shares and selling them immediately with the prospect of purchasing later at a lower price and thus earning a profit.

Small Investor Protection Agency (SIPA)   A private organization that acts in the interests of retail investors, alerting its members to investment risks and acting on their behalf to influence regulations and procedures.

Strip bond   A bond with interest coupons removed, or the coupons themselves. Strip bonds are sold at a discount to the face value of the bond or the coupons; the discount and the maturity date (or due date) of the bond or coupon determine the annual interest earned.

Trailer fee   A fee (actually, a commission) paid annually to a financial advisor by a mutual fund company whose units the advisor has sold to clients who continue to hold them.

Value fund   A mutual fund that purchases shares in a company on the basis that the share price is less than its true value.

Volatility   Wide swings in the value of an investment over time. High volatility brings increased potential reward at an increased level of risk.

ACKNOWLEDGMENTS

The goal of this book was to go beyond the familiar RRSP investment guides and address the hazards faced by Canadians with substantial assets and limited investment knowledge. To achieve this, I needed actual experiences from real people telling their real stories, holding back neither the mechanical details nor the emotional trauma. Their cooperation, more than anything else, made this book possible. My debt to Stan Buell, Patricia Cosgrove, Sandra Gibson, Joe Killoran, Carol MacKinnon, Jocelyne Robidoux, Stephen Gadsden, and Helen Rentis is enormous; those who were just as forthcoming but prefer to conceal their identities know of my gratitude.

Others provided an essential fount of information, views, sources, and commentary. Among them are John De Goey, Larry Elford, Ken Kivenko, Robert Kyle, Hans and Shannon Merkelbach, Jim Roache, Glorianne Stromberg, and Jeff Thomson. Thanks as well to Matthew Elder at Morningstar Canada; Larry Wade, for his lectures on RRSP investing; and Bill Sloper and Neil Gross for their professional insights. Paul Bourque of the Investment Dealers Association and Michael Lauber, Ombudsman for Banking Services and Investments, were gracious with their time, as were a quartet of sources at the Ontario Securities Commission: Wendy Dey, Eric Pelletier, Perry Quinton, and Susan Wolburgh Jenah.

I have been associated with Penguin Group (Canada) for almost 20 years and over that period their high publishing standards have never wavered. I am indebted to Editorial Director Diane Turbide for her initial confidence in the idea. For this edition, copy editor Sharon Kirsch and senior production editor Sandra Tooze maintained Penguin's tradition of professionalism and attention to detail—my thanks to them as well.

Finally, love and appreciation to my agent Hilary MacMahon of Westwood Creative Artists, whose warm outlook never fails to lift my spirits; and to my wife, Judy.

INDEX

Numerals in italic indicate charts, graphs, etc.